WITHDRAWN

This Side of Despair

This Side of Despair

How the Movies
and American Life
Intersected during
the Great Depression

Philip Hanson

Madison • Teaneck
Fairleigh Dickinson University Press

Associated University Presses
2010 Eastpark Boulevard
Cranbury, NJ 08512

The paper used in this publication meets the requirements of the American National Standard for Permanence of Paper for Printed Library Materials Z39.48-1984.

Library of Congress Cataloging-in-Publication Data

Hanson, Philip
    This side of despair : how the movies and American life intersected during the Great Depression / Philip Hanson.
        p.   cm.
    Includes bibliographical references and index.
    ISBN 978-0-8386-4129-3 (alk. paper)
    1. Motion pictures—United States—History.   2. Motion pictures—Social aspects—United States.   3. Motion pictures—Political aspects—United States.   I. Title.
PN1993.5.U6H343 2008
791.430973′09043—dc22

                                                                2007028415

10 9 8 7 6 5 4 3 2   13 12 11 10 09
PRINTED IN THE UNITED STATES OF AMERICA

For Cindy,
who on any number of occasions
has kept me from going under.

Contents

Preface

IN THE 1930S, THE HABITUAL AND PREVIOUSLY OFTEN INVISIBLE economic processes and transactions that made daily life run were suddenly stripped bare and thrust before the eyes of the world. Economics, it became painfully clear, accounted for a lot, perhaps nearly everything. Who you were was not quite the result of the private act of choosing or of privileged birth, as it once had seemed. These beliefs were now revealed to have been largely illusions. One day you might be an engineer, the next day you were not; one day you were a farmer, the next a bum; one day you were housed, the next cast out. Perhaps you were a teenage girl at home with your parents; soon thereafter you could be prostituting yourself out on the rail lines. The crisis became so severe that democratic countries went Nazi or fascist. And the movies, partly by intention, partly dragged kicking and screaming, took notice. Several studios experienced the Depression in its purest form: they went into receivership. Some were managed by bankers, the very people Franklin Roosevelt, in his riveting inaugural address, had called "the money changers who had fled the temple." No less than the Globe Theater of Shakespeare's day, the movies houses of the American thirties carry an imbedded history of their times, and especially of the defining crisis of the decade.

Movies represent a convergence point of the Depression era: they do not offer an unmediated view of their times, rather they represent a view of their era through a diffused and prismic sociological lens. Deflecting elements include what was largely an immigrant body of studio owners, mostly Jewish men sensitive to the resistance to their being accepted in American society, men careful to abide by at least a semblance of censorship publicly aimed at protecting the mainstream. Simultaneously, movies represent efforts to read the market, to win at the capitalist game, to give the masses what they want. And they become entangled with societal prohibitions on race and gender representation. They exist between the desire to glorify the outlaw of the period, the gangster, and to sustain established prohibitions against

9

doing so. They start out punishing fallen women, then give in to market demands (which themselves converge with the rise of a new discipline, sociology) to sympathize with the victims.

And because they cannot do otherwise movies record, directly and indirectly, developments in American life. Films become intimately entwined with isolationist issues of the early thirties, only to become as equally entwined with reconverting Americans to war ends in the later thirties. And movies struggle, as America struggles, to come to terms with the damning issue of race. At a time of bitter national debate over anti-lynching legislation and in the midst of open Jim Crow practices, a few films sincerely attempt to get beneath the surface of race issues; many others work to maintain the status quo. As male economic power is jolted, women sometimes emerge empowered, or at least more empowered than they had been at the decade's start: thirties films present the most verbally dexterous group of actresses in film history. Near decade's end, national nausea rises at the prospect of the continuation of world war at precisely the moment the New Deal runs into its own crisis: at this very dark moment in the national consciousness film noir emerges. Often remakes of the period illustrate how much films are a product of their moment: *The Maltese Falcon* was made twice before it became a true example of film noir. And noir literature existed long before film noir. Only an intimate knowledge of the period explains the phenomenon: the marketplace had to have been reconditioned for such changes to take place. And films which tag the thirties with the mistaken concept of escapism reveal themselves as unable to escape. This at the same moment that the conflict of a free society possessed of democratic free speech clashes with capitalist concerns marked by special interests, a conflict played out in mass market films which deflect anxieties and misgivings over undemocratic capitalist self-interest onto a spate of films about America's fourth estate, the newspaper business.

Acknowledgments

I WISH TO THANK RICHARD GOODER AND ANN NEWTON AT CAM-
bridge University, Norma Jenckes at The University of Cincinnati,
Karen Raber at The University of Mississippi, Andrew Johnstone at
The University of Birmingham, S. Jay Kleinberg and John Maitlin at
Brunel University, and my colleague at the University of San Francisco, Kim Connor, for reading and commenting on various parts of
this manuscript while it was in progress. An early version of chapter 5
first appeared in *The Cambridge Quarterly*. A version of chapter 6
appeared in *The Journal of American Studies*. I used fragments of previously published articles to illustrate points in chapter 3. Those articles on *The Emperor Jones* and *Imitation of Life* first appeared, respectively, in *American Drama* and *Journal X: A Journal in Culture &
Criticism*.

This Side of Despair

1

Ducking Prostitution

The Anxious Decade

ONE OF THE MOST POTENT IMAGES OF IDENTITY APPROPRIATION triggered by the Great Depression appears in a striking episode in the 1932 film, *If I Had a Million*, which concerns a dying millionaire who decides to bypass the leeching heirs around him and leave his money — a million per person — to strangers chosen randomly from the phone book. One of his choices is a young prostitute, Viola Smith. First seen in the film, Viola is working in a dingy bar, being pawed by an obnoxious sailor. In the midst of Viola's debasing herself, she receives her check for a million dollars. She disengages from the sailor and goes alone to her hotel room. There she painstakingly smoothes out the blankets on her bed, clearly aware of its greater space when used by just one. Luxuriating in solitude, in reclaiming proprietorship of her body, she lies down and deliberately removes her garters, both accessories for her trade and a reminder of her being constrained by the need to sell herself, and tosses them off. Her face radiates relief as she spreads out on the bed to experience not sharing the space with a customer.

The image makes points with which a Depression audience could identify: Viola is not a prostitute by choice or even necessarily as a result of moral shortcomings — however much a zealot might condemn her. Forces larger than she have taken over her existence. She is a prostitute. She gets a million dollars. She stops being a prostitute. Her identity, as well as her body, is at the mercy of economic conditions. For some of those closest to the economic bottom during the thirties, literal prostitution, of the sort represented in *If I Had a Million*, materialized as a personal threat. Writing in 1934 about the castoff teenagers who roamed the country during the Depression, Thomas Minehan, a graduate student who in the early thirties donned old clothes and traveled the country among homeless youths to gather material for a thesis, described homeless teenage girls who had resorted to prostitution for survival. Noting that almost one-fourth of all conversation among the teenagers focused on food, Minehan remarked, "Two girls entered

15

Having received a surprise $1 million check, the now ex-prostitute of *If I had a Million* removes the trappings of her former trade (Paramount, 1932).

a jungle where thirty or forty men were cooking. . . . Then they made a proposition. There was a box car on the tracks near by. They would go there and the men in pairs would follow. If the men had money a nickel or a dime would be appreciated because one of the girls needed shoes." As a result, "All afternoon the girls received the men and boys in the box car. Some men doubled back on the line and repeated. Others visited both girls." When "the girls quit [they] demanded their supper, divided the seventy cents in cash, and caught a freight train for the East." Of young homeless men, Minehan remarks, "One of the first lessons that a boy learns on the road is to beware of certain older men. . . . These men become friendly with a lonely boy and attempt to seduce him."[1] Martha Gellhorn, who traveled the country for the Federal Emergency Relief Administration reporting on social problems, told of "little boys earning pocket money by perversion."[2] Aside from making prostitutes of children, the dominant trauma of the period could appropriate one's identity in other ways. Thirties reporter Edward Webster remarked of young people who were suddenly getting married that "the marriage of a considerable number of transient relief clients may involve an economic motive," meaning that they married just to get the government relief money available to married couples.[3]

No decade ever made clearer the relationship between identity and economics. The dramatic shift away from twenties prosperity that resulted from the stock market crash threw into relief the reality that for many who one was was due to one's degree of economic stability. Sociologist Mirra Komarovsky established in a study conducted in the mid-thirties on the effects of economic calamity on families that an undercurrent of anxiety marked every family she interviewed, even if one did escape rock-bottom degradation. Her study illustrated how fears of loss of autonomy, some version of being prostituted, sexual or otherwise, haunted the dreams of many Americans during the thirties.[4] One woman wrote to Eleanor Roosevelt, insisting on her identity in national terms, "We are *American* born citizens and have always been self supporting. It is very humiliating for me to have to write you. Asking you again to pardon the privilege I am taking. I am hoping I may hear from you without publicity by ret. post." "Another, writing to Franklin Roosevelt, addressed the issue of the effect of the Depression on her son's identity, "We have a boy 17 yrs. old who . . . is an excellent French horn player, I have been told by good musicians he is a professional now. O, president, my heart is breaking, as I see him go from home with half enough to eat . . . to be sure he could beg his lunch but he's too proud to beg as long as he can help it."[5] In 1932, a Mrs. Clare,

Prostitutes beckon to prospective customers from a house of ill repute in Peoria, Illinois. May, 1938. Arthur Rothstein, Library of Congress.

who had possessed a million dollars in investments, suffered at the demise of the stock market, which cost her all her money and her home. Her loss of identity involved a complete change in class status. She "dropped clear through the middle bracket into the proletariat, from which it is unlikely that either she or her descendants will emerge for some time."[6] Langlan Heinz, who had graduated from the University of Colorado and worked as a civil engineer until the early 1930s, was arrested in 1932 for vagrancy. He had up until his arrest been subsisting on the charity of Brooklyn locals who fed him and that of the local fire department who "gave him occasional shower baths."[7] He had gone from being a civil engineer to being a bum and a jailbird.

Wrapped up as identities are in profession and finance, having one's identity revised against one's will was a frequent and bitter occurrence in the thirties. In cases where a revision was not absolute, the threat, in the form of reduced job hours, potential layoffs, or plant closings, created persistent tension. Film, as an art form of the masses, both captured and participated in this tension. Vulnerable to the negative impact of the decade's economic trauma, thirties cinema, responding to its mass market consumers, left a history of personal and national anxieties. The movie house, as a place for negotiating interrelated issues of film profit and consumer desire, becomes a site where the imprints of the powerful or of powerful economic forces on individual identity materialize. Films of markedly differing sorts ruminated on the threat of loss of one's self posed by economic upheaval. People are used, turned into things against their will, commodified, or simply discarded by economics or established forces which, in the process, soullessly violate traditional definitions of personal or class identity.

Early in *The Grapes of Wrath,* the shock of having one's family's generations-old identity exposed as existing at the pleasure of others hits Tom Joad (Henry Fonda). The Joad family identity is wrapped up in its relation to the land. Back after a stint in prison, Tom finds his family home empty. Muley, a family friend who has been hiding from the authorities, recounts the people's eviction from the land. The Preacher's situation personalizes the account. His only name is Preacher. But he says he cannot be a preacher anymore because he has lost his certainty due to the irrational uprooting of the community around him. When Tom introduces him to Muley, Tom says, "You remember the Preacher don't you?" The Preacher interjects, "I ain't a preacher no more." And Tom has to amend his question, "All right, you remember the man?" Such identity revisions multiply once the Joads hit the road in search of work. The Joads had shared in a philosophically constructed and economically grounded group identity—tenant farmers, hard workers, self-sufficient—and forces outside of the

The state, in the form of a bulldozer, about to eradicate community identity in *The Grapes of Wrath* (Twentieth Century Fox, 1940).

family erased this identity without putting a satisfactory new definition in its place. When a gas station attendant disrespectfully assumes the Joads do not have money to buy gas, Tom upbraids him: "ask right. You ain't talkin' to bums, you know." Herman Schubert, a supervisor of research and vocational guidance in upstate New York in the 1930s, surveyed some 20,000 of the estimated 250,000 teenage transients who took to the rails in response to the Great Depression. Addressing the question of their identity, Schubert asked, "Are they bums? . . . Not unless one wants to classify a goodly section of the remainder of the country as such."[8]

THE GLOBE AND THE MOVIE HOUSE

American anxiety over loss of autonomy during the Depression characterized both life and the movies. One of the central theories about the nature of film production in the thirties is founded on studio anxiety that materialized after several of the studios went into receivership early in the decade as a result of contractions brought on by the Depression.[9] What happened in the studios as they recovered from their receivership trauma supplies one of several important elements necessary to understanding the relationship of thirties movies to thirties America. Such anxiety within the film community was fueled by other sources. Many of the studios were led by Jewish executives, who had themselves been immigrants or were the sons of immigrants. While anti-Semitism in Germany was raging, in the United States, as late as 1938 a poll revealed that "sixty percent of Americans objected to the presence of Jews in America."[10] Additionally, movies had been under pressure from moral groups to censor potentially explicit material, and by 1934 existing censorship codes were significantly toughened up in the form of the Hays Code. The studios went along because the alternative meant intervention from the outside, which was likely to be coupled with an assault on their block booking practices.

In his seminal work on the studio system, Thomas Schatz has explained that an assembly line system, heavily dependent on churning out films in proven film genres, emerged from the receivership crisis.[11] Tino Balio remarks that receivership almost cost some studios their identity: "When motion-picture firms went under . . . bankers installed themselves in the top management positions and took charge of the distressed companies."[12] Burned by economic trauma, and threatened with a loss of their own identity, studios sought to reduce risk by adopting a safer approach to production. Such production of proven genre material was intended to reduce risk and maximize profit. It worked, in the words of Rick Altman, so "that every successful film not already identified with a specific filmic genre triggers a process of attempted genre constitution in which the studio tests a series of hypotheses regarding the specific source of success. . . . when a successful formula is discovered, it never escapes other studios, thus leading to the constitution of an industry-wide genre." At the same time, films are circumscribed by censorship, powerful interests, and predictable for-profit production practices.[13] The studios exercise maximum control of content. But such control could not erase the cultural transactions that went on every day in every movie house in the United States. If the teams of people who made movies did so under constraints imposed from a constellation of power centers, they were not entirely powerless to negotiate what appeared as a final product on the screen.

Such cultural transactions tell us much about power relations in the thirties (whether they be political, economic, racial, sexual, or aesthetic). One cultural analyst, writing about theaters, reaches the following conclusions, which help illuminate how moviemakers negotiated film content while at times under extraordinary external pressures from those with political and economic power to circumscribe what made it into the movies: "art does not simply exist in all cultures; it is made up along with other products, practices, discourses of a given culture. . . . 'made up' means inherited, transmitted, altered, modified, reproduced." Regarding what goes on in a theater, "there was actual construction of a building, the charging of admission . . . the set of regulations governing what could and could not be presented . . . no one was actually to be killed or tortured, no one was to have sex . . . no one was really cursing . . . The writing of scripts . . . could be screened ahead of time by the censors." The writer adds, the "cunning of the theater is to make its spectators forget that they are participating in a practical activity, to invent a sphere that seems far removed from the manipulations of the everyday."[14] While all of these things pertain to movie houses of the thirties, a student of the New Historicism may recognize that the writer is Stephen Greenblatt, and he is discussing the power dynamics not of thirties movie houses but of Renaissance theater. Yet his remarks illuminate thirties power dynamics. He goes on to explain how the theater of Shakespeare's day negotiated its content with external Elizabethan power centers. He argues that censorship was erratically enforced; it could represent forbidden subjects as long as it did so with an eye to potential interference from power centers, and, by the use of synecdoche or metonymy, it could skirt the censors and treat the forbidden by offering a part to stand for the whole, a practice which also worked in thirties film and persisted into the sixties, when for example, Hitchcock conveys the sex act between Cary Grant and Eva Marie Saint in *North by Northwest* by having Grant reach for Saint at the exact moment the train in which they are riding is immersed in the darkness of a tunnel, a strategy of which Hitchcock remained proud to the end of his life. We see only the reach, but we know the meaning of the darkness.

If one considers thirties social dynamics for a moment, two Greenblatt questions illuminate the on-screen content which results from the studio encounter with the censors: "What governs the degree of displacement or distortion in theatrical representation? Whose interests are served by the staging?" The response to these questions can be found embodied in the concept of contingency, which is the focus of this book. What contingencies—racial, gender-based, aesthetic, economic and or political—explain what one sees on the thirties screen? Additionally, as one uncovers the contingencies that result from negotiating disparate values and ideas, what does what one sees on the screen illuminate about thirties America? A few examples, which also serve as an introduction, help flesh out the meaning of the answer to these questions.

INTIMATIONS OF DISASTER

The growing awareness of a threat to individual identity brought on by national economic trauma emerges as a struggle in films, with marginalized characters embodying early versions of identity reversals. Initially one can see movies working literally to shake off events that portended greater economic disaster to come. No film illustrates this better, and perhaps more unexpectedly, than the 1929 Marx Brothers vehicle, *Cocoanuts,* a film that appears almost at the moment of the stock market crash, but deals not with the crash at all, but with land deals that had been going on throughout the twenties down the coast from the New York Stock Exchange in Florida, deals described by Frederick Lewis Allen as a rehearsal for the crash up the Atlantic coastline that was soon to follow.

Florida land in the mid-1920s and Wall Street stock at the end of the twenties shared a common quicksand-like feature. Each represented the illusion of being on solid ground. The rise of the automobile in the early twentieth century had made Florida more accessible to East Coast cities. The climate had always made it an attractive place for vacations or hotel investment. Until the mid-twenties, like stock, the price of real estate represented something like its actual value, and, just as stocks had, until the mid-twenties, the land had been purchased for its actual value. But the Florida land deals began to fulfill a desire for riches through speculation rather than through investment based on the reality of worth. In 1925 the vice president of a bank wrote for the *Miamian,* "Go to Florida. Where enterprise is enthroned. Where you sit and watch at twilight the fronds of the graceful palm, latticed against the fading gold of the sun-kissed sky.[15] Connecting "enterprise," "palm trees," and "gold" represents a careful choice of images. In retrospect the Florida experience exists as a harbinger of what was to happen to the stock market just a few years later. Increasingly, during the Florida land boom of 1924–26, buyers had no intention of ever occupying or even holding onto the land they had purchased. Rather, they had come to believe that appreciation was a permanent and natural condition of Florida real estate.[16]

Soon, in some of the worst-case scenarios, investors were buying and contributing to driving up prices for land that was worthless. The sale of swampland came to be a kind of mythic joke that arose from the period. A buyer would purchase land as an investment with the expectation of its appreciation in worth, selling it to another buyer with the same expectation, driving up prices for land that was worthless. "The trick was, though, to ride with the expansion as long as possible and get out before the collapse." So expansive was the Florida land boom that by 1925 the *Miami Herald* carried more advertising than any paper anywhere in the history of the world ever had before.[17] In 1926, the bubble burst; deflation set in and, for the rest of the twenties, until the ominous year 1929, while the rest of the country boomed, Florida's economy stagnated.

George S. Kaufman and Morrie Ryskind, the two writers who worked on *Cocoanuts* in the infamous crash year, could not have known what to make of the Florida land experience. They exploit it for comic purposes, treating it as one in a history of snake-oil land deals, a result in the film of crooked dealings on the part of a not very sophisticated crook, Hammer (Groucho). But *Cocoanuts* captures and preserves the last incandescent moments of the flappers. Hammer, manager of an empty hotel, is desperate for business. And the future of the film's love interest couple, Bob Adams and Polly Potter, depends on Bob's getting work as an architect, a vocation dependent on further development in Florida. The couple's romantic identity as lovers, as husband and wife, depends on the economics of real estate. Harpo's persistently stealing the shirts off the backs of various characters in the hotel reinforces the film's environment of being a shark tank of petty crookery: you could lose your shirt down there. When Hammer tries to sell land, he uses the logic of the Florida boom period: it's accessible from the Northeast, and the weather is beautiful. As Groucho pitches the idea of helping to Chico, the jokes materialize as derived from the Florida land bust. He asks Chico, "Do you know what a lot is?" Chico responds, "Yeah, it's too much." Of course, Bob buys a lot, for his future home with Polly. To save their marital identity, the plot has a millionaire miraculously send news that he's coming to the hotel with four hundred guests and plans to build.

Released in 1929, *Cocoanuts* could not know what was in store for the country. It finishes off its rickety plot with a belief in the quick recovery of Florida's economic future, making the need for chicanery in selling the land a moral and temporary problem. As a record of its time, *Cocoanuts* provides a mixture of images of hedonistic flappers and frantic land auctioneering, in retrospect a mix of what was to be the crashing end of one era and the torturous onset of another. The novelty songs, "Monkey Doodle Doo," "He Wants His Pants," "The Skies Will all be Blue," convey a careless ease that would be regarded retrospectively with bitter irony by F. Scott Fitzgerald. From the historical perspective of the filmmakers, the enormity of what exactly their satire confronts remains unseeable. The practice of buying on margin, paying only a part of an item's worth with the intent never to pay the full price, but to sell when the price goes up, a land and stock market practice in pre-Depression America, materializes in the film.

Cocoanuts offers an early glimpse of connections between romance and finance that the Depression was just on the verge of exposing. The first could be easily enabled or blocked by the second.

INSTITUTIONAL IDENTITIES: THE CRIMINAL AND THE MADMAN

The Criminal

As the Depression deepened, films expressed a deepening suspicion of societal institutions, most notably the prison, which possessed the authority to rewrite individual identity. A deeply glum film arose out of the American, or more specifically, the Southern justice system and tapped into particularly historically based fears of loss of self to powerful interests, which expressed themselves in the form of the prison. *I Am a Fugitive from a Chain Gang* (negotiated down from its book title, *I Am a Fugitive from a Georgia Chain Gang*, so as not to offend Georgia) confronts American fears of a growing gap between the realities of the law and justice, doing so through a specifically Southern institution, the chain gang, which by the thirties had established its own peculiar place in Southern labor history. The contingencies exhumed by the film go deep into central contradictions in the American enterprise, with its claims for liberty and its undermining history of colonial and regional slavery and Jim Crow. The chain gang serves as a vestige of the slave system, a point Robert Burns returned to time and again in his autobiographical account of his experience on a Georgia chain gang (upon which the film is based), characteristically remarking, "the chain-gang system of Georgia . . . is a different code. Born and raised in the system of slavery, life is cheap and of little value. . . . Feuds, lynchings, intolerance, illiteracy and hatred have survived through that one word: revenge!"18 The film generates its plot out of the possibility of one's losing one's self to punitively repressive authority. If economic deprivation creates desperate need, the authorities are there to squash any effort at desperate action. Though some of the time it covers takes place in the period between World War I and the Depression, its drawing from Southern history makes it a paradigm charge against Hoover era inequity. What had been a race-based system of oppressive treatment was exposed as a broader class war against people at the bottom (true also of the way the slave and Jim Crow systems had kept poor whites at the bottom in the South). The period's economic crisis revealed the frightening potential for an expansion of such harsh expressions of power.

American slave history demonstrated that the law had taken over the persons of the powerless before. The evolution of the chain gang can be traced from the Southern slave system forward. When emancipation ended the old hierarchy of the labor-intensive plantation slave South, the planter class experienced a crisis of labor. The plantation hierarchy addressed this crisis in a number of ethically unsatisfactory ways before hitting on a solution. Initially the dominant class in the South relied on Black Codes, a system of petty racist laws that sent newly freed African Americans to prison for minor offenses. This practice enabled the convict lease system (represented in *Gone With the Wind* when Scarlett acquires laborers by renting them from the state penitentiary). The history of the convict lease system is reflected in J. H. Jones's characterization of it as "the product of human rapacity grafted upon conditions that a defunct slavery had left behind it."[19] Because the numbers of available convict laborers remained insufficient, the South eventually settled on tenant and sharecropping systems as a means to address their labor problems.[20] However, convict chain gang labor was not abandoned.[21] Though African Americans and poor whites who were interviewed during the Depression often remarked that they could hardly see any difference in the way they had been living (pre-Depression), *I Am a Fugitive from a Chain Gang* appealed to thirties audiences on two related levels. First, it was one of Warner Brothers' social consciousness films. It addresses a social injustice for a generation hungry to see exposed the powers they believed responsible for their woes. Second, it specifically demonstrated that the law, rather than being an impartial code, could be irrational, and more sinister—an expression of class and political power, especially when addressing the powerless person at the bottom. That the film is based on Burns's actual life account intensified the emotional reaction it received. The irony of Jim's (Paul Muni's) remark, "I steal," as he disappears into the dark at the film's end, in Pauline Kael's words, "haunted a generation."[22]

The film also connects its chain gang injustices to those widely perceived as having been visited upon the Bonus Army of World War I veterans who had marched on Washington in 1932 out of economic desperation, only to have Congress turn a deaf ear to their entreaties and to have someone else—someone with more power—decide their fate. The justice gap of serving with MacArthur in World War I and then being routed by him in Washington is evoked by Jim's receiving a medal in the war and then having to sell it when he cannot get work. Jim gets into trouble when he follows a fellow indigent to a small diner for a handout and he's forced by the indigent at gunpoint to help with a robbery. He receives ten years on the chain gang.

   Inside the prison camp, the guards' sadism suggests the danger of unrestricted authority, which was made more real by disclosures of chain gang abuses during the period. Photos exist of the sorts of torture Southern work farm penitentiaries visited on inmates, such as staking them out in the hot sun (as we see in the film, with one inmate fastened in a crucified position). One eyewitness of the period described chain gang convicts in knee-deep water "held together by chains that fretted in their flesh, compelled to attend to the calls of nature in line as they stood day in and day out and their thirst driving them to drink the water in which they were compelled to deposit their excrement."[23] Julius Adams, an African American sentenced to a Mississippi work farm when he was convicted of petty larceny, "and unable to pay his fourteen-dollar fine," recounted being forced to work until his fingers froze and skin peeled off his hands down to the bone. He acquired gangrene and the boss took him to a chopping block and chopped off the frozen fingers one at a time.[24] The film clearly shows the racial segregation that occurred in such chain gangs. And many of the horror stories that came out of the history of Southern work farms came from African Americans. The system's ugly (specifically slave) history, is evoked when the black convicts sing a work song. When they employ old African call-and-response devices, the structure of the Old South

A visual of the state's proprietorship over the inmate's body in *I am a Fugitive from a Chain Gang* (Warner, 1932).

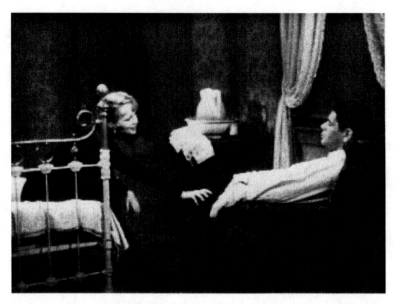

Representing the democracy of those at the bottom, a young prostitute in *I am a Fugitive from a Chain Gang* offers herself to recent chain gang escapee, James Allen (Warner, 1932).

system, with its slave roots, materializes for a moment.[25] In his book Burns recognized this point, remarking, "the tempo and speed [of chain gang work] is regulated by the chanting of Negro bondage songs."[26] James C. Cobb remarks that the convict-lease system "clearly benefited powerful Delta corporate and planting interests."[27] This point is echoed in the film by the powerful in the state of Georgia abusing their authority by making deals with Jim to return to Georgia after his escape, then breaking their promises after he honors their terms.

The film also conveys what became a widely accepted democratic ethos during the Depression: the down-and-out would help each other when the powerful would not. Jim receives help from fellow convicts. On the verge of escape, he is given the seven dollars an aging convict has left. Once he has successfully fled from the penitentiary, he is given asylum by another ex-convict, who himself runs a risk for doing so. He has made his escape with the help of a black convict who has a reputation on the chain gang for never missing with his sledgehammer. And while hiding out at the fellow convict's apartment, a young prostitute gives herself to him for free for the suffering he has endured. The array of people who help him, eventually adding a Christian hue when his brother, a reverend, lends support, offers a claim for a version of

American democracy, one that eschews Mayflower pedigree in favor of racial and class inclusiveness and help that is given outside of capitalism-for-profit rules of exchange. When the state of Georgia double-deals and Jim has to escape a second time, the film drives home the point that the system's advertised claim to rehabilitate exists as a perversion. Jim has become a successful engineer during the years after his first escape (the real Burns had started an advertising firm and later became a tax consultant).[28] Georgia's betrayal drives him to steal. The state writes criminal identity where one need not have existed.

The Madman

If the prison in the thirties could not be trusted with identity production, the asylum was also suspect. And this at the moment the effect of the economic crisis on mental health had become a public concern. During the Depression "the psychological problems for the unemployed remained devastating." Karen Horney, a psychiatrist in the thirties, broke with Freud by claiming that neuroses should be more closely understood within the social context of their occurring. She saw the economic upheaval of the thirties as an important factor in psychological disorders: "Hence, in speaking of a neurotic personality of our time, I not only mean that there are neurotic persons having essential peculiarities in common, but also that these basic similarities are essentially produced by the difficulties existing in our time and culture."[29] Harry Hopkins, Franklin Roosevelt's director of the Federal Emergency Relief Administration (FERA), felt a growing "concern for the psychological health of the unemployed." He sent out reporters who worked for FERA, who "sought information in particular on the mental outlook of the jobless." FERA reporter Louise Wilson described "a wild-eyed young man [who] was holding his child as his wife tried to get someone to pay the rent." The man told Wilson, "You can't expect a man to keep sane under these conditions." Wilson recalled, "I didn't think he was a sane man as he talked to me. He was a husky man with lots of initiative, crazy to work." Sociologist Glen Elder concluded that the social stigma of sudden loss of self-sufficiency and status led, in the middle class, to "more incidents of neurotic behavior." A psychiatric caseworker found of an unemployed man given employment, "The mere fact of his having responsibility and a pattern of routine for existence completely changed the man. He went around whistling."[30]

The problem of dealing with possible psychological maladies brought on by economic crisis was complicated. After World War I Freud had questioned what a psychiatrist would do if civilization itself had "become neurotic." Freud's interest was in evaluating competing versions of civilization. But the problem he confronts concerns how to determine a healthy model against which to evaluate unhealthy civilizations. A worry in the thirties was that neuroses would become widespread, in a sense that neuroses would become a national characteristic. One goal of the FERA interviews was to determine a model of sanity. But a constellation of mental health problems confronted authorities. Making the issue more of a problem was the state of the mental health establishment in the decade. The confidence at the end of the nineteenth century that had characterized a powerful coterie of asylum superintendents who had promised 80 percent cure rates had eroded. Patients released as cured had been returning to asylums in large numbers in the early decades of the twentieth century. By the thirties short funds and asylum failures lead to scandal. James Michael Curley, governor of Massachusetts, visited Boston State mental hospital for women, and left claiming the women were not being properly cared for. Increasingly the asylums were becoming warehouses. As such, they took a more disciplinary approach to patients. Inside the asylums hierarchies developed and inmate obedience, rather than a cure, became the desired goal.[31]

Unable to cure the chronically mentally ill, the psychiatric establishment turned to addressing more marginal behavior, a shift with political consequences. Mental health historian Gerald Grob elaborates, "The new concern with conduct disorder was an indication that the traditional psychiatric preoccupation with the severely and chronically mentally ill was diminishing, and that behavior perceived to be outside acceptable social norms was coming under psychiatric jurisdiction." What is abnormal then carries a stigma, and the psychiatric establishment was seeking to identify the abnormal outside of the asylum (as Grob sees it, a play to expand their power), a threatening development since the abnormal can be punished with confinement.[32] Elaine and John Cumming remark, "mental illness . . . is a condition which afflicts people who must go to a mental hospital, but until they go almost anything they do is normal." Erving Goffman argued that the mental health establishment "institutionalized" the "mandate" to decide who is ill, with the consequence of a straining to prove someone mentally ill and why that someone must be confined.[33]

The very shadowiness of defining mental illness could serve political ends. Roosevelt's program for giving aid to Depression victims brought on charges he was a traitor to his class. And beyond that, he was charged with being insane. Illustrating how deciding insanity can be as much a political move as a medical move, Arthur Schlesinger Jr. explains that during the war over government control of utility companies, it was suggested to the president of an electric company they start a "whispering campaign designed to create popular suspicion that the 'new dealers' and especially the 'New Dealer-in-Chief' are either incompetent or insane."[34] The combination of medical authority, self-interest, and a haziness surrounding certain definitions of mental health conferred a potential for abuse, one which reveals as much about public fears of authority as it does about problems of psychiatric certainty. *Mr. Deeds Goes to Town* is a film that builds its sentimental core out of the issues connected to potential abuses by psychiatric authority and anxiety over potential psychological problems afflicting the public. Capra and his writers create a standard of sanity, one which they identify with a morally healthy small-town America. They demonstrate how Depression conditions can cause a complete reversal of values, which can lead to mistaking insanity for sanity. In the process the film introduces a new term into the American vernacular: "pixilated." It means insane.

In spite of Capra's own misgivings about FDR's social welfare policies, Longfellow Deeds's sanity in the film is questioned on the basis of his desire to give to the poor, not as straight charity but as investment money to help them get a new start. The charge against Deeds is articulated in his sanity hearing by a wealthy lawyer, John Cedar, who tells the packed court Deeds's "incompetency and abnormality shall be proved beyond any reasonable doubt." Referring to Deeds's "mental quirks," Cedar charges, "in these times with the country incapacitated by economic ills and in danger of an undercurrent of social unrest, the promulgation of such a weird, fantastic, and impractical plan as contemplated by the defendant is capable of fomenting a disturbance from which the country may not soon recover." He attributes Deeds's desire to give his twenty million dollar inheritance to down-and-out farmers as the act of a "diseased mind." It would be hard for a thirties audience not to see this film as putting Roosevelt's social welfare policies on trial. Deeds began his charitable enterprise after being threatened by a farmer with a gun. The man had lost his farm and could not feed his wife and children. In that respect the film replays the drama of the early thirties, which started with militant actions by angry farmers, who in some cases blocked highways to prevent the delivery of goods.

Before the sanity hearing, the film has already introduced us to Deeds as morally and psychologically healthy, especially in comparison to the city dwellers he encounters when he comes to the city after inheriting a fortune from a dead relative, a banker. When the banker's lawyers search for Deeds in his hometown, a local tells them, Deeds is a "fine fellow, very democratic." In the city Deeds is confronted by Mencken-like literati, who ridicule his *Saturday Evening Post* poetry and manners. At the trial we learn he has supported two destitute old

The state's witness, the psychiatrist, gives testimony that threatens to put Long-fellow Deeds under the power of the state in *Mr. Deeds Goes to Town* (Columbia, 1936).

women, who, nevertheless, testify that he is "pixilated" because he whistles to himself. The subjective nature of sanity is foregrounded by their charging that everyone they meet is pixilated. The psychologist testifies that manic depressives can go for years without being detected, and echoing later critics of psychology, he adds, "assuming we are normal," the very assumption Freud struggled with, that is, finding a model of normality. The trial ends with the judge proclaiming Deeds sane. Unlike John in *Fugitive*, who is twice turned over to prison authorities, Deeds narrowly escapes losing himself to the mental health experts who would have awaited him at the asylum. *Deeds* writes insanity as an identity construction of experts who have strayed too far from essential, small-town American values, which in turn blocks their seeing the way to help the country recover.

BERKELEY'S PROSTITUTE

Social message films became popular in the thirties because they afforded an opportunity to examine tensions between individual hardship and national economic retraction. Since movies represented an art

form for the masses, films presented a sympathetic treatment of outsiders or the oppressed. Explorations of what it meant to be prostituted
picked up where *If I Had a Million* left off. *Blondie Johnson* (1933),
for example, examines the making of a female gangster. The film opens
with Blondie (Joan Blondell) appealing to a relief administrator for aid
for her ailing mother. He turns her down when he learns she earlier
quit her job. However, she quit her job because her boss was sexually
harassing her.[35] For the film's relief administrator, the circumstances of
one's hardships do not matter. The harsh logic of financiers and politicians who simply believed the economy was undergoing a natural
adjustment manifests itself in film representations of people in power
refusing to consider the role of national trauma in personal tragedy.
When Blondie returns home, her mother has died of pneumonia after
being turned out onto the street by her landlord for not paying the rent.
Blondie seeks help from a lawyer, who will not take her case because she
has no money. Blondie becomes a prostitute and a gangster.[36] But she
has not entirely chosen to be those things; her identity is at the whim
of external forces.

   Easy Living, written by Preston Sturges, differs from *Blondie Johnson* in tone, but it demonstrates that two quite different films can be
derived from the same period-rooted economic logic. Its anxieties,
used to comic effect, match those of many films of the period. Though
Mary Smith (Jean Arthur), the central character, becomes neither a
prostitute nor a gangster, that she is repeatedly taken for a prostitute
generates the film's comedy. Early in the film Mr. Ball, a millionaire,
and his wastrel wife argue atop a skyscraper penthouse about a fur coat
she has purchased. They struggle and the coat flies over the wall to the
street below, landing on Mary's head and breaking the feather in her
hat. Discovering what has happened, Ball gives Mary the coat. At her
office, Mary is fired because her boss believes she has prostituted herself for the coat. Soon Mary is breaking open her piggy bank for change
to buy food. Mr. Louie, a hotelier in debt to Ball, believes he has
learned that Mary is Ball's mistress. He makes up a story and offers her
a suite at the hotel, intending to blackmail Ball. Soon real prostitutes,
believing Mary has hit on a successful formula, began booking rooms
at Mary's hotel. Mary is not a prostitute, but she is not so far removed
from prostitutes either.

   A persistent exploration of the conditions under which hard-pressed
people can be prostituted exists in Busby Berkeley's thirties musicals.
Prostitution dangles as a threat throughout these films. If one sells oneself, particularly if this happens against one's will, Berkeley, through
his choreography of dance numbers in the films, examines the conditions out of which such sales arise. The Depression intensified the pres-

sures on many to sell themselves in ways they might not have imagined possible. Berkeley's *Gold Diggers of 1933, Footlight Parade, 42nd Street, Dames,* and *Gold Diggers of 1935* all consider ways people can be converted into commodities. His dance routines seem intentionally separate from the rest of the films, serving as a subconscious of economic realities that the saccharine main plots deny.[37] Thus, Berkeley's choreographed dance numbers exist as the purest versions of modernist technique to be found in thirties commercial film. Aesthetically they function as interventions in the linear-narrative success stories these films so confidently offer. As the Horatio Alger plots of the main narratives unfold, they are interrupted and commented upon by song and by the abstract, often nonrepresentational dance numbers, which are intentionally filmed from a number of disorienting camera angles. In this respect they function as do several modernist experiments of the twenties and thirties: they make tired subject matter new by a visually disorienting view of their subjects (recalling Picasso's paintings, Pound's "make it new," and William Carlos Williams's intentionally disorienting treatment of a rose in *Spring and All*); they serve to expand perspectives on subject matter as Faulkner does through multiplying narrators in *The Sound and the Fury* and *As I Lay Dying,* and they work as a subconscious of a reality not in evidence in the primary plots, as Freudian influenced stream-of-consciousness narrative worked in Joyce, Woolf, and Faulkner.

Any number of modernist aesthetic theorists could be quoted on the "higher realism" modernists assigned to abstract art. In their attacks on representational art, modernists argued that the abstractions of Expressionist and Cubist painting penetrated to a higher reality, which Expressionist painter Wassily Kandinsky connected to an "inner truth," meaning a truth superior to representational realism.[38] In his dance numbers Berkeley discovers a way to comment on the false reality of the Algeresque plots of the films. He can dissect the economics of entertainment and of identity narratives by his abstract choreography and camera angles. This enables him to expose entertainment as an economic enterprise and identity as at the mercy of economic forces.

The film *42nd Street* is one of the bitterest commentaries on economic threats to selfhood in the thirties. The theme song for *42nd Street* contains an invitation, "Come and meet those dancing feet / On the avenue / I am taking you to / Forty-Second Street." As the song progresses, the audience is promised an introduction to ladies who are "indiscreet." Berkeley's Cubist vivisecting of the women (recalling Picasso's *Les Demoiselles D'Avignon*) in the visual treatment of female body parts suggests two things. First, the frequent visual severing of the women into legs, arms, and heads leads to an interchangeableness of the "girls" (rarely are they called women). This depersonalizes the showgirls both as performers and potential lovers. Second, in a way suggested by Chaplin's *Modern Times,* when the tramp falls into the giant machine works in the factory and becomes a part, a cog, in the machine, the girls in the elaborate Berkeley chorus lines and in the kaleidoscopic visual patterns comprised of women's bodies, are reduced to parts of a money-making machine, the show itself. As in Cubist painting, or in the explicit claims of William Carlos Williams's poetry, Berkeley's numbers insist on the viewer experiencing the women and the dance as alien to the plots. "The Machinery Ballet" number that opens the second act of Berkeley's 1928 Broadway musical, *Earl Carroll Vanities of 1928,* was "inspired, the programme asserted, by a visit to a Ford automobile plant."[39] Like machine parts, the women are advertised as interchangeable, as when Dorothy Brock (Bebe Daniels) the star of the musical Julian Marsh (Warner Baxter) is putting on, in the film must be replaced by Peggy (Ruby Keeler).

The economic machine extends to the show's director, Marsh. Marsh has had a nervous breakdown because of an earlier show. The show's producers are worried that he might crack again. Though he should be rehabilitating, Marsh tells the producers, who have flattered him with remarks about his reputation, "Say, did you ever try to cash a reputation at the bank? I'm in this for one reason: the money." One of the producers tells him, "With all the hits you've had, you ought to be worth plenty." Marsh counters, "I ought to be but I'm not. Did you ever hear of Wall Street?" Depression economics charge *42nd Street* with an omnipresent tension. In all three of Berkeley's musicals of 1933, the shows stagger along in jeopardy of shutting down for lack of money. Marsh, like the women in the show, must do things he would rather not do.

The film's first scene featuring Dorothy, the show's star, suggests the unpleasant economic dynamics of her star identity. The scene opens with a close-up of Dorothy's contract. This should be a good thing. But it is not a reality that comes unencumbered. The show's rich backer, Abner Dillon (Guy Kibee), holds the contract. He doesn't know much about contracts, but remarks, "it looks good to me." As he speaks, we see Dorothy, but not as a whole person, instead as a pair of exposed legs dangling over the edge of the bed. It is Abner's gazing at the legs the camera follows; his words have a double meaning. Dorothy becomes a sexual object, the "it" of his sentence. Dorothy tells him, "It's the biggest contract I ever signed, thanks to you, Mr. Dillon." The relationship between Dorothy's contract and Dorothy as sexual object clarifies. Being a star is dependent on Abner's goodwill. The film plays with the notion of Dorothy prostituting herself. As they discuss the contract Abner puts his hand on Dorothy and tells her, "You could have your choice of any show." She responds. "Not with this Depression," clinching the connection between economic need and sexual bartering. Later, after Dorothy has broken her ankle, Abner replaces her with another girl, Annie, also known by the suggestive nickname, Anytime Annie (Ginger Rogers). Annie refers to her making a deal with Abner "over breakfast," intimating that she too paid to play.

The film *42nd Street,* due to censorship codes, must steer clear of the implications it dangles before its audience. But in a characteristic Berkeley strategy, a musical number late in the film exposes what has been repressed. The "42nd Street" number, typical of Berkeley, injects subversive doses of higher reality. It sets itself off stylistically from the sunny songs of the show by being delivered by Ruby Keeler in a nasal wised-up Bessie Smith / Mae West manner. The lyrics tell us 42nd Street is "where the underworld can meet the elite," the sort of occurrence which is a matter of money. The street is covered with people rushing to work and the unemployed selling apples. The visual distance separating them is nothing. The camera pans across sidewalks of jovially dancing people to hesitate on the headline of a newspaper, which concerns a murder case, collapsing the separation of acceptable and destructive behavior. In rapid succession, the camera captures a cop, African American street kids dancing for coins, and a tacky apartment where a seedy lookout tips his hat to entering prostitutes. The happy music is subverted by the focal point rapidly moving to an upstairs room, where a prostitute is sadistically assaulted by a rapist. She jumps from a window into the arms of a man in the crowd below and joins the dance, only to be stabbed in the back by the assailant. The song ends with a close-up of the smiling soon-to-be newlyweds (Dick Powell and Keeler). But the formal closure that fixing the camera on the two lovers should give has been unsettled by rape, murder, and prostitution. The number reminds that March, Dorothy, Annie, and others have only narrowly escaped streetside degradation.

Coming into the Depression, out of the prosperous twenties, marriage and birth rates had been booming. But this changed. "Marriage and birth rates fell dramatically in the early 1930s." According to one source, "By 1938 . . . 1.5 million people had been forced to postpone marriage due to hard times." Gender roles themselves seemed to have been partly vacated: "one woman observed, 'They're not men anymore, if you know what I mean.' " This shift away from traditional gender roles arose from "feelings of inadequacy on the part of the male and lack of respect for the unemployed man from his wife."[40] No one in popular culture raised more penetrating questions about the economics of romantic "realities," the economic underpinnings of marital identity itself, than did Berkeley.

The stylized rape that opens *Gold Diggers of 1933* illustrates this point. At stake is personal identity. The women are either performers who earn a living or, if they can't, they're prostitutes. One of the chorines remarks, we'll "have to do things I wouldn't want on my conscience." The show for which they are rehearsing opens unsubtly with the girls singing "We're in the Money." Their costumes are facsimiles of giant gold coins, visually transforming the women's bodies into currency. The Depression-soaked song concerns saying goodbye to breadlines and being able to look the landlord in the eye. Surprisingly, the song addresses the bitter political debates of the period involving the United States going off the gold standard as a means of recovering prosperity. In September 1931, Great Britain had gone off the gold standard, and Americans, fearing the United States would do the same, began to hoard gold. In February 1932, Congress passed the Glass-Steagall Banking Act. Its intent was to ease credit restrictions on banks and make some of the government's gold available to business. By this point gold and currency hoarding had become a problem. And silver "aroused deeper passions" than gold. The "remonetization of silver, it was argued, would not only ease the debt burden at home but would ease the purchasing power of silver using countries . . . and open up great new markets for American products." Ginger Rogers sings, "The long lost dollar has come back to the fold. With silver you can turn your dreams to gold." Though some economists, chiefly John Maynard Keynes, argued that "the curse of Midas would fall on countries which clung to gold," Hoover fought hard in the closing period of his presidency to retain the gold standard. In Roosevelt's campaign rhetoric, going off the gold standard was presented as one cure for the country's financial angst; doing so would enable more fluid management of money.

When Ginger Rogers (whose name is Fay Fortune, a play on words for the financially threatened chorus girls, as is her name when delivered as Miss Fortune), sings the song in Pig Latin, we get a demonstration of how hard-pressed women will twist themselves into knots to make a living. Her admonition, "Let's lend it, spend it, roll it around," states a Keynesian point repeatedly made in Capra's *American Madness:* prosperity comes from putting money out there, circulating it, making it work. In its historical moment, this concept comes out of criticisms of Hoover's policies and is reiterated in Keynes's economic theories. When one listens to the particular lines, their detailed connections to economic debate of the period suggest the intense desire for economic solutions to the Depression. However, the fragility of

The stylized rape of *Gold Diggers of 1933*. When the Depression hit show cannot pay its bills, one of the sheriff's men rips the costume off Fay's body (Warner).

being "in the money" (literally and figuratively) is exposed by the sheriff's arriving to confiscate the scenery because the show's producer couldn't pay for it. The sheriff's men tear the costumes off the girls' bodies, a fusion of economic and physical rape. When a deputy tears a configuration of coins off Fay's body, she cries, "Well, at least give me car fare!" He responds, "What for?" In the mock economic transaction, his remark asks of the semi-nude girl something suggestively sexual for the car fare. The screen image implies the illusory nature of the space between freedom of choice and being commodified. Soon the unemployed chorines are sleeping until 10:30 a.m., wisecracking about starving, and going through a man's pants for money (the latter an act associated with prostitutes). Trixie (played by Aline MacMahon), whose name puns prostitution, steals the neighbor's milk.

Later, the film presents an extended misunderstanding that casts the women as prostitutes. This development plays out the precariousness of their identity without having to actually present prostitution. When a wealthy man mistakes one of the chorus girls for his brother's fiancée, he tries to buy her off, remarking, "Just tell me how much." The girl, Carol (Joan Blondell) responds, "Sorry, no price on me." His class bias and remarks about the low morals of chorines irritate Trixie and Carol, who decide to "take the two men for a ride." Their actions mock prostitutes working johns. Trixie orders expensive hats and manipulates the men into paying. Much is made of the delivery boy's term—c.o.d.— "Cash on delivery," a joke about prostitutes. The girls manipulate the men into buying them corsages and champagne. In a nightclub, Trixie puts her hand on the leg of the lawyer (Peabody) under the table. Later the other man, J. Lawrence, gets drunk and falls asleep in Carol's apartment. In the morning Trixie makes him believe he's slept with Carol. Trixie tells him, "Call it payment for a night's lodging if you like." She charges him $10,000. When he first offered only $5,000, Trixie asked, "What do you think Carol is?" In the process of playing with Peabody (played by Guy Kibbie, who was fifty-one but looked seventy), Trixie manipulates him into marriage. She lays out a scene of domestic bliss, even as she hustles him for champagne and a pet lapdog. Her manipulations expose the line between wife and prostitute, since it is hard to believe she would marry him if he didn't come with money.

At the film's climax, Berkeley generalizes the plight of the women into a bitter comment on the effect of the Depression. Collapsing the fate of the Bonus Army and that of the women in the final number, Berkeley has Carol appear as a streetwalker. Approaching a homeless man, she shares a cigarette with him. Looking at the hobo, Carol remarks, "I don't know if he deserves a bit of sympathy. Forget your sympathy." Then indicating the remark is meant to puncture complacency, she adds, "I was satisfied to drift along from day to day, til they came and took my man away." Of her own man, she sings, "You put a rifle in his hand." The song explains he was sent overseas as a soldier. Earlier he cultivated the land, she explains, against background images of the farmer and the fiasco of the Bonus Army, which could have been dubbed the army of forgotten men.[41] The "Forgotten Man" number, marked by images of soldiers, recalls that Berkeley had attended a military academy and served in World War I as a field artillery lieutenant. His training had been "as a choreographer of military parades and marches."[42]

The camera pans across windows of other lonely women and lights on a sleeping hobo, whom a cop harasses into getting up off the sidewalk. Like Jim in *I Am a Fugitive from a Chain Gang*, the hobo displays a war medal. The look of hate Carol visits on the cop recalls the national response to Hoover and MacArthur for using force against American veterans. The number juxtaposes scenes of a marching army, the American flag, wounded soldiers, and soup lines. In the soup lines, demonstrating an ethic that was to symbolize that of the down-and-out, the men democratically share cigarettes. The number ends with an extravaganza of marching soldiers, soup-line men, and beseeching women. Out of the crowd Carol appears singing lines from the song, calling on those in power to "bring him back again." By presenting Carol as a prostitute in the film's last song and tying her condition to the plight of several groups of hard-luck men, Berkeley employs the number to comment on the earlier mock prostitution, which, ironically ended in marriage. Carol loses the musical's man to World War I and winds up a streetwalker; in the main plot, she gains a husband, but one who first took her for a prostitute. A cynic could see her marriage as his commitment to pay for her.

National Identity

In 1932, at a low point in the Depression, a group of prominent citizens popped in on Herbert Hoover with a proposal. According to one report, "86 eminent persons including Edsel Ford . . . petitioned President Hoover [and] argued that a dictatorship was the way out of the Depression." This was not to be the only time the concept of a dictatorship would be raised as an issue during the Depression. In a political fight over the Guffey Bill, Franklin Roosevelt's opposition "fell into fits of professed apprehension over the immanence of dictatorship." In January of 1933, just prior to Roosevelt's taking office, Walter Lippman urged him to confront the Depression crisis with this solution: "The situation is critical, Franklin. You may have no alternative but to assume dictatorial power." The forcefulness of Hitler and Mussolini in Europe had led some Americans to believe that a shift to a dictatorship might be a good idea. Al Smith, former governor of New York, remarked that "even the iron hand of a national dictator is in preference to a paralytic stroke."[43] The Depression made more than just individual identity an issue. National identity, captured in Thomas Paine's famous dictum that the people should govern themselves, would have been radically altered had a president followed this advice. But the concept illustrates a desperate national anxiety. The tensions concerning a potential change in national identity are reflected in magazine articles of the period. In its April 1930 issue, *American Mercury* carried the title, "The Collapse of Democracy." Its June 30 issue of the same year listed the article "Elective Monarchy in America." *The New Republic*'s June 1, 1931 issue contained the article "Toward an American Fascism"; and that same journal, as late as October 2, 1935, offered "The American Plan: It's Rise and Fall."

Films participated in anxiety over threats to traditional identity and in their plots explored solutions to such threats. They exemplify a national meditation on a crisis of American identity. Writing about Hollywood interest in U.S. history in the thirties, Paul Vanderwood

remarks on the desire to find solutions to the economic crisis by looking "backward into the national consciousness to discover how their
predecessors had survived the pressures of their most difficult times."[44]
Vanderwood's point extends much more broadly to such films, which
cumulatively represent an engagement with the economic (and therefore political and social) crisis confronting the thirties. Films of the
period sift through Western and American history, as well as through
thirties global and national politics, in search of persons and strategies
on which to model a response to the Depression.

   Heroes for Sale (1933) exemplifies this point. Like *Gold Diggers of
1933* and *Gabriel over the White House,* it encapsulates the bitterness
over the Bonus Army and the harshness of authorities while the masses
suffered unemployment. The central character's World War I heroism
is falsely claimed by another, the son of a banker (at a time when
bankers were the nation's villains), and he becomes a drug addict as a
result of the morphine he takes for war-wound pain. The hero loses his
business to big business and automation, and his wife is killed in a labor
riot. Yet *Heroes* finds its way through its multiple miseries to closure
by the central character's quoting from Roosevelt's inauguration
speech as an answer to the pain the film has exposed. In its effort to
close off anxieties over national issues, *Heroes* resembles *Wild Boys of
the Road* (1933), which features homeless teens who ride the rails, one
of whom is subjected to an assault by a rapist and another who loses
his leg to a train. After *Wild Boys* spends eighty-six minutes of running
time showing the miseries of the teenagers, it sends them to court
where in two minutes a judge solves their problems by finding them
employment. *Wild Boys,* like *Heroes,* looks to American institutions
for a solution to the country's trauma.

   Unlike *Heroes* or *Wild Boys,* Capra's films explicitly find authoritative American tradition in the small town; they do so by connecting
the town to paradigm moments in American history. Capra's *American Madness* (1932) foregrounds one of the most public enactments of
economic trauma, the bank run. In a *Harper's* article from 1932,
George R. Clark described the psychological effect of the failure of
two banks in a small town, "The collapse of two banks within four
days brought a shock more profound than the loss of the money, which
was in itself considerable: It unsettled all their fundamental beliefs."[45]
As an allegory of economic crisis, *American Madness* finds its solution
in a mixture of thirties cutting-edge economic theory and American
history. Its central character, bank president Thomas Dicksen (Walter
Huston), like Longfellow Deeds, demonstrates his moral fiber by
democratic behavior: he jokes with the lowliest bank employees as he
enters the bank each morning, tipping the security guard's hat, telling

the janitor he deserves a new uniform. Rumors that the bank cannot cover its deposits provoke a crisis.

American Madness articulates public impatience with traditional economic theory. The theories that guided Hoover and his predecessor Coolidge were those of eighteenth-century Scottish economist Adam Smith and late eighteenth–early nineteenth-century French economist Jean-Baptist Say. Smith argued that if market forces were allowed to operate without government intervention, then "an invisible hand" would keep the economy in balance. He saw a national economy as a natural phenomenon, one which maintained its own balance, as long as no artificial interference upset it. Say, best known for his "law of markets," claimed that supply creates demand. If production occurs, people will buy. In the period leading up to the Depression William Trufant Foster and Waddill Catchings challenged classic economics.[46] They asserted that sometimes variables interrupted the flow of money to the populace. They argued that an industry which increases production without increasing the flow of capital is a bad thing: so sometimes government must interfere to increase income to consumers. When business became sluggish, government should engage in more public spending, even if this meant increasing the national debt (which could be paid off in times of plenty).[47] In sum, they concurred with the soon-to-be-dominant theories of a rising star in economics, John Maynard Keynes.

Capra makes it clear that Dickson represents people from outside the circles of power. His creditors have immigrant names. The film presents a tension between Dickson, under pressure from his board of directors to end his liberal policies, with his tendency to give unsecured credit and to make loans in tight economic times, and the blue bloods of the bank's board. Further, Dickson asserts to the board that in order to get prosperity back money has to be in circulation. This theory is countered by the board who want to merge with a banking giant and pursue a much more conservative fiscal policy, one, the film implies, that will only loan money to "the haves" (to use the term Huey Long made popular) and not to "the have-nots" that Dickson apparently has been specializing in. Dickson explains that if he doesn't loan money to an employer, and that employer can't pay his bills, then that man's employees will be out of work, and they won't be able to pay their bills. In essence, Dickson believes such a policy created the Depression. His statement of economic theory, embedded in a vehicle of popular culture, underscored the anxiety filmmakers and audiences brought into the movie house in the thirties, since it draws from economic theory in the air at the time. Dickson finds precedent for his actions in American history, citing the example of Alexander Hamilton, who made loans based on "character." Similarly, in *Deeds,* Longfellow Deeds falls back on Ulysses Grant, who started out as an "Ohio farm boy." In *Meet John Doe,* Doe is talked out of participating in a wealthy fascist's political plot to win the White House by being reminded of the examples of Washington, Jefferson, and Lincoln. In *Mr. Smith Goes to Washington,* Jefferson Smith draws authority for his politics from the Lincoln monument, a statue of Hamilton, and a painting of Jefferson signing the Declaration. Characteristic of all three of these Capra films, when the bank board refuses to help Dickson, the working class and immigrant investors—the little people, he has trusted—come to his rescue. Capra's films find essential American identity by looking back to the small town and connecting its values to those of American icons at what Ezra Pound would have called "luminous moments" in history. In such points of convergence Capra finds authority for national identity. His films expose one strain of the American mind of the thirties: one represented by dislike for modernity. On this point Capra shares values with T. S. Eliot, who posited the small parish as the ideal social structure, as opposed to the new twentieth-century metropolis, which he characterizes as "a small and mostly self-contained group attached to the soil and having its interests centred in a particular place . . . [the] ideal of a community small enough to consist of a nexus of direct personal relationships." Louis Brandeis held a similar view, asserting "localism was . . . a moral preference . . . [and] . . . only the national government could exorcize the curse of bigness."[48]

Unearthing the internal ideology in Capra's movies exposes the political complexities in the thirties ideological struggle over national identity. Capra's films seem to cohere with a liberal's view of the common people. But Joseph McBride has pointed out that Capra's work, often taken as a cinematic expression of New Deal ideology, comes from a director hostile to Roosevelt's social welfare programs. McBride notes that Capra was especially hostile to using taxes for welfare purposes. Notably romanticizing the forgotten man in Capra's films comes with the occasional objection that commoners are undependable and possess the capability of becoming a "mob," the exact term Eliot used in expressing his anxieties over spreading democracy, an updated characterization of Matthew Arnold's Philistines. Capra had to tone down presenting the commoners as a mob before the studio would release *John Doe,* and even then they come across in that film as easily swayed. Even as *John Doe* settles on the rightness of a national society of John Doe clubs, it argues against any political leadership for such a network—in other words against any role for a big centralized government that might serve as a watchdog against capitalist business for the interests of the little people.[49] *Deeds* appears to argue for a New Deal-like social welfare system, a giving to the forgotten man to get him back up on his feet. But examined closely *Deeds* emerges as of a piece with Capra's other films, an argument for personal rather than government charity, precisely Herbert Hoover's position, and, as Eric Hobshawm has noted, precisely Ronald Reagan's position in the eighties. *You Can't Take It With You* argues for personal charity, as when the family takes in the bank clerk, but against taxes to support the government institutionalizing charity. *Lost Horizon,* a film about utopia, embodies Eliot's dream of a parish-like community, one with the right sort of people in charge.

In sum, Capra's films reveal the undercurrent of resistance to big government that never entirely went away in the decade and reemerged near decade's end to shut down the social welfare revolution the New Deal had started. Conservative anxieties over fundamental changes in America eventually burst forth late in the decade in the form of the House Committee to Investigate Un-American Activities (HUAC), which shut down the New Deal Federal Theater Project and charged such New Dealers as Frances Perkins and Harold Ickes with being communists. Within Capra's films one can still see the traces of the daily political negotiations over national identity which took place in the thirties: a romanticizing of the forgotten man, Capra's liberal writer, Robert Riskin, pushing for a society that takes care of the little man, an audience deeply sympathetic to characters set upon by frightening external forces, and a conservative director against big government and with at least a modicum of distrust for the commoner. In Walter Houghton's majestic study, *The Victorian Frame of Mind,* he persistently reminds his readers that the Victorian mind, taken collectively, was not a neat thing but was rife with internal ideological contradictions and frictions. An analysis of thirties films demonstrates his point applies equally to the Depression and its movie houses.

2

The War over World War I

IN ROBERT BURNS'S AUTOBIOGRAPHICAL ACCOUNT OF THE PERIOD
covering his time as a soldier in the First World War through his arrest
and time on a Georgia chain gang, during which he witnessed miserable conditions and torture, he makes sense of his Depression-era
experiences by referring back to the trauma of the war and the way he
was treated once back in the United States. Upon his discharge from
the army, he found his job gone and his girlfriend taken by someone
else.[1] In the film version of Burns's book, *I Am a Fugitive from a Chain
Gang!* (1932), the desperate central character attempts to hock his war
medal. Burns's inclination, from the perspective of the early thirties of
the Depression, is to see the war as a source of his ills. His view represents a central current of sentiment among the U.S. populace, one
which materializes in early thirties cinematic treatments of the Great
War. In *Heroes for Sale* (1933) a World War I veteran becomes an addict
after taking morphine for pain suffered from war wounds. After the
war he is put in prison for narcotics addiction. The veteran pilots of
The Lost Squadron (1932) wind up unemployed, alcoholic, and riding
the rails throughout the thirties. The pacifist of *Ace of Aces* (1933)
becomes a killing machine in the war and suffers subsequent psychological problems. National doubts over World War I would evolve in
the thirties into an intense isolationism, which in turn would deepen
with the onset of the Great Depression. *I Am a Fugitive from a Chain
Gang, Heroes for Sale,* and *The Lost Squadron,* thirties films primarily
focusing on Depression-era unemployment woes, all open with scenes
on World War I battlefields. Summarizing the perspective that the Great
War was somehow a source of the Great Depression, Herbert Hoover
opens his memoirs with the words, "In the large sense the primary
cause of the Great Depression was the war of 1914–18."[2]

With respect to World War I, thirties cinema was part of a larger field
of aesthetic representation, a point illustrated by Evelyn Cobley's
study of World War I literature. She explains that the vast body of fiction written about the war until 1937 was almost "universally protest

literature," reflecting an "anti-war bias," with the single exception of work by Ernst Jünger. Of interest is her conclusion that this current of subversive thought remained consistent until deep into the decade, 1937 (a year after Germany violated the Versailles Treaty by remilitarizing the Rhineland). Although she does not explore the historical implications of this remark, her finding coheres with the shift the United States was about to experience. She borrows a term from cinema to describe the rhetorical strategies used by writers who criticized the war in fiction: the antiwar fiction was produced during "a period we now associate with high modernism." But in ant-war literature "realistic modes" rather than modernist modes continued "to dominate" until 1937. In fact, such writers adopted "the same conventions of realistic discourse as the documentary writers."[3] By the end of the thirties, Senator Gerald Nye, a staunch isolationist throughout the decade, who chaired a Senate committee investigating World War I munitions companies charged with profiteering, remarked of a shift in late thirties films depicting World War I: films were not showing soldiers "crouching in the mud . . . disemboweled, blown to bits." Instead, one saw "them merely marching in their bright uniforms, firing the beautiful guns at distant targets."[4] From Nye's perspective cinematic realism treating World War I had been replaced with something else, something attractive.

Realism, as an aesthetic strategy, reveals much about its own present. Margaret Drabble once remarked that realism was a "term so widely used as to be more or less meaningless except when used in contradistinction to some other movement."[5] Her remark coheres with recent critical treatments of realism. Writing about the use of realism in the nineteenth-century French panorama, Maurice Samuels concludes that the aim was to "produce the most accurate possible representation of the historical referent." Samuels argues that the power of the realistic historical spectacle to hold its viewers spellbound in creating an interpretation of the overwhelming historical past (the French Revolution, in this case) could undermine "that society's possibility for continuing the narrative into the future. For what hope for continuing forward, politically or socially, the text [he refers to *Adieu*] asks, exists for a society fixated on its past?"[6] Realism as a representation strategy may undermine an ideological position by appearing to oppose fact to theory. Discussing realism in the late nineteenth and early twentieth centuries, Robert Weimann explains that writers of this period place realism in contradistinction to existing liberal assumptions, which had been working to reinforce established power and a societal status quo. He characterizes this as a "critical realism" which seeks to subvert established views.[7]

In contradistinction to *what* did thirties filmmakers place what they took to be realistic representation? Both Winston Churchill and Nazi Alfred Rosenberg "found it easy to conceive of the events running from 1914 to 1945 as another Thirty Years' War and the two world wars as virtually a single historical episode."[8] Thirties filmmakers could not know there would be a Second World War, but they feared as much and sought to define the First World War in such horrific terms that they could arrest any progress toward a second. They wished to undermine the ideological foundation of the First World War by attacking the assumed verities upon which it was built. Paul Fussell argues that World War I "reversed the idea of Progress." His capitalization of "Progress" conveys that going into the First World War, progress was understood as a "natural" verity. Fussell quotes Henry James on World War I at the moment of James arriving at a more realistic view of progress: "The plunge of civilization into this abyss of blood and darkness . . . is a thing that so gives away the whole long age during which we have supposed the world to be . . . gradually bettering, that to have to take it all for what the treacherous years were all the while really making for and meaning is too tragic for any words."[9] In *A Farewell to Arms,* Hemingway summarizes the effect of the First World War on demolishing traditional verities: "abstract words such as glory, honor, courage, or hallow were obscene beside the concrete names of villages, the numbers of roads, the names of rivers, the numbers of regiments, and the dates." Commenting on Hemingway's words, written in 1929, Fussell remarks, "In the summer of 1914 no one would have understood what on earth he was talking about."[10]

By the thirties, they knew. Thirties World War I films set out to make Hemingway's position stick. Such films assault three "natural" verities in their "realistic" subversions: first, the rightness of traditional authority, second, the concept, which can be traced back through Western civilization all the way to the Roman Empire, by way of Horace, that "Dulce et decorum est / Pro patria mori" [It is sweet and honorable / to die for one's country] (which has implications for the concept of sacrifice as it had been presented throughout U.S. history), and, third, in a concept it shares with the Legal Realism movement of the decade, that property ownership (with its attendant suggestions of class privilege) is a natural condition, either on the individual or national level, in the latter case, that of a defined country. The consequences for films seeking to assert a negative definition of World War I play out throughout the Depression decade, as political events make such films increasingly dangerous to evolving U.S. war aims. By the end of the 1930s filmmakers, in the service of impending U.S. war interests, felt compelled to retract from the "realism" of treatments of the war in such films as *All Quiet, Ace of Aces, Today We Live, Journey's End, The Lost Squadron, The Last Flight,* and *Men Must Fight* (and the earlier silent World War I film, *The Big Parade*). As they did so, in later films, *The Roaring Twenties, The Fighting 69th, Men against the Sky,* and *Sergeant York* (all made before December 7, 1941), they sought a pre-political, natural, and therefore transcendent source of authority upon which to ground their countering redefinition of the war. In that respect, they faced the same problem faced by Modernists who had sought some transcendent grounding for art, and they arrived at a similar solution.

The cinema assault on traditional verities was part of a larger battle that raged throughout the decade. One can better understand the point of cinematic depictions of the First World War if one understands the debates of the period. If Churchill and Rosenberg could see the period from the outset of World War I to the end of World War II as covering a continuous struggle, an event that occurred during the Hoover administration helped crystallize a perceived continuity of leadership errors that ran from World War I through the Hoover years of the Great Depression. In 1932, some twenty thousand World War I veterans and their families scraped together the little money they had to travel to Washington to petition the government to grant them promised bonus checks early, since the Depression had reduced them to critical circumstances. The by then bedraggled group of World War I veterans who called themselves the Bonus Expeditionary Force, and who were covered as "heroes" by *Time* magazine, were met with hostility by Hoover, who, claiming a communist plot, had them forcibly evicted from their makeshift shacks by General MacArthur. With this action, Great War and Great Depression leadership merged in the national consciousness.[11]

In 1919, having attended the Versailles Peace Conference, John Maynard Keynes argued that leaders of the victorious Allies had established a set of dynamics with "an almost fatal bias toward the *status quo*," suggesting that the goal of Versailles leadership had been to reestablish the prewar dynamics that had provoked the war in the first place.[12] Anger over national leadership that had seeds in the Great War was reignited by perceptions that failures of leadership caused the Depression. This deepened resentment over the war and resistance to a resumption of U.S. participation in European hostilities. Herbert Hoover, in particular, was singled out for national wrath. By 1930 he had been echoing his vice president in remarking that "prosperity is just around the corner." He had repeatedly refused to use government funds for public relief, though he did use them for private industry — a fact that enraged the American public.[13] Instead, he remarked the Depression would test the mettle of the American people, suggesting

Bonus Army demonstrators clashing with police in Washington, D.C. July, 1932. Associated Press, National Archives.

their own moral weaknesses needed correcting. A little more than a decade after the Depression another child of the thirties, novelist Thomas Berger, looked back and summarized Hoover: "old Hoover, starched collar, pickle-faced, the personified *No.*"[14]

The economic failures of the thirties supported a widespread sense that class-based leadership had failed from the Great War to the Great Depression. The logic connecting the period from World War I to World War II is summed up by Woodrow Wilson's bitter post-Versailles remark, "I can predict with absolute certainty that within another generation there will be another world war."[15] After predicting that the unrealistic reparations the Allies assigned to Germany would lead to a chaos in Europe that would "submerge civilization itself," John Maynard Keynes concluded, "We are at the dead season of our fortunes."[16] John Kenneth Turner's book, *Shall It Be Again?* charged, "Wilson had led the United States into war to preserve Wall Street investments."[17] Films of the early Depression decade participated in an antipathy to the leaders who got the world into the war and damaged the men who fought and managed to survive it, summed up in Gertrude Stein's remark that Hemingway and others of the post–World War I era were a "lost generation." And economic circumstances of the period, suggesting why the Depression provided a particularly sympathetic vantage point from which to view the veterans of the First World War, led one social worker to apply the term to the unemployed youth of the thirties, calling them a "lost generation."[18]

Distrust of American industrialists and businessmen lay at the core of Senator Nye's committee from 1934 to 1936 "investigating the propriety of relationships between bankers, munitions-makers, and government officials and the forces that might have led America to war in 1917."[19] Such sentiments led to the Neutrality Act of 1935, which was renewed in 1936 and 1937 and to a pronounced mood of isolationism throughout the United States until late in the decade. Nye called the bankers who had financed the munitions industry during the war "profiteers" and "merchants of death." As such they had sacrificed young soldiers for their own gain. His characterization was made more palatable during the Depression. One might compare Franklin Roosevelt's 1933 inaugural address remarks, which referred to bankers as "unscrupulous money changers [who] stand indicted in the court of public opinion."

David Kennedy articulates the connection between Depression concerns and isolationist hostility to World War I. Isolationists came to believe World War I had been fought "not to make the world safe for democracy but to make it safe for Wall Street bankers and grasping arms manufacturers." Isolationists called World War I "the European War." And, postwar history confirmed that "far from being redeemed by American intervention, Europe swiftly slid back into its historic vices of authoritarianism and armed rivalry." This logic "fell on receptive ears, especially in the anti-business atmosphere [created by] the Great Depression."[20] In the area of cynicism over leadership between the wars, one can see Kennedy's point exemplified by comparing the bitter characterizations Keynes offers of Versailles leadership with the equally acerbic language with which John Kenneth Galbraith characterizes Wall Street leadership at the time of the crash. Keynes calls Wilson "incompetent" at Versailles, refers to his advisors as "dummies," and summarizes the claims of leaders at Versailles as the "unveracities of politicians."[21] Of leaders Galbraith holds accountable for the Great Crash, he calls Andrew Mellon a "passionate advocate of inaction," Congress's knowledge of special interests groups "obscene," and Federal Reserve Board members "mediocrities."[22]

One product of a growing hostility to war leaders was a sense of class exploitation. The soldiers' sacrifices came to be perceived as having been sold out by political, economic, and, in some cases, military leadership (a point illustrated by MacArthur's role in the Bonus Army episode). Soon the nation was questioning national leaders, accusing some of war profiteering. "Revisionist literature in the 1920s" had already begun to

discredit "traditional explanations of the origins of the First World War."
As late as 1938, isolationist sentiment remained strong enough that
"Representative Louis Ludlow of Indiana sought to force out of committee his proposed constitutional amendment that would have made a
national referendum on a declaration [of war] mandatory."[23] The economic trauma that made money scarce was aggravated by the inability,
perceived as unwillingness, of European war allies to pay the United
States money owed for World War I debts.[24]

Of wartime leadership, Paul Fussell remarks of Sir Douglas Haig,
commander of forces in France, "in a situation demanding the military
equivalent of wit and invention, Haig had none. . . . one powerful
legacy of Haig's performance is the conviction among the imaginative
and intelligent today of the irredeemable defections of all civil and military leaders." Describing the 1916 disaster on the Somme, Fussell sees
one cause as "traceable to the class system. Upper-class military leadership "entertained an implicit contempt" for soldiers "recruited
among workingmen." Officers "assumed that these troops . . . were too
simple and animal to cross the space between the opposing trenches in
any way except in full daylight and aligned in rows." Leaders believed
the "troops would become confused by more subtle tactics like rushing from cover to cover."[25] The effect, of course, was that the men were
more easily machine-gunned by the outnumbered Germans.

When Hemingway used the term "hallow" to illustrate the transcendent concepts used to justify World War I, he probably avoided the
more common term "holy" to avoid too openly assaulting someone
else's sacred cows. Nevertheless, neither he nor Henry James was alone
in believing that the "real" could expose the falseness of traditional pre-
political abstractions. Especially in the effort to define property, the
Legal Realists, a school of legal scholars, had emerged by the thirties
holding similar views about employing what they took to be realism
to subvert what legal theorist Felix Cohen at one point called "those
otherworldly abstractions haunting Classical Legal thought" and at
another point acerbically termed "the "heaven of legal concepts."[26]
Legal Realism developed during the same period Weimann associates
with an increasingly critical stance for the literary realists. Their views
were embedded in their assault on class privilege and theories of Natural Law that governed property rights. World War I caused the generation of the Legal Realists to "lose much of the pre-war faith in reason, both as a reliable source of moral understanding, and as a powerful
internal guide to law." The prosperous twenties nearly drove the Legal
Realists from the field, but Classical Legalism failed to reestablish dominance because the Depression provoked a new wave of sentiment for
a break from the old status quo: "Just as economists were attempting

to reimpose an apologetic mode of natural equilibrium on the system—the Great Depression encouraged the view that, far from being neutral and natural, markets were social constructs."[27]

Through most of the nineteenth century, legal theory held to a belief in "Natural Law." While Legal Realism may now seem an ideology lost to time, the terms of its anger illuminate many of the complaints embedded in thirties war films. The Legal Realists had reached the conclusion that "The law had come to be out of touch with reality." Two central concepts at the core of Legal Realist interest concerned property, and, especially triggered in the Depression era, government intervention in the economy, or from the Legal Realist perspective, in property rights. Morton Horowitz explains, "the orthodox idea of property was that it was a pre-political, Lockean natural right not created by law." By this reasoning property transcends human construction or challenge. Such a view supported existing class interests. Classical theories of law were deeply embedded in notions of natural order and often embraced Social Darwinism: Whatever is—class, inequality—existed as a result of the fittest having risen to the top. One can see conceptually related logic in classic economics in Adam Smith's notion that an "invisible hand" guided the economy, with the consequence that neither government nor the law should interfere, to do so would be unnatural. By the logic of Natural Law any intrusion of the law upon property rights would be a subversion of Nature. Law comes to embody a set of principles resistant to change, especially in the form of any threat of class leveling, with the resulting conceptual offspring of classical economic theory, laissez faire. If one already owned property, having inherited it, one was permanently in a power-superior position when it came to making contracts. Therefore, Progressive economist Robert T. Ely argued, "an increasingly concentrated and unequal distribution of wealth had resulted in the 'coercion of economic forces.' "[28]

The elements of this debate also take shape as concepts in the struggle between Hoover-style Republican opposition to government intervention in the economy and Roosevelt-style use of the government as a variable to intervene. Hoover's reluctance to give financial relief to people at the bottom arose from a faith in laissez-faire economics, a belief that such interference would unbalance natural economic laws. But legal scholar Cass Sunstein makes the point, "We can speak as confidently as we like of natural or God-given rights, but without public protection of private property, people's holdings are inevitably at great risk. . . . legal protection is indispensable to make rights real in the world. Those who complain of 'government [intervention],' arguing that they merely want to fend for themselves, ignore this point at their literal peril."[29] Horowitz suggests that Legal Realism then gains force through an unwillingness to accept what the Depression was making the new status quo. If one had been secure through investment or employment, suddenly one's circumstance, who one was, had been destabilized, a point hard to accept as natural. In political terms, Hoover represented the status quo, and Roosevelt represented the Legal Realist position. Roosevelt's position argued that status built on property holdings itself was a construction, rather than a pre-legal, pre-political condition. Little wonder, Sunstein explains, that "many of the Legal Realists found prominent positions in the Roosevelt administration."[30]

The distrust of World War I leadership, the suspicion that soldiers had been sacrificed for ends other than those claimed when the war began, and the sense that claims made in the name of altruistic motives were carried out in behalf of class and property interests, all show up as argument in World War I films of the decade. After the reformed pacifist of *Ace of Aces* joins the air force, the men of the air squadron introduce him to their commander: a chimpanzee. The undercurrent of bitterness that marks the joke captures a central current of early thirties treatments of the First World War—an assault on the authorities who run the war. In the futuristic *Men Must Fight,* which in 1933 predicts a resumption of World War I, the women of the film associate war authority with male leadership. At one point the central female character, a leader of pacifist demonstrations, threatens that women won't give men any more men, will stop having children so no more men will be born. Near the film's end the grandmother of a young man flying off to war remarks that women should rule the world so there will be an end to warfare. The bitterness toward the promises of politicians emerges when Wilson's words, that World War I had been "the war to end all wars," are repeated at a peace rally. Similar bitterness marks *The Lost Squadron,* in which fighter pilots return from the war to hear a politician promise they will find "everything as you left it. And your services will never be forgotten." Soon a series of newspaper headlines flash across the screen documenting how entirely authorities have forgotten the war veterans. The headlines, covering the descent of the veterans' fortunes over time, read, "Nation Welcomes Soldiers Back," "Congress Disputes Bonus," "Soldiers Clean City Streets," "Service Men in Breadlines." The pilots soon learn one's job has been taken and another's girlfriend is marrying someone else.

World War I had begun with the belief that duty dictated answering the call of national leaders to fight the war. As the war ground on, Philip Gibbs recalled the deep hatred soldiers had acquired through the war experience for civilian authority: "They loathed the old men. . . . They desired the profiteers should die by poison gas." In a war poem, Siegfried Sassoon concludes that the job the soldiers wanted was to

Soldiers running into machine gun fire in the smoke of a World War I battlefield in *All Quiet on the Western Front* (Universal, 1930).

"clear those Junkers out of Parliament."[31] In *All Quiet on the Western Front,* as the soldiers on the front lines are being steadily annihilated, one of them returns to his home village and encounters his father and other village elders who insist the soldiers on the field ought to show more initiative by going on the offensive. Their advice is so ridiculous he aborts his leave and returns to the front where he confides in another veteran that only the men at the front understand "reality." *All Quiet* explores several avenues for exposing the falseness of authority's claim to certitude. Rather than accept existing authority as part of a natural hierarchical state, the film anatomizes how authority works to subvert trust in traditional wisdom. Fussell cites the case of a Captain Neville, who had absorbed and blindly followed the English public school ethic of war as a "sporting" affair. Participating in this ethos, Neville engaged in an odd practice that had made its way onto the battlefield, that of kicking a football toward the enemy while attacking. Captain Neville led a charge on the enemy lines, "as he did so he kicked off a football. . . . That seemed the signal to advance." The episode ended as "Captain Neville was killed instantly."[32] In *All Quiet* the village mailman, Himmelstoss, is made a drill sergeant. Uncritically accepting jingoistic war truisms, he becomes a manic basic-training instructor. When he at last comes to the battlefield, he is at first frozen with fear.

But at the oft-repeated phrase, "push forward," a concept built on the false foundation of "natural" German superiority (the schoolteacher has called them the "iron men of Germany"), he madly charges into battle where, like Neville, he is blown up. Unable to distinguish reality from traditional national wisdom, Himmelstoss exemplifies tragically fallible authority.

After several episodes of *All Quiet* have exposed the vicissitudes of leadership, the men sit down and attempt to redefine the essential nature of their leaders. They criticize the gap between the ferocious war rhetoric and the leaders remaining far behind the lines. They begin to strip authority of its mystique by replacing the aphorisms of war leadership with political motive. This critical strategy matches the Legal Realists' insisting that the law was not some neutral entity existing outside of politics, ideology, or self-interest. As they grope to replace the natural wisdom of the traditional account of authority, they impute un-metaphysical motives to their national leadership. Of the Kaiser one suggests, "Every full grown emperor needs one war to make him famous. Generals too." Anticipating what in a few years will be the Nye Committee's investigation of profiteering by wartime weapons makers, another adds, "And manufacturers, they get rich." Having de-authorized the leadership, one veteran suggests, "They should rope off a field, sell tickets. Take all the kings, and their cabinets, and their generals and put them in the center in their underpants, and let them fight it out with clubs." In their exploration of national leadership, they move from accepting an account of an elevated, politically disinterested, and wise leadership to one which reduces it to politically interested and ludicrous.

Just as acidic is the assault of films on the concept of sacrifice, indemnified as it is by Western civilization's time honored concept that "Sweet and honorable it is to die for one's country." *Lost Squadron* assaults this idea as the opening credits still roll: behind the credits we see a flag with a skeleton holding a scythe. In *Today We Live* (1933), a soldier suggests, "War does in good chaps," implying it leaves behind the bad ones. Echoing Gertrude Stein's remark to Ernest Hemingway that "You are all a lost generation" (meaning those who have survived the war), after the war a woman, Nikki, in *The Last Flight* (1931) tells a veteran pilot who, along with his friends, has been losing himself in drink in Paris, "You're all lost." Of the pilots in *The Last Flight*, a doctor remarks, "they are unfit . . . Their nervous systems are deranged, disorganized." Another man characterizes them as "Spent bullets." Late in the film, Nikki asks a pilot, "Can't you cry, Cary?" and he responds, "Without them [his fellow pilots, who have been dying off or losing

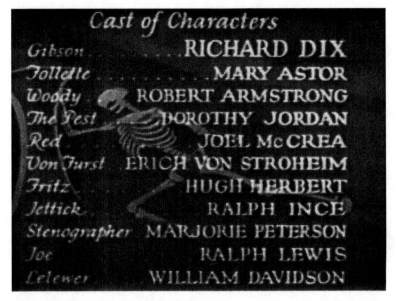

Behind the credits of *The Lost Squadron*, one can see the image of the grim reaper (RKO, 1932).

their sanity after the war] nothing matters. Comradeship was all we had left. And now that's gone too."

In *All Quiet* a schoolteacher at the film's outset seeks to convince his classroom of boys that they should enlist. As did British authorities, he predicts, "I believe it will be a short war with few casualties." But at the war's outset a volunteer had to be at least five feet eight to be accepted. Huge losses reduced that height within just months to five three.[33] The teacher repeats Horace's apothegm: "Dulce et decorum est / Pro patria mori." Late in the film, after a great deal of combat experience at the front lines, one of the soldiers returns to the classroom and directly addresses the class, telling them, with the benefit of his own front-line experience, it is neither sweet nor beautiful to die for one's country. "It is better not to die at all." "What good is it?" he acerbically asks.

On the question of property ownership as a natural condition, early thirties films repeatedly make the Legal Realist point. Filmmakers integrate questions about property into war films as evidence of coercion by established power. Until shortly after the Civil War the core example of property in American law had been land. Trespassing "was the essence of legal interference with property rights." Definitions of

Shells have opened up graves in a cemetery in *All Quiet on the Western Front*. Sitting in a grave, Paul talks to a now-dead soldier (Universal, 1930).

the legal status of property shift in the late nineteenth and early twentieth centuries toward what Supreme Court Justice Noah H. Swayne termed "everything which has exchangeable value." Legal Realists recognized that property represented certain rights protected by law. That property ownership could not be outside the law was demonstrated when the government exercised rights to buy land, even from unwilling sellers, for the public good. Private rights had to be balanced against the public good. Existing power, enabled by holding large amounts of property, might be challenged by a redefinition of property as in the words of Yale law professor Wesley N. Hohfeld, "a bundle of legal relations" rather than as a preexisting natural circumstance outside human law.[34] Filmmakers were also uncovering the way such insights exposed coercive practices. Applying the issue of natural-versus-constructed boundaries to countries, one soldier in *Today We Live* remarks, "Countries are silly things." In *All Quiet* a soldier complains that his wife cannot run a farm back home by herself. But when another asserts he is in a similar situation and says he should just go home, a veteran tells him if he tries to do so, he will be shot. The war circumstance underscores that what one can and cannot do with one's property is a matter of coercion. The bodies of the men themselves become, in effect, national property, to be disposed of as authorities see fit. The implications of this point extend beyond the soldiers. Shortly after a soldier has rhapsodized about girls back home, the young soldiers encounter a group of French girls. The women are willing to host the men overnight. The camera creates a small story that explains this willingness. Access to the encounter is confined by a camera close-up of an American soldier stroking the hand of a young French woman. This seems like the ideal romance he has fantasized. But the camera revises this piece of narration to give us the filmmakers' reality. As the camera space widens, we see the girl. She appears to focus her attention on the American. As the camera pulls back we see she is not looking at him at all. Rather she's ravenously devouring the food he has given her to gain entry. A later close-up, of what would become a stereotypical joke gift in wartime—nylons hanging on a railing—reveals the heart of this male-female relationship. Interpreting it as romance gives way to interpreting it as transaction. The girls have had to redefine themselves as marketable property. Like the young farmer who has had his farm removed from his reach, the girls have been commodified; they sell themselves to survive. The war pushes into the foreground the point that their status as property is subject to coercion by those in power. Property, rather than existing as a pre-political entity, exists as an extension of constructed power.

Efforts to redefine authority, sacrifice, and property as constructions vulnerable to political coercion, rather than as natural verities, persisted well into the mid-thirties. Howard Hawks's 1936 film, *The Road to Glory*, presented French soldiers at the front lines in a manner virtually identical to that of *All Quiet*. In 1938, the bitter antiwar film, *Dawn Patrol* (first filmed in 1930), was remade in response to public demand, as though with a second war becoming imminent the public wanted another look at the reality of the first—before authorities could make their realties change. But within a year representations of World War I were undergoing an enormous shift. To realize the historical intricacies of this shift, one must work out the full implication of what was at stake in Horowitz's conclusion that the Legal Realists had resorted to science in their challenge to Classical Legal theory. This meant de-authorizing presumed verities with scientific facts. The Legal Realists' "realism" is placed in the service of criticism. The account the Legal Realists wind up with is intended to be based on science. But that is not their central aim. Their primary desire is to deauthorize Classical claims to pre-political truth. The Classical claims serve whatever group is in power because they argue for maintenance of the status quo: whatever is, is natural. This explains why Horowitz asserts that Classical Legalism was making a comeback throughout the prosperous twenties. When one's property or circumstances are secure, pressure to change diminishes. (For example, Roosevelt believed he could only achieve the social revolution he embarked upon during a Depression.) The trauma of the period made potential supporters more amenable to social change.[35]

By the end of the twenties, the Legal Realists had begun to lose out to Classical Law. But the advent of the Depression reversed this trend and reinvigorated Legal Realism. Cinematic realism, in portraying the war, persists until world events of the late thirties provoke American leaders and the film community to shift to a strategy of redefining the war in terms of the pre-1914 verities. The problem this presented for them concerned the persuasive power of the World War I films that had already been established throughout the thirties. Like modernists, who had struggled with finding transcendent authorization for their art throughout the early decades of the century, filmmakers would have to discover a strategy for redefining World War I and reconverting the American populace to a resumption of that war's issues. Put another way, if the isolationist argument, including representations of World War I in early thirties films, had created a powerful definition of the war which was stripped of the pre-political verities used to indemnify it in the first place, late thirties filmmakers needed to find a way to re-indemnify the war, to restore the ideological verities that had been used in 1914 to justify it.

Slowly world events of the late thirties made a resumption of the war inevitable. On September 1, 1939, Germany invaded Poland, and two days later Britain and France declared war on Germany. By this time, China and Japan were engaged in full-scale war. But to revise the United States position and resume a war over the issues of World War I, it became necessary to convert the American public to support of the war. This would not prove to be an easy task. Like much of the rest of the country, Roosevelt had begun the thirties, or at least his presidency, as an isolationist, and he publicly resisted becoming an interventionist for as long as he could. In 1932 he had "dismayed internationalists by ... announcing publicly that he opposed American entrance into the League of Nations." And throughout the early thirties many American leaders felt that, given the flaws of Versailles, Hitler's "pleas for 'living space' appeared not unreasonable and his desire to unite all Germans under one flag seemed to some a more faithful application of the principle of self-determination than Wilson had achieved at Versailles."[36] When Roosevelt gave his "Quarantine Speech" in 1937, charging totalitarian governments with "lawlessness," the British wrongly believed the United States would intervene in China. Roosevelt told his emissary, Norman Davis, to instruct the British that "there is such a thing as public opinion in the United States." Referring to the lack of enthusiasm of the populace for intervention in foreign affairs, Roosevelt said of the coolness to his Quarantine speech, "It is a terrible thing to look over your shoulder when you are trying to lead and find no one there." In the election of 1940, both Roosevelt and Willkie bowed to public pressure and took noninterventionist positions on the war. Roosevelt's policy after the election was that the United States would be the "arsenal of democracy" and would do "anything short of war" to aid the democracies of the world. But by the end of that year, he felt compelled to offer "his countrymen a basic primer on American national security," remarking, "if Great Britain goes down . . . the Axis powers will control the continents of Europe, Asia, Africa, Australia . . . and they will be in a position to bring enormous military and naval resources against this hemisphere. . . . all of us, in all the Americas, would be living at the point of a gun."[37]

But films had so effectively contributed to making the "abstract words" cited by Hemingway "obscene," an undoing of the national image of World War I as a profiteering opportunity for the "merchants of death" and a tragic failure of leadership became necessary to convert young men and the nation to a willingness to sacrifice again. At decade's end filmmakers had shifted to enabling a reconversion of the public. The nation would have to be reconvinced of leadership's authority and of the words of Horace which embodied the transcendent values of sacrificing oneself in the interests of one's country. Such a sacrifice included one's self and one's property, or at least the self-interests that led to property accumulation. By the end of the thirties, filmmakers found themselves faced with the problem of finding more than pedestrian meaning in history or of history's being merely a nightmare from which one could not awaken. Modernists had struggled with this problem for decades. And filmmakers would find a modernist solution.

In her study of modernist poetry, Carol Christ argues that "much Victorian and Modernist poetry seeks to discover in history a teleology that gives value and direction to past and present . . . they seek in some way to establish an absolute basis of historical valuation, whether it be a positivist science of history, a mythological structure, or even both. . . . modern poems seek frequently to establish a historical context which they then can absorb into some ahistorical structure." Of Pound, Christ remarks, "Pound develops a positivist theory of history whereby significant facts are sufficient carriers of their own meaning. . . . He calls it the 'Method of Luminous Detail.' Certain facts give one a sudden insight into circumjacent conditions, into their causes, their effects, into sequence, and law." These luminous details result in the artist being able to discover universal "laws"; in other words, they enable the artist to imbue art with transcendent value. The late thirties war films' efforts on this point represent a continuation of a struggle to invest not art but World War I with transcendent meaning that had been destabilized by the critical realist assault. By the late thirties filmmakers portraying World War I, to use Christ's term, wanted to restore an "ahistorical" value to World War I. Writing in 1939, Walter Benjamin summarizes the problem for any art that wants to make a more than secular claim on its audience, "philosophy has made a series of attempts to lay hold of the 'true' experience as opposed to the kind that manifests itself in the standardized denatured life of the civilized masses. . . . What they invoked was . . . most recently, the age of myths."[38] The logic of the late thirties World War I films suggests that the Hollywood establishment perceived the problem of bitterness over national authority and World War I sacrifice, by then deeply ingrained in post–World War I America and fostered by early thirties World War I films, as a problem requiring the sort of transcendent indemnification of history sought by modernist poets.

To address skepticism directed at national leadership, filmmakers of the late thirties sought to introduce a transcendent authority that would authorize national authority. No film did this more effectively than *Sergeant York* (1941), which represented participation in a national reconversion strategy and itself enacted a conversion experience onscreen. Alvin York, who is converted to becoming Sergeant York, must be made to see the error of his ways regarding authority, sacrifice, and the essential meaning of property. Our first sight of York occurs when he and his friend noisily make trouble outside of the community's country church. Inside, the film's first ideological point is being made: church members are loudly singing "When the Roll is Called up Yonder, I'll be There." That the call to duty comes from inside the church begins the process of revising the source of national authority for this film. One of the major voices of authority in the film will be that of the local reverend. No major World War I film of the early thirties had a central character who was a member of the clergy. But both *York* and *The Fighting 69th* (1940) include one. Both films quote from the biblical parable about a shepherd leaving his flock to go after a sheep who has gone astray. This logic works to revise the relationship of characters in early thirties films vis-à-vis authority. Instead of the war being presented as an error in judgment committed by incompetent or corrupt authorities, or Senator Nye's "merchants of death," the error is that of the soldiers or potential soldiers who resist traditional authoritative wisdom. In *York*, *The Fighting 69th*, *The Roaring Twenties* (1939), and *Men Against the Sky* (1940), prospective soldiers, soldiers, or veterans who have ignored the wisdom of authority have to atone for having done so. The soldiers in films of the early thirties who were sinned against by a war brought on by national leadership have now been reconceived as having sinned against authority. The later films offer a lesson to isolationist America and serve the interests of reconverting the populace to a pre–World War I understanding of that war and of its looming resumption. This occurs by presenting the wisdom of authorities as existing on a foundation of pre-political verities. The central allegory from late thirties World War I films to December 7, 1941, is that of the soldier being converted to this position.

Sergeant York works to reauthorize national authority in the debate over World War I by employing a set of carefully chosen "luminous" moments from America's past which are combined with the transcendent authority of the pastor. Alvin York is disinterested in both world events and religion. He needs the guidance of authority to see the light. American history and national mythology become so entwined in *York* that they point to a deeper authority; no accident, it is a conclusion the film sets out to achieve. As the pastor counsels York out on the countryside, the camera moves to a nearby tree, which bears the inscription, "D Boone cilled a Bar on the tree in year 1760." The film then cuts to York and his brother out hunting, tying them to the Boone mythology. When York is cheated in a land deal, he gets his gun and heads out for vengeance. But supernatural intervention prevents York's murdering anyone: lightning starts up and hits his gun, bending the barrel. York strikes out and soon finds a horseshoe (God's given him luck), and passing the church, hears singing from inside. They're singing "That Old Time Religion" (with near hysterical fervor), and York joins in. The "old time" of the religion argues for meaning more teleological than early thirties current events or cinematic representation. York has fulfilled an earlier prophecy of the pastor's that he'll get religion suddenly rather than come to it gradually. We can see that York's fate (to become a World War I soldier) is being guided by higher authority. York is becoming both a participant in and an example of a transcendent national mythology.

Whereas early thirties films portrayed a complaint on the part of front-line soldiers that officers and other authorities (the Kaiser, for example) were far behind the front lines, officers in late thirties World War I films regret they cannot go to the front. The commanding officer expresses this wish in *The Fighting 69th*. Unlike the incompetent Himelstoss of *All Quiet*, a lieutenant of *The Fighting 69th* is described as being hard on the men "for their own good." In *The Fighting 69th* a priest tells Jerry (James Cagney) a cowardly soldier that prayer will help him overcome fear, thereby redefining the earlier films' depictions away from war leadership being the cause of the soldiers' insufferable condition and toward a depiction of a transcendent leader alleviating it. The stupidity of the town fathers in *All Quiet* agitating for the soldiers who are being annihilated at the front to charge forward is replaced by the wisdom of the clergy of *Fighting 69th* and *York.*

Such wisdom is entwined with select moments of American history. And this history, in turn, merges with national mythology, so that the entire process seems to acquire the status of myth. York's Daniel Boone-like shooting in boot camp gets him an offer of promotion to corporal, which he initially turns down on the basis of his religious objections. Two of his superior officers reason with him, drawing from a potpourri of "luminous" historical moments in American history, which they yoke to various biblical scriptures to offer a transcendent counterargument to York's reluctance to fight. The company captain argues that Daniel Boone fought for freedom. In *York,* the unreliable confidant of *All Quiet* is replaced by confidants who can explain a transcendent cause. The captain and a lieutenant send York home to meditate on what is right in fighting for the World War I effort. Quite Jesus-like, Alvin goes up onto a mountain where he fasts and meditates. He takes with him, not the expected Bible, but a book of American history. On the mountain he experiences his conversion to wartime aims, a conversion authorized by United States history and scripture.

On the issue of sacrifice, the end of decade films attack the early thirties representations on almost a point-by-point basis. Gertrude Stein's aphorism that those who survived the war were a "lost generation," repeated in the prologue at the outset of *All Quiet* and again by Nikki in *Last Flight,* is directly revised in *The Fighting 69th.* A priest eulogizes the soldiers killed in World War I, calling them the "Lost Generation," redefining Gertrude Stein's term away from the disillusioned (or the "destroyed" men who escaped the shells of the *All Quiet* prologue) to the once enthusiastic and patriotic soldiers who have died in combat. In *The Lost Squadron, Journey's End, Heroes for Sale,* and *The Last Flight,* soldiers and veterans turn to alcohol or drugs to deal with the war experience. But by the late thirties, the boozing of York and his friends at the film's outset is a moral flaw that has to be eradicated with the help of authorities. In *Men Against the Sky,* the World War I veteran pilot's alcoholism is his own fault, evidence of his lack of appreciation for having been a war hero. Being sacrificed to substance abuse as a result of war trauma is transformed into moral weakness. The recognition of the futility of war on the soldiers' part in *All Quiet,* which leads to their criticisms of authority and the war, becomes pure cowardice when a soldier makes the same complaints in *The Fighting 69th.* The mirage of all the pre-political justifications of the war uttered early in *All Quiet,* then revealed to be false late in the film, are transformed in York. As one officer solemnly characterizes it, "a great responsibility rests on us." By the end of the decade sacrifice in World War I was no longer an example of one's having been carelessly exploited; rather it was redefined as a sacred trust.

The redefinition of property that occurs as part of the rewriting of the First World War points to the ideological scale of the conversion enterprise at work at the end of the thirties. In an essay on the sociology of modern theater, George Lukács tracks the shift from a classical period in drama, which he characterizes as having had a foundation of "mystical religious emotion," to a modern period in which the new man "feels he wants, and is aware of wanting, to come together—and knows he is incapable of it." The new man lives in a time which "lacks a mythology." Lukács demonstrates that the confidant in classical drama exemplified a sealed and certain universe: "all Hamlet's actions and all his motives are rightly regarded and valued by Horatio, in their original sense."[39] But when a Paul, near the end of *All Quiet*, attempts to resort to the classical universe and put his faith in a confidante, the effort collapses. He has abandoned his leave and returned to the front where things are "real." But he has not fully realized how penetrating this truth can be. His confidant, Katz, is the only old veteran left from the young soldier's arrival at the front. He tells Katz that as long as

Ghosts of the soldiers, whose faces are superimposed on a cemetery of the dead soldiers, look back regretfully in *All Quiet on the Western Front* (Universal, 1930).

Katz is alive, nothing bad can happen. Katz is wounded and the young soldier carries him on his shoulders, confiding in Katz that all will be well. But long before the soldier stops talking Katz has died, leaving him confiding in a dead man. Katz's real condition subverts the resort to a confidant as a possible certainty.

In this vein, in the earlier films property is merely subject to partisan coercion by those in power. Late thirties filmmakers are left with the problem of restoring the meaning of property in the classical universe. In the classic universe conversion and sacrifice are rewarded. In *The Roaring Twenties* (1939), a World War I veteran who has turned to gangsterism after the war has to atone for his cynicism (the same cynicism expressed by soldiers in the earlier films) by giving his life to save that of a veteran who stayed inside the law. The latter veteran prospers. In *York*, when York returns from the war, having totally giving himself over to authority, the state of Tennessee, as a kind of deus ex machina, intervenes and gives him his long-coveted farm, making property part of the spiritualized universe in which his conversion took place. As the United States confronts its own impending role in a resumption of the "European war," Hollywood has helpfully restored the classic universe of certain verities.

But Jerry's ghost, his face superimposed beside a war monument, having changed his ways smartly salutes the priest (Pat O'Brien) at the end of *The Fighting 69th* (Warner, 1940).

Such a restoration becomes a central image in the reconversion films. In the closing seconds of *The Fighting 69th*, Jerry, the once rebellious and complaining soldier who has redeemed himself by sacrificing his life in the war effort, now returns as a ghost. He is part of a parade, which is accompanied by rousing music. As a ghost, he stops and offers a smart salute, not to the expected superior officer, but to the priest. World War I has been returned to the transcendent crusade it had been promised it would be back just before August 1914.

3

Racial Constructions of the Thirties

COLONIAL FILMS AND
INTERNATIONAL RACIAL DYNAMICS

IN THE MID-1930S IN THE SYMBOLIC BIRTHPLACE OF THE GREAT Depression, New York City (the place where the Market had crashed in 1929), Mayor Fiorello La Guardia was pressuring Robert Moses, architect supreme of the city, to build playgrounds for black children, who were among the most impoverished in a city devastated by economic trauma. In Riverside Park, Moses had built dozens of playgrounds for use by white children, but he initially refused doing any for blacks. Finally, under pressure from La Guardia, on the Harlem side of Riverside Park he put one up, but "into the ornamental iron trellis outside its public rest rooms" Moses ordered his laborers to "fashion iron sculptures of monkeys," thereby embedding in the project a small monument to the racial dynamics of the period.[1]

Such dynamics can also be found embedded in the films of the period, which, when viewed as a body of work, expose the contradictions in ethics, the containment strategies, and the occasional surprise history lesson which characterized thinking in traumatized America during the Depression. From the outset of the American enterprise race practices had contradicted the ideals of the nation's architects. More than a century and a half after the nation's inception this persisting contradiction took strange forms in national culture. In a November 2, 1936, *Time* review of the film, *Charge of the Light Brigade,* a loose cinematic adaptation of the Tennyson poem heroizing colonialism, the reviewer commented on the "mystery" of the American film industry waving "the British flag so much more effectively than its own."[2] At the bottom of this mystery one finds an issue the reviewer never mentioned: race. Some films celebrated colonialism and some did not. Whether they did or did not is almost wholly determined by their racial dynamics. *The Last of the Mohicans, Drums along the Mohawk,* and *The Howards of Virginia* all deal with colonialist history and all treat colonialists as villains. *Charge of the Light Brigade, Gunga Din,*

66

The Last Outpost, Sanders of the River, Another Dawn, The Golden Dawn, Stanley and Livingstone, Shanghai Gesture, Trader Horn, The Sun Never Sets, and *Under Two Flags* all also present colonialists, but favorably. The first group of films treat colonialists as oppressors of colonized Americans. The second group treat colonizing a native people, when they are people of color, as necessary. In America of the thirties, popular taste for heroes and villains was color coded. That the United States had once been a colony was only a bad thing in a relative sense.

In the area of race, the Depression had both domestic and global consequences, intensifying hostilities already present. In the American South, the "Great Depression intensified racial animosity by heightening competition for a share of the dwindling economic pie." The number of lynchings each year of African Americans had been falling going into the Depression, but in 1930, they began to climb.[3] Globally, the British Empire was feeling pressure from the Depression, and its iron hold on its colonial possessions began to loosen. For the British, the thirties became "the age of appeasement." In colonial India, Indian activists began to talk back to the British. Gandhi organized resistance to the British Raj. Winston Churchill remarked, "It is alarming and also nauseating . . . to see Mr. Gandhi, a seditious Middle Temple lawyer . . . striding half-naked up the steps of the Viceregal palace, while he is still organizing . . . a defiant campaign of civil disobedience, to parlay on equal terms with the representative of the King."[4] Elsewhere, about to invade Ethiopia, the Italians first seized Libya, where the "Sanuisiyya Muslim Brotherhood of the eastern Libyan desert . . . organized a brilliant guerilla campaign which fought the Italian invaders until 1931." In the process of ending resistance the Italians imprisoned "hundreds of thousands of civilians in concentration camps.[5] Then in 1935, Italy invaded Ethiopia. Ethiopia, a member of the League of Nations, and its emperor, Haile Selassie, "expected the other member states to protect his country from Italian aggression." They did not, and the country fell.

In exile Selassie addressed the General Assembly of the League of Nations. He argued, " 'International morality' was at stake."[6] But neither of the major powers of the League—the British or the French—would intervene. In the United States, once a colony itself, the complicated response to the Ethiopian experience contains the same contradiction one finds in the New York City trellises. *Time*'s coverage of the Italian invasion of Ethiopia, motivated as Mussolini was by the intention to colonize Ethiopia, offers insight into the conflicted values audiences brought to colonial films of the period, what were acceptable language and behavior racially in the public sphere. On the

"Ungo-uc-tiyaki SARÁKA"

Says gay ULI-ALI *of* TIMBUCTOO
(Meaning "*No-No-Me no need* SARÁKA")

But . . . Millions of civilized people do need SARÁKA and hundreds of thousands use this NEW DISCOVERY upon Doctors' advice for thorough and safe relief from habitual

CONSTIPATION

Uli Ali's active outdoor life and the natural fresh foods she eats precludes her suffering from constipation. But for you highly civilized people, whose sedentary lives and refined foods make you the victim of habitual constipation, there is good news for you in this new discovery.

Developed from the sap of a tropical tree—tested and perfected for many years by a famous laboratory—Saráka* was first introduced through the medical profession.

Samples of Saráka were sent to doctors all over the United States. Tests were made by tens of thousands of physicians. They, having satisfied themselves as to its merits, began recommending Saráka to their patients.

Today, people all over the country use it, at doctors' advice, for relief from habitual constipation.

Saráka is now on sale in most drug stores in large and medium size and in the 10¢ trial-size. If your doctor has not given you a trial package, get one from your

Costs 10¢ to Try

druggist or mail the coupon below. See what a safe and pleasant way Saráka is to gain relief from habitual constipation.

*Trade Mark Reg. U. S. Pat. Off.

Copyright 1934
Schering Corporation

SCHERING CORPORATION
Dept. T-7, Bloomfield, N. J.

I'd like to try Saráka. Enclosed is 10¢ to cover postage and mailing of trial package.

Name_____

Address_____

City_____ State_____

Advertisement (*Time*, July 30, 1934).

one hand, *Time* made Selassie man of the year in 1935, remarking in admiring language, "In 1935 there was just one man who rose out of murky obscurity and carried his country with him and up into brilliant focus before a pop-eyed world." Yet soon the *Time* writer slipped into period-centered characterizations of Ethiopia as a primitive country: "In the wake of the world's grandiose Depression, with millions of white men uncertain as to the benefits of civilization, 1935 produced a peculiar Spirit of the Year in which it was felt to be a crying shame that the Machine Age seemed about to intrude upon Africa's last free, unscathed and simple people. They were *ipso facto* Noble Savages."[7]

Beyond simple cultural insensitivity, in an article published a few issues later, *Time* covered Selassie's European exile with the racially insulting title, apparently intended to be witty, "Jig Up?"[8] During the era, *Time* also makes an odd use of the word, "blackamoor," which is a synonym for Moor, but also means "devil," using it as a kind of unpleasant aphorism for "rascal," as in a 1936 issue that covers the burning deaths of a group of black convicts in the back of a prison truck in Alabama.[9] In that article (cavalierly titled "Blacks Aflame") the writer refers to the convicts, in carefully chosen quotation marks, as "bad niggers," interspersing that term with "blackamoors."[10] The term "bad nigger" was meant in the African American community at the time to signify one's being dangerous. But the *Time* writer uses it mockingly, suggesting the men think they are "bad," but they are really simpletons. The writer describes the prison guard who unlocks the back of the truck to free the men, who happen to be burning alive, as saying, "Jump out you fools! Jump!" Thus the oddly lightheartedly titled article revises the men's identity from dangerous to foolish. Adding a layer of absurdity to the race history of the period, in the same year, *Time* covered a contemporary play, *George White's Scandals*, which featured Selassie as a character. Conflating minstrel stereotypes with Selassie's character, when the Italians invade the play's Selassie cries, "Boys, our country am menaced. What is we gwine do?" The play's Ethiopians settle on a bizarre choice: "His Majesty and guardsmen execute a hilarious tap dance." The play's audience responds with "applause which almost stops the show."[11]

Thirties audiences approached colonial films with a shared racial history. Shared racial assumptions meant the mythology of colonialism could be presented to Americans, the descendants of colonized people, but also the descendants of colonizing nations, without hesitation. As an example, *Sanders of the River* (1935), about British rule in Africa, begins with words on the screen which inform its audience of "Tens of millions of natives . . . governed and protected by a handful of white men." In the film's trailer, Sanders, the colonial commissioner, is located in a setting where "one white man ruled millions of savages." *Another Dawn* (1937), also about the British in Africa, opens with a written introduction, which refers to the colonial outpost in North Africa as "a long way from Tipperary" where "a handful of the king's best preserve peace amongst the warring natives" at "the cost of much British blood spilled in the sand." In the filmed operetta, *Golden Dawn* (1930), set in East Africa, the written prologue to the film characterizes the British and Germans who have waged war for colonial Africa as "victors and vanquished held together to keep the natives in peaceful subjection." The film then contributes to a longtime colonial construction of white presence in foreign countries as a matter of duty, taking up Kipling's "white man's burden," to lesser people. Without the colonizers the savages would virtually annihilate one another.

On this point, the films cohere with the history of the European colonial experience. Examination reveals how thoroughly colonizers created identities for themselves and for those they dominated. In colonial India, the British regularly described themselves or their actions with such terms as "godly," "virtuous," "industrious," "pluck," "dashing," "devil-may-care," "sporting," "fair play," steady," "cool-headed," "presence," "gentlemen," "noble spirit," "derring-do," "gallantry," "self-sacrifice."

Conversely, Indians were "naturally submissive," "savage," "childlike," "obsequious, " "swindlers," "dissemblers," "feeble and unwarlike," "unconcerned as to who ruled them," "barbarous," "too indolent to be enlightened," "uppish."[12] One can easily infer how power relations contributed to the logic behind these identity creations. They also differ hugely from the definitions those governed applied to themselves and to those who governed them. Yet the claims often survive unchallenged in movies of the thirties, a popular reification of centuries of historically created racial views. At times, the film industry even willfully resists counterdefinitions of racial identity, as when John Colton's 1926 play, *Shanghai Gesture,* is completely bleached of its bitter racial critique for the 1941 film version.

Often films of the period present colonized peoples as either savages or lackeys, with the latter category given ethical preference. As the thirties undergo political shifts, films shift as well. In the early thirties, they show more of the racial confidence that had characterized colonial and general Euro-American experience of times past; as the Depression wore on and Europe experienced threatening changes, the colonial films undergo a transformation: they evince an us-against-them structure (which also happens in films depicting Native America), with the colonialists often battling uneven odds against savage locals. Made early in the decade, 1930, *Trader Horn* demonstrates how white expertise results in white dominance in Africa. *Trader Horn* works as a thirties film primer for the white experience in Africa, with white expertise as central to the colonial enterprise. One justifies one's presence in another's country by claiming one is needed. In India, British accounts of their role are rife with claims that they brought law and government to the Indians; they saved the Indians at the bottom from the mismanagement of those at the top. Horn (Harry Carey), the white trader of the title, is a Stanley type who has explored much of Africa. He remarks he was the "first white man to set eyes on the river." The voice of white experience in Africa, Horn has a young trader with him who is in Africa for the first time. Horn guides both his young protégé and the film's audience through Africa. In a paternal manner, he explains cannibalism and aborigine life. Horn's relationships with the native Africans offer a paradigm for black-white relationships. The central black-white relationship in the film is that of Horn and his foreman, Wanchero, who is a "good" native. We soon see why. Horn describes him as "half bulldog and half watchful mother." Horn is Wanchero's whole universe. Wanchero faithfully protects Horn and obsequiously waits on him, seeming to have no independent desires of his own; at one point he pulls a sliver out of Horn's toe.

Harvard Sitkoff suggests the eugenics movement of the first three decades of the century, which was about to be put to tragic use in Nazi Germany, had a symbiotic relationship with Jim Crow racism, a point that manifests itself in the second half of *Trader Horn*.[13] When Horn and his protégé encounter a white missionary woman, she informs them she is searching for her long-lost daughter. Soon the missionary turns up dead and Horn vows to finish her search for her. It appears *Trader Horn* will turn into a rescue film, with the white men saving the white girl from brutality. Instead the film makes the move Tarzan films make: in black Africa race tells. When found, the white girl turns out to be ruling the blacks. Even without the benefit of an explorer's expertise this film tells us, racial hierarchy will prevail. When the girl intervenes with the tribe on behalf of Horn and the protégé, the tribe turns on her, and we get a primal colonial moment. As the tribe pursues the whites, Horn stays behind to hold them off and save the others. Wanchero will not leave his beloved master, and of course he sacrifices himself so that Horn can survive. He is therefore the perfect colonial subject, a forerunner to the Arab woman, Cigarette (Claudette Colbert), in *Under Two Flags* (1936), who gives herself up to save a group of French Foreign Legion soldiers (though she has been romantically spurned in favor of an Englishwoman by one of them), and of the film version of "*Gunga Din,*" the quintessential native sacrificer, who would appear in 1939.

The trajectory of representation of colonialism in the thirties generally follows global developments. Early representations of the colonial establishment do not exhibit the underlying anxiety resulting from threats to established order that characterize a spate of late thirties colonial films. Those of the mid-thirties begin to display nostalgia or defensiveness over European colonial experience that give way in the late thirties to plots about bands of colonial soldiers encircled and threatened with annihilation. *Morocco* (1930) hardly confronts the colonial establishment as an entity governing people foreign to those in power. Power simply is. Money and the military are not presented as threatened. Rather people find their way around these things to acquire a measure of freedom. The French Foreign Legion is present in Morocco because of French imperial aims on North Africa, but one would have to know regional history coming into the film to see the politics of the struggle. Local resistance to the Legion exists as a secondary plot device in the attraction between Mademoiselle Amy (Marlene Dietrich) and Tom Brown (Gary Cooper). Two things preoccupy Josef Von Sternberg in this movie: the moral freedoms possible in locales far from European centers, and the democratic possibilities at the social bottom. Amy shows inclinations to break from societal restrictions throughout the film. In her cabaret act, she roams around the audience and kisses a young woman flush on the mouth. One might infer she is world-weary in the sense of a Hemingway character who has seen too much of "civilized" behavior in the World War I and postwar period, but the film's tensions do not involve the system's possible demise. The old established powers remain entrenched. Amy is kept, up to a point, by a wealthy European, but at the film's end she follows the democratic example of the native and poor European women and tosses her shoes off to follow Brown and his regiment. Coming at the end of the prosperous twenties, *Morocco* offers its mass audience a reassuring gesture of one choosing love over money. The film does not express an anxiety over the colonial establishment that will mark later films because after the Allied victory in World War I and the ensuing prosperity of the twenties; the Depression hadn't yet threatened the old order.

Nor does *Morocco* demonize people of color, especially those who would rule in the place of the colonizers, as do mid-to-late thirties films. Whereas the 1936 film *The General Died at Dawn* presents Americans in civil-war-torn China as carriers of democracy, increasingly mid-thirties representations of colonialism contrive to defend the need for white rule over people of color. As these films materialized, events in India were suggesting the instability of the old colonial makeup. From the early thirties, India had been agitating for more self-rule. Early in the decade, the Indian National Congress "voted by a virtually unanimous majority [to] dissolve immoral ties which bind them to the British system."[14] In England, concern grew over the possibility of losing India. Lord Rothermere, proprietor of *The Daily Mail,* "dictated a series of explosive editorials under the general title 'If We Lose India—!' " Winston Churchill claimed "England, apart from her Empire in India, ceases for ever to be a Great Power."[15] By 1937, Hitler advised Britain's Foreign Secretary, Lord Halifax, how to deal with Indian revolt: "Shoot Gandhi, and if that does not suffice to reduce them to submission, shoot a dozen leading members of Congress; and if that does not suffice, shoot 200 and so on until order is established."[16]

Clive of India (1934) demonstrates the need for colonial administration of Indians. Historically speaking, the Robert Clive who conquered and administered India for the British wrote from India to London in 1764, "I can assert with some degree of confidence that this rich and flourishing kingdom may be totally subdued by so small a force as two thousand Europeans . . . [The Indians are] indolent, luxurious, ignorant, and cowardly beyond all conception." Of Clive, Niall Ferguson remarks, "The impulse of a man like Clive was simply to plunder—and plunder he did, though he later insisted that he had been 'astonished at his own moderation.' A man so violent in his disposition that in the absence of foes he thought at once of self-destruction, Clive was the forerunner of Kipling's dissolute empire-builders in his story, 'The Man Who Would Be King.' "[17] At least twice Clive did attempt suicide, ultimately successfully. In the film, on his second venture into India, words on the screen tell us just why colonial rule matters: "A madman sits on the throne of Northern India." The reference is to Siraj-ud Daula, Nabob of Northern India. We get a demonstration of Siraj sadistically whipping a woman, and soon we see his order to confine English, Dutch, and Portuguese prisoners in a tiny room (afterwards called the Black Hole of Calcutta), with the intent to suffocate them. Of the incident, Lawrence James explains, "For the British, 'the Black Hole of Calcutta' was an atrocity which demanded vengeance. . . . [Yet] Siraj may not have been directly responsible, and one Indian writer has blamed the incident on Eastern 'negligence, indifference, and inefficiency.' "[18] Nevertheless the film's treatment of Indian torturers justifies the need for civilized Anglo intervention.

A year later, *Sanders of the River* appeared, its plot constructed out of values embedded in the culture. As the Depression stretched British resources and taxed their ability to silence challenges to the colonial establishment, films of the mid-thirties become more assertively apologies for the necessity of colonialism. Such apologies represented nostalgia for an order being shaken by both the Depression and fascism in Europe. At the bottom of *Sanders* lies the claim for white rule over black Africa. Historically, colonial management within the British establishment took two racially determined forms. In one category, "there was the tradition of self-government which had been evolved in the colonies of white settlement (Canada, Australia, New Zealand, etc.). Fundamental to this tradition was the belief that each colony was a separate unit which ran its own affairs with minimal supervision from the centre." The second tradition was characterized by "autocratic government which had developed in British India and in a number of colonies in the tropics since the 1790s." The second tradition was racially determined: "In such places neither British laws nor representative forms of government had been thought suitable because the inhabitants were for the most part neither British nor European."[19]

Sanders means to create its plot sympathies out of the dynamics of colonial values. After announcing in writing its claim that the natives are "protected" by the colonialists, the camera cuts to a close-up on a spinning globe, which stops at Nigeria and reveals Commissioner Sanders's domain. We first spot Sanders consoling a homesick white civil servant, reminding the man of his duty to his "black children." Soon Sanders is rehabilitating the unpleasantly named Bosambo (Paul Robeson), who has been convicted of habitual petty larceny. Bosambo aspires to be chief of his people, and Sanders tells him to be chief he must serve the British king. Bosambo bows down before the whites, and he is given the medallion authorizing his position. Typical of colonial claims, the film stresses Sanders taking an antislavery position and helping Bosambo eliminate it in his region. Words on the screen tell us that for five years the natives "enjoyed primitive paradise under Sanders' " rule. When Sanders resigns to get married his replacement immediately mucks things up. He and Bosambo wind up prisoners of a new chief. War and theft thrive. Sanders returns to restore order, doing so in a manner historically consistent with the colonial experience. He appears with a Maxim machine gun and opens fire on the spear-wielding natives. He restores Bosambo to his role as chief, and Bosambo responds he has learned Sanders's secret to good governance. But Sanders corrects him to say it is a "British secret."

By the late thirties, as war in Europe became increasingly certain and traditional world order was thrown into question, colonial anxieties heightened. Three films, *Stanley and Livingstone, The Sun Never Sets,* and *Gunga Din,* exemplify this point, none more than *Gunga Din* (1939). Set in India, this film presents the same problem that *Amos and Andy* would later present as a television series in the Unitd States. The dominant representations of the Indians in *Gunga Din* contain no positive role models; Indians are either subservient (Gunga Din) or members of the *thagi* strangulation cult.[20] Their religious rituals and strangulation practices justify British presence in India. Indian politicians, who by the thirties were agitating for independence, are not represented. Without them, the *thagi* serve as straw men for the pro-colonial argument: If these people represented Indian India, then some sort of power enforcing order was necessary.

Though *Gunga Din* foregrounds both a secret Indian society and strangulation cult, the *thagi,* and the faithful Gunga Din; the latter, until the film's end intended to be a comic Indian Stepin Fetchit sort; we do get glimpses of the Indian soldiers who served the British. But they appear only briefly and function primarily as targets whom the *thagi* can kill off without removing any of the white principles. *Gunga Din* opens with written words informing us that the portions of the picture dealing with worship of the goddess, Kali, those featuring the *thagi,* rest on historic facts. The film declares its special status as entertainment and education, with the consequence that the historical portions indemnify sympathy for colonial order.

Gunga Din carefully communicates its politics. Our primary view of Indian ideology occurs in the form of the strangulation cult. Early in the film an Indian member of the cult cuts British telegraph wires. Soon an Indian implores British soldiers to protect him, only to betray them by signaling to others who murder them in their sleep. When Sergeant Archibald Cutter (Cary Grant, with a joke about his real name, Archibald Leach), sneaks off to steal gold from a temple, he stumbles upon a *thagi* cult meeting. The film collapses differing historical time periods in scenes of the cult rituals by putting some of Ghandi's anticolonial ideology into the mouths of the cult's leader (of this scene in the film, Lawrence James points out of the *thagi* "fanatics, one . . . in his simple dhoti bears more than a passing resemblance to Ghandi"), which conflates Ghandi's ideology with that of the *thagi,* or of presenting to a mass American audience, who would know little of India, a vision of Ghandiesque revolution mixed with sadistic ritual.[21] The cult's high priest tells his zombie followers, "We have been kicked, spat upon, and driven to the hills like wild things." The high priest reveals his plan to ambush the British and, after offering a history lesson in Indian civilization, sarcastically asks Cutter and other British soldiers, "Who is this ugly little savage to snarl so boldly at the British lion?" He adds, "fine generals, friends are not made of jeweled swords and moustache wax." To this Cutter responds, "You're mad." But much of the exchange, including Sergeant MacChesney's (Victor McLaglen) calling the High Priest an "ape," encompasses the debate and ideology occurring inside of British India in the thirties.

   The film's only Indian alternative to the *thagi* is Gunga Din, a water carrier for the British army. Early in the film, Din approaches MacChesney with a request that he be made a soldier. MacChesney responds, "Don't make me laugh." Cutter, however, amuses himself by putting Din through an army drill, laughing at Din's efforts to ape the soldiers. To impress Cutter, Din plays the bugle, but in an amateurish fashion. Late in the film when the British army marches to rescue Cutter and two other soldiers, Din climbs atop a building and plays his bugle, warning the army of an impending ambush. He dies in the effort. After the British army routs the *thagi*, Kipling writes his "Gunga Din" poem and stands beside a colonel as he reads it at Din's grave. Like Cigarette of *Under Two Flags*, Din is rewarded posthumously by being appointed a corporal. He has done the right thing by dying for the colonialists. The film ends with the company's colonel reading from the poem. Din's emotional funeral serves to close off challenges to racial dominance raised by the High Priest, buried though they were in scenes of Indian torture and strangulation practices.

   Gunga Din exists as the paradigm thirties representation of British soldiers being outnumbered and surrounded by superior numbers, and in this respect contributes to a colonial mythology that sprang from the small number of British who governed the gigantic Indian population. The three principal soldiers of the film are trapped in a tower room by hundreds of screaming *thagi*. The *thagi* intend to ambush the main body of the British as they come to rescue the trapped soldiers. If the British go, the way of life they represent goes with them. This point makes more sense if one compares *Gunga Din* to a slightly later film and one that seems far removed from colonial concerns. In 1940, Alfred Hitchcock's *Foreign Correspondent* was released. *Foreign Correspondent* presents free Europe represented by Great Britain as in danger of eclipse by external attack. After the central character, a reporter (Joel McCrea), uncovers a plot that is part of a larger war effort against the British, he delivers an address into a radio microphone that is meant for Americans. He pleads, "It's death coming to London. . . . It's too late to do anything here now except stand in the dark . . . but there are still lights on in America. . . . Keep those lights burning, cover them with steel, ring them with guns." The lines represent Hitchcock's plea for the United States to enter the war on the British side. *Gunga Din* participates in the same nervousness that was by then permeating the globe. It suggests what is at stake in the empire. If the empire is lost, it will not just be a European matter; elsewhere the globe will be overrun by savages and mental deficients.

   The Sun Never Sets (1939) presents an anticolonialist millionaire who broadcasts criticisms of the Empire from his own secret radio station. For doing so, the film deems him mad. In *Gunga Din* such criticisms are discredited by being put in the mouth of the sadistic priest. *Stanley and Livingstone* offers as justification for European presence in Africa what Conrad's colonialists in *Heart of Darkness* termed the "redeeming idea," the concept that was "behind it all." Without the redeeming idea colonialists are merely plunderers, savagely looting native peoples. The Christian idea of bringing civilization to the natives, "light to dark places," runs through *Stanley and Livingstone.* Stanley (Spencer Tracy) serves as a surrogate for the mass audience of the film. Initially he appears as a crass American interested in going to Africa to get a story for the *New York Herald.* He specializes in for-profit yellow journalism, responding to his publisher's remarking that finding Livingstone will be "the greatest story in the history of journalism" with the claim that if Livingstone is dead he will "bring him back in alcohol for Barnum's new museum on fourth street." His remarks set up expectations of sensational entertainment to be found in the form of savage and exotic Africa.

At one point the publisher remarks that Africa is a "dark continent unchanged since the dawn of time." Anxieties about the dangers for whites in Africa are allayed somewhat when Stanley encounters Mr. Kingsley, a white man, and his daughter (whose servants are all blacks). The order we are introduced to is that of white dominance over blacks. Stanley's sidekick (Walter Brennan) Americanizes the racial dynamics of Africa when he repeatedly connects them to those of his days as an Indian fighter in the Dakota Territory. When native Africans menace Stanley's expedition, Brennan tells him, "Don't stand there in the open. This is Injun fighting." Stanley cries out, "If only we could tell them we come in peace."

After Stanley encounters Livingstone, he finds one of the natives of Livingstone's group going through his possessions. He beats the man and knocks him down. Livingstone intervenes, telling Stanley, "You should never strike one of those simple people." This is the beginning of Stanley's conversion to paternalism. He ceases being in Africa as a kind of yellow journalist P. T. Barnum and begins to take seriously his responsibility as one of the bearers of light. He witnesses Livingstone and the natives singing "Onward Christian Soldiers" and the film presents it as a spiritual experience. Though, historically speaking, a British traveler reported that the natives Livingstone tried to convert ridiculed him: " 'the tribe's favorite pastime' was 'imitating Livingstone reading and singing psalms. This would always be accompanied by howls of derisive laughter.' Not a single Makololo was converted."[22]

But Stanley is converted away from crass profiteering in Africa, and the thirties audience is meant to see that this film means more than mere commercial entertainment. It offers an education in the meaning of a white presence in Africa. Livingstone repeatedly spells out white responsibility to civilize the natives. En route out of Africa, Stanley again encounters Miss Kingsley. She tells him he now has the "same look" as Dr. Livingstone. Back in England addressing the British Geographical Society, Stanley's account is doubted. He completes his conversion experience by informing the society, which thought him an American, that he too is of the British Empire, born in England. He is of the colonizing nation. He has gone from being a profit-driven American engaged in crass sensationalist enterprise to being a Christian believer in the civilizing colonial mission and a member of the empire. By this point the audience can see themselves as having come to a higher understanding of the colonial enterprise. Though in reality Stanley became an agent for King Leopold, who practiced genocide in the then-Belgian Congo, in the film he becomes the ideal representative of an appropriate paternalist racial order.[23]

As these films were playing on American screens, a war was being waged in the United States over a politically hot racial issue. The "Great Depression intensified racial animosity by heightening competition for a share of the dwindling economic pie." The number of lynchings increased and, as white workers lost jobs, they began to pressure black workers to force them to vacate their jobs so that whites could take them. "A reign of terror swept through the lower Mississippi Valley" as whites sought to oust blacks from jobs. As the mid-thirties approached, "every civil rights leader" considered anti-lynching the "most persuasive moral issue."[24] Just as FDR was reeling from losing his battle to pack the Supreme Court in 1937, an anti-lynching bill hit the Senate in 1938 and set off a vituperative fight.

Liberal Northern Democrats, who supported anti-lynching legislation, found themselves battling with Southern Democrats and Republicans, the new conservative coalition. Roosevelt carefully supported the bill and "virtually every Southern Senator denounced the President's meddling in the matter." Southerners filibustered and Republicans came to their aid and "voted ten to three against stopping the filibuster." Soon the bill was dead. Allen J. Ellender of Louisiana recounted "in great detail the battle to subjugate Afro-Americans." He remarked, "It was costly: it was bitter, but oh, how sweet the victory." Unintentionally offering a lesson in the global nature of racism, during the debate Theodore Bilbo of Mississippi "unveiled his scheme for the African colonization of American Blacks."[25] The trauma of lynchings, combined with the fight to free the Scottsboro Boys, the battle against the poll tax, and a constellation of fights over unequal treatment of blacks were all played out as Hitler steadily increased his influence in Europe. The similarities of fascist racial views to those of United States racists did not escape American civil rights activists. "The widely pub-

Eleanor Roosevelt at Works Progress Administration African-American nursery in Des Moines, Iowa. June 8, 1936. Franklin D. Roosevelt Library.

licized boast of Mussolini's son that he exulted in the 'magnificent sport' of watching his victims blow up like 'a budding rose unfolding' helped to clinch American support for the hapless Ethiopians and their diminutive emperor, Haile Selassie."[26] Recognizing the hypocrisy of condemning Hitler and Mussolini when African Americans were being lynched in the United States, Harvard Sitkoff remarks, "The constant references to violence against Afro-Americans as a form of Nazi atrocity heightened the sense of shame and guilt the NAACP strived to instill in white America."[27]

Resistance to longtime racist practices suggests white America in the thirties was not a racist monolith. A political coalition of conservatives and Southern Democrats had kept efforts to undo racist policies from succeeding. But a group of white senators from the mid to the late thirties made a genuine effort to pass anti-lynching legislation, which had become the number one goal of the NAACP in the decade. Senators Edward Costigan and Robert Wagner fought throughout the decade for an anti-lynching bill. Eleanor Roosevelt made public displays of opposing segregation, on one occasion at a conference in Alabama refusing to observe segregated seating by moving her chair to a halfway point between the white and black sections. Later she went into the air with black Tuskegee airmen to subvert the racist point that blacks could not fly planes. And Franklin Roosevelt employed thousands of blacks in New Deal projects and appointed William Haste as the first black federal judge. By decade's end the thirties had served as a kind of dress rehearsal for the "second reconstruction" that would take place in the sixties. African Americans had moved from supporting the Booker T. Washington "separate but equal" position to fighting for the integration that would begin to emerge in the early fifties with *Brown v. the Board of Education.* The period's films reflect both a growing awareness of black history and an entrenched establishment resistance to significant change (the strength of which was illustrated politically by the defeat of anti-lynching legislation). Science in the thirties was beginning to argue that behavior assumed to be racial was often conditioned rather than genetic. Thirties history reveals how thoroughly ignored this point was. Ironically, racial constructions of the period, rather than race itself, proved to be the result of economic and political factors, a reality preserved in the decade's films.

Several Paul Robeson roles illustrate the dissenting voice that was struggling to be heard throughout the thirties. His film *The Emperor Jones,* an adaptation of the Eugene O'Neill play, at least made African American hemispheric history available to mass audiences, and offered a counter to prevailing subservient roles. Conversely, the 1934 film, *Imitation of Life,* offered in the form of a corporate model establishment resistance to change in U.S. racial dynamics.

African America:
The Emperor Jones, A History Lesson

Filmed in 1933, O'Neill's play *The Emperor Jones* had been written at the end of the first real era of United States expansionism, one which had begun with Kipling's advice to the Unitd States to "take up the white man's burden" by colonizing Latin American countries. In 1898, Spain ceded Puerto Rico to the United States. The same year American troops occupied Cuba. In 1903 Theodore Roosevelt took Panama and in 1905 established a customs receivership in the Dominican Republic. The United States occupied Nicaragua in 1909 and purchased the Virgin Islands in 1916. In 1915 the United States took Haiti and remained there until 1934.[28] The announced reason for occupying Haiti was the violent overthrow of Guillaume Vilbrun Sam, one of the Haitian presidents cited by Eugene O'Neill as a model for the title character in *The Emperor Jones*.[29] In 1920, the year the Provincetown players put on *The Emperor Jones*, O'Neill's theater group was enacting much the same logic that was being played out in the political theater of western hemispheric relations.

The contiguous relationship between the tragedy of Brutus Jones, Haitian political history, and U.S. racial tensions materializes at the very outset of the play, in lines that do not appear in the film, in the politically charged language of O'Neill's stage directions that read, "The action . . . takes place on an island in the West Indies as yet not self-determined by white U.S. marines. The form of native government is, for the time being, an empire." O'Neill's language is loaded with political irony and pessimism. The fragility of self-rule and native government are conveyed in the phrases, "as yet not self-determined" and "for the time being." Nevertheless, the choice of an island in the West Indies as the setting evokes a hemispheric history of imperialism which began with Columbus's landing and the subsequent initiation of an Indian slave colony.

Audiences seeing the film in 1933 were seeing a particular sort of African-Haitian tragedy which shared a history with both black and white America. Treated by O'Neill with the deterministic logic of naturalism, Jones's tragedy emerges as the collision of centuries of accumulated tragic African American history with the local experience of the black descendants of slaves from the era of Dessalines and Toussaint L'Ouverture.

Brutus Jones, a railroad porter, who has a pained history with Jim Crow practices in the United States, winds up on a Caribbean island that resembles Haiti and becomes emperor there. References in the film to Jones's American experiences suggest the connection between Jones's exploitive behavior on the island and his shaping American past. The racial irony of Jones's experience on the island emerges when he explains to Smithers, the English capitalist entrepreneur, why he struggled to become emperor: He did it neither for the glory nor the people, but for the money, "the long green." He adds, that's "me every time."

Jones tells Smithers there are two kinds of stealing on the island: the little stealing Smithers does and the big stealing Jones does. The film turns to explaining the environment in which Jones absorbed such a philosophy, putting the words in Jones's mouth: "If dey's one thing I learns in ten years on the Pullman ca's listenin' to de white quality talk, it's dat same fact. And when I gets a chance to use it I winds up Emperor in two years." In an historically ironic sense, Jones has learned his business ethics and methods from the very class whose ancestors, socioeconomically speaking, enslaved Jones's ancestors. Jones's profit incentive matches the logic of capitalist investors. Given the terms of the U.S. occupation of Haiti, ironies multiply. Hans Schmidt reports, "Anti-imperialists argued that imperialism profited a privileged minority of American businessmen, while the expenses of conquest and military occupation were borne by all people. . . . James Welden Johnson [and others] charged that the marines invaded Haiti as bill collectors for the National City Bank of New York.[30]

Once there, the marines introduced a form of slavery, a corvée, in which native Haitians were forced to work on the roads (the same work done by chain gangs in the United States during the first three decades of the century). This quasi-slave system, resembling as it did nineteenth-century slavery in the United States and occurring in an area where Columbus had enslaved Tainos to gather gold and where African slaves eventually replaced the Tainos on sugar plantations, further enraged critics of the marine occupation. The intervention in Haiti took place within the context of the larger U.S. claims to a liberal-progressive foreign policy, which had as its declared goal introducing democratic liberalism to technologically "deprived" peoples. But racism complicated the United States approach to Haiti.

Marines shocked the mulatto elite of Haiti by referring to Haitians as "niggers." In 1920, the year *The Emperor Jones* was first produced, an atrocity story published in the *New York Times* provided an evocative connection between Unitd States race history, the race history that was unfolding in Haiti, and the events of O'Neill's theatrical tragedy. The paper reported "how American marines, largely made up of and officered by Southerners, opened fire with machine guns from airplanes upon defenseless Haitian villages, killing men, women, and children in the open market places; how natives were slain for 'sport' by a hoodlum element among the same Southerners."[31] Their remarks virtually repeat those being made by Mussolini's son during the Italian assault on Ethiopia. Ironically, Jones, a product of Jim Crow, practices the methods of his oppressors upon fellow blacks on the island.

At points in the film it becomes apparent Jones has been marked by vestiges of the Southern slave system. In an attempt to intimidate Jones,

Smithers reminds him of race practices in the United States. Smithers tells Jones he's heard it isn't healthy for a black man to kill a white man: "They burns 'em in oil, don't they?" Jones responds, "You mean lynchin'd scare me?" Explaining the societal stake white enforcers of Jim Crow laws had, Neil R. McMillen remarks, "lynching was deemed necessary because Black[s] could not otherwise be trained to subordination."[32] Jones's remarks suggest he has committed crimes. But the film argues his actions and his identity cannot be separated from his racially based experience and his race's history in America. That the flow of what Stephen Greenblatt calls "social energy" was not merely one way (that is into the film) is illustrated by the effect *The Emperor Jones* had in the South.[33] O'Neill recalled that when the company performing *The Emperor Jones* ventured into the "South proper" they were "warned by the Ku Klux Klan jackasses not to venture further." In the thirties it was common for Southern movie theaters to refuse to show films that did not depict blacks in subservient roles.

Judging by the film, O'Neill's interest in Guillaume Vilbrun Sam (in addition to Sam's being a black exploiting blacks) arose out of three apparent factors: Sam's vicious methods for maintaining power, the violence of his overthrow, and the pretext made by the United States of intervening to keep order in Haiti because of the unrest caused by Sam's overthrow. In the words of Hans Schmidt,

> The overthrow of Sam was exceptionally bloody and repugnant to public opinion both within Haiti and in the United States. Sam, in office less than five months, was implicated in the massacre of 167 political prisoners. . . . After the massacre of the prisoners . . . Sam took refuge in the French legation. . . . Enraged mobs violated the legation's [special status] and killed both Sam and Etienne. Sam was dragged from the French legation and publicly dismembered. Portions of his body were then paraded around the streets of Port-au-Prince in a grotesque spectacle accompanied by vindictive cries of the mob.[34]

Sam's overthrow took place in July 1915. While U.S. officials expressed shock at the sadism of the treatment accorded Sam, in the United States the *Boston Guardian* reported that in Marshall, Texas, "Charles Fisher, a Negro youth, was recently badly mutilated by a mob here. . . . the mob sheared off the youth's ears, slit his lips and mutilated him in other ways below the belt." The *Cleveland Gazette* reported in December of 1914 the story of a mob in Shreveport, Louisiana, of "200 white men" who took Watkins Lewis, a black man accused of murdering a white, and bound him to a tree trunk. "Fallen trees and branches were heaped about him. . . . 'I didn't do it' [Lewis] screamed as the flames leaped about him." In 1915, just months before

Sam's overthrow, the *Chicago Defender* connected widespread race
violence at home to expansionist desires abroad:

> The United States is sending missionaries to teach the heathen . . . but here
> in the South the same dastardly crimes are committed. . . Today the busi-
> nessmen are trying their hardest to go into South America, and the Latin
> countries are only going to allow them in under certain conditions. Race
> discrimination and lynchings will be no upholders there. The people there
> brand Americans as lynchers, and it will be hard for the Americans to con-
> vince them otherwise.[35]

Those who showed up for the film in the thirties may have understood
the irony of Jones's personal tragedy relevant to the account in the
Chicago Defender: His not comprehending the historical connection
between the lynchings Smithers uses to intimidate him and the exploitive
tactics he employs to profit from the natives who share his ancestry.

Just as references to lynching are charged with historical meaning,
so the image of the black man on a chain gang being whipped by a white
carries a particular regional history. In the United States in the immediate postbellum period the ex-slaveowners of the South sought to
reassert their former hold over their ex-bondsmen and bondswomen.
By the late thirties, a Georgia Baptist Convention commented on such
strange labor strategies, "there are more Negroes held by these debt
slavers than were actually owned as slaves before the War Between the
States."[36] Jones tells Smithers that his being whipped on the chain gang
provoked his escape. Connecting Jones to the existing Southern chain
gangs deepens the film's sense of the historical scars Jones carries with
him, given the chain gang's ugly connection to black history and slavery in America. At the close of the Civil War, A. Philips, a future warden of a Mississippi penitentiary made an ominous prediction: "Eman-
cipating the Negroes will require a system of penitentiaries."[37] His
connection, rather than addressing the needs or potential of ex-slaves,
focuses on control. Seeking to reassert power over its newly freed
workforce, the dominant class of ex-slaveholders experimented with
several methods of labor control. In addition to the labor gangs of the
immediate postbellum period and the more successful resort to sharecropping, former masters benefited from the convict-lease system,
which gave way to chain gang labor of convicts. The racial nature of
chain gangs made the connection to slavery all the more troublesome.
Vernon Lane Wharton documents this point: "The general method of
handling prisoners in the various jails was to place them in the munic-
ipal chain gang for work on the streets. Even the Negro women were
often included in such groups. In the black-belt towns these chain

gangs quickly assumed a racial character. The feeling that no white man should be included in them caused mayors to remit fines or white citizens to collect funds for their payment."[38]

Edward L. Ayers remarks, "To planters used to managing slaves, the bound labor of convicts must have seemed a welcome opportunity to return to accustomed ways . . . Obviously the roots of such forced labor reached into slavery."[39] Jones's connection to the chain gang, with its image of whipping, echoes the complicated reality of blacks imprisoned in the South in the half century following the Civil War. The irony of Jones's historical blindness is borne home by the image of a local black woman attempting to steal from the emperor near the beginning of the film. The old raggedly dressed woman is discovered by Smithers sneaking around the opulent emperor's palace. Smithers threatens her with his riding whip.

Jones, like many of the actual Haitian emperors, having absorbed European biases, discounted the value of the African-based Vodoun or (Voodoo) religion. Vodoun was for much of Haiti's history a religion of the peasant, a religion that helped the poor cope with their social afflictions. Jones rejects it because he believes native non-Westerness makes them ignorant and heathen. His action recalls the suppression of African religion and customs by Southern plantation owners, who also banned the use of African drums (out of a fear that drums could be used to send messages and thereby facilitate a rebellion).[40] When the marines took Haiti, one of the things they forbade was the use of drums. Referring to the split between the traditional ruling class of Haiti (up to Duvalier), with its emphasis on lighter-colored skin, Harold Courlander writes, "For the elite, Vodoun has often been an embarrassment and a tribulation. They have felt the need to apologize for its existence . . .They have tended to equate it with the darkness of race, without really perceiving that it helps to satisfy essential social needs for which the elite, so often in political power, have never been able to supply more than superficial answers."[41]

The film ends with a rapid succession of visions that take Jones back to his African roots. He is whipped on a chain gang, sees slaves on an auction block in the South, sees Africans in a slave ship, and encounters a witch doctor. Only when he joins the Africans in a religious dance does he die, in other words after he has acknowledged his ancestry. His tragedy results from a cumulative regional past. The entire film has been a trip back into hemispheric history. It insists on the interrelatedness of exploitation, chain gangs, and slavery. By 1933 O'Neill had established himself as a significant literary figure. Tino Balio points out that Hollywood liked to do the occasional "serious" picture; this offered credibility in the form of redeeming social value. *The Emperor*

Jones did not make much money (and the film version was somewhat watered down), but it did illustrate that America was not a racial monolith. Lessons in global history showed up side-by-side with films like *Trader Horn* and *Stanley and Livingstone*. For mainstream film of the period, however, threats to admitting and confronting this history (say in the form of anti-lynching legislation or joining the communist party, as Robeson did) were met with strategies of containment, as in the 1934 film version of Fanny Hurst's novel *Imitation of Life*.

IMITATION OF LIFE:
A Corporate Model for Racial Status

By the socioeconomic lights of the 1934 film *Imitation of Life* something is visually unnatural about African American Delilah (Louise Beavers) standing at the back door of a house, while white "Miss" Bea (Claudette Colbert), a single mother, struggles to bathe her child and get ready for work. The scene's unnaturalness arises not from Delilah standing at the back door, in terms of 1934 racial dynamics the right place, but from a perfectly good black servant being wasted while the white lady has to care for her own child. Of course Bea doesn't see that; she's too distracted. But Delilah recognizes the natural solution to her own problem, finding domestic work where she can bring her own child along. While Bea is upstairs attending her daughter, Jesse, Delilah, though she has known Bea for about two minutes, takes it upon herself to lay out breakfast for Bea and Jesse. Typical of the flattering self-image the film takes of black-white relations, Delilah's conversation concerns only Bea's problems, in spite of Delilah's being homeless, having no job, and having a child of her own.

Had the film explored Delilah's problems in more detail, her circumstance would have revealed the nurturing kindly face at the back door to have been at the least a survival strategy. For the already difficult situation of black workers in the United States during the period was disproportionately worsened by the onset of the Depression. The New York State Department found that during the Depression "a woman worker living at home with her family" had to earn "$1,056 a year, or over $20 a week, in order to achieve a minimum 'adequate living budget.' " This figure assumed income from a spouse. If the woman was alone, she would need to earn $1,193 per year. A close match economically to Delilah, one Mrs. Johnson, an African American "thirty three year old day domestic, earned between $4 and $ 6 a week."[42] Conditions for domestic workers in New York in the 1930s illustrate the hardness of life for such a woman: "a 'slave market' for domestic workers developed in which black women stood on street corners in the Bronx and Brooklyn while white women auctioned for their services." Little wonder that Delilah's negotiating position is difficult to spot.

And Delilah is hired for room-and-board only. Yet in a short time she has a place in the "family." She is quickly known as "Aunt" Delilah, a southern servant's familial role that has migrated north as a consequence of the large post–World War I out-migration of blacks from the South and the effort to contain them. Regarding this oddity—a New York white woman in the 1930s adopting a familial address for an African American woman that had its origins in the apologist arguments of pro-slavery ideologues—Eric Sundquist explains that the landmark Supreme Court decision in the 1883 *Civil Rights Cases* extended "racial dualism." The "reunion of North and South necessitated political and legal separations that turned the 'Negro problem' over to the South . . . using the South to further what were in reality national inclinations. . . . There was throughout the North not only acquiescence among the white population in the 'Southern Way' of solving the race problem but a tendency to imitate it in practice."[43] The South's household economy, with the big house existing as both family residence and economic center, became the locus for blacks to be part of the white family. In the antebellum era, they were slave and family members, first as the patriarch's "children" then as "aunts" and "uncles"; in the Jim Crow era, they were "servant/family members." In the thirties African Americans were aware of the demeaning price one paid for being a member of a white "family. Six anonymous black men wrote the *New York Times* in the mid-1930s, "Negroes like to be addressed by the customary titles of polite and civil society, Mr., Mrs., Miss. [They] dislike being called 'boy,' 'girl,' 'aunty,' 'uncle' . . . A sentimental tale about one's 'old black mammy' will prevent or destroy rapport with a Negro audience."[44] Nevertheless, Harvard Sitkoff writes, "the leading voices of Northern liberalism increasingly voiced indifference to the plight of Blacks, disenchantment with radical reconstruction, and opposition to their former goal of a racially egalitarian nation."[45]

For African Americans in white families Hollywood had constructed an appropriate family identity from early in film industry. The Mammy of *Birth of a Nation* (played in blackface by a white actress) internalizes the emotions of her white family, even as family members ride out in Ku Klux Klan robes to prevent, among other things, the threat of ex-slaves soiling white women by rape. Yet throughout Depression-era America conditions threatened to upset the racial order envisioned in *Birth of a Nation,* the title referring to a vision of a new national order enforced by the Klan. The Depression triggered economic forces that gave birth to the liberal-black alliance that would form the core of the modern civil rights movement. Uniting black causes with other agendas recurs throughout the 1930s, with blacks becoming an identifiable force in the popular front.

In an address at Howard University Franklin Roosevelt had stated "that among American citizens there should be no forgotten men and no forgotten races."[46] Such talk would eventually cause a rift in the Democratic Party and contribute to the House on Un-American Activities Committee, which would connect the black-communist alliances and the New Deal–black alliances of the thirties in order to launch its attack on New Deal social programs. A potential black-union alliance also did not sit well with movie studios, which were anti-union. Hollywood had "rampantly discriminated against African Americans," and the studios used the black list as a weapon against union organizers. Eventually the Conference of Studio Unions "came to see that the illiberalism that sustained Jim Crow was the same one that sustained the blacklist."[47] The message of *Imitation of Life* coheres with a resistance to change confronting African American demands for opportunity in the period. It argues for the go-slow attitude that even Southern liberals had counseled.[48]

Beatrice Pullman's problem in *Imitation of Life* seems impossible, and her eventual solution a fantasy with moral and economic lessons. Widowed with a child, she has about nineteen dollars when she decides to rent a dilapidated store on the boardwalk in New York to go into business selling pancakes. Without consulting Delilah, Bea uses Delilah's secret recipe (and eventually Delilah's face on a billboard) to launch the business — against all odds. Out of money, Bea must talk skilled laborers into trusting her and waiting until she succeeds before she pays them back. She persuades the painter and the man who supplies her fixtures. When she pays her last installment to the fixture man, he offers a capitalist lesson for the Depression era audience, telling her, "It does you good to see someone go right ahead and make a success. . . . You paid nothing down on the store because you agreed to put the improvements in and you got the improvements because you had the store. I guess about the only cash you put out was on my fixtures, and when I came to collect, you talked me out of that!"

For a down-on-its-luck audience it would be hard not to interpret this as both a call for patience and a recipe for success. Until 1933 many American corporations had dealt with the Depression through "welfare capitalism," subsidizing labor to maintain order and retain workers until better times would arrive.[49] This view accorded with the Hoover administration's pleas for the American public to be patient in trusting establishment governmental authorities to achieve prosperity. Neither Bea nor Delilah challenge the system. Rather they work inside the system, and inside the establishment racial order, to better their economic situation.

When Bea takes pity on Elmer Smith, a hungry out-of-work man loitering outside the diner, and gives him some pancakes, he imparts another capitalist secret. For more food he'll give her a million-dollar idea in two words. He tells her that Coca-Cola used to peddle Coke for five cents a glass across a counter. He gives her the two words, "Bottle it," meaning mass produce the pancakes on an assembly line. In this film following the lead of two of America's largest corporations, Coca-Cola and Ford Motors, and by the thirties, the studios themselves, ends economic woes. Later we see boxes of pancake mix roll off the assembly line as proof of success and as an intended "imitation of life," here in the form of a dominant corporate practice.

Anticipating advertising strategies of later corporate assembly line giants, a sign lights up the sky announcing, "32 Million Packages Sold Last Year." The act of advertising, a central presence in this film, occurs more than once. If one takes the force of the Bryant and Dethloff insight that advertising encompasses the twin results of "standardization of American culture and the solidification of consumerism as a major factor in the national economy," then advertising in *Imitation* standardizes both a model for success and a racial hierarchy. Given the use of Delilah's likeness in the ads, it is a force for mass producing her "appropriate" identity, or to use an old term which carries negative connotations, her "place" in the social hierarchy. This latter point applies to the function of the film itself in constructing African American identity. The power of advertising as a cultural force is articulated by David Potter, who concludes that "advertising compares with institutional religion and the school system in the magnitude of its social influence."[50] Arguing for such a role for advertising, Walter Benjamin asserts, "It cannot be overlooked that the assembly line, which plays such a fundamental role in the process of production, is in a sense represented by the filmstrip in the process of consumption."[51] *Imitation,* serves the same function as an assembly line in delivering a mass-produced role for African Americans to its consuming audience. Benjamin adds, "Mechanical reproduction of art changes the reaction of the masses toward art. . . . The progressive reaction is characterized by the direct, intimate fusion of visual and emotional enjoyment with the orientation of the expert."[52] Ford and Hollywood merge in arguing for status quo capitalist paradise.

The precise model for the corporate and racial order was embedded in Hollywood's own thirties relationship to United States corporate practices. Henry Ford had perfected the assembly line.[53] Robert McElvaine writes that "The automobile was so central to the economy, in fact, that most authorities identify Henry Ford's decision to shut down production for six months while he shifted from the Model T to the Model A as the chief cause of the recession of 1927."[54] In his autobiography, Ford described the relationships of men on an assembly line: "Some men do only one or two small operations, others do more. The man who places a part does not fasten it — the part may not be fully in place until several operations later. The man who puts in the bolt does not put on the nut; the man who puts on the nut does not tighten it."[55] The importance of the automobile to the successful United States economy of the 1920s cannot be overestimated. Keith Bryant and Henry Dethloff remark that "The coming of the automobile set forces in motion that helped establish a consumer-goods economy. The car manufacturers introduced new production and marketing methods — the moving assembly line, installment buying, for example — that changed the national economy."[56]

The three ingredients of Bea's success foregrounded in the film come right out of corporate economic history of the period: she buys on time, she advertises, and she uses the assembly line. The Depression-era movie industry had several good reasons for pointing to such factors in creating a carefully conceived multiracial but hierarchical narrative of success. The 1920s had been good to Hollywood. Coming into 1930, the Big Eight studios had a combined profit of over $55 million. By 1931 that figure had dropped to $6.5 million, and in 1932, as the American economy plummeted toward bottom, they "showed net losses totaling $26 million." Thomas Schatz reports, "The industry hit bottom in early 1933, with the five integrated majors — Paramount, MGM, Warners, Fox, and RKO — hit the hardest. Three of the five — Paramount, Fox, and RKO — went into bankruptcy or receivership in early 1933, and in all, the stock value of the five majors fell from nearly a billion dollars in 1930 to under $200 million in 1933."[57] Tino Balio remarks that Universal (the studio that made *Imitation*) by 1933 "had gone into receivership."[58] Buhl and Wagner point out that these losses represented a

> trend that accelerated consolidation and control by Wall Street [a trend] that was already under way from investment in equipment for the new sound films. . . . Movie people soon resumed operations at higher levels, but with a newly burnished corporate style bureaucracy firmly in place, turning Hollywood from a society of semi-mavericks into a complex and carefully structured system designed to turn out and (just as important) to market a more regularized product.[59]

Schatz comments that under such conditions "Harry Warner saw himself in the early 1930s as the Henry Ford of the movie industry, and the studio as a factory that produced consistent, reasonably priced products for a homogenous mass of consumers."[60] Darryl Zanuck thought of working at Twentieth-Century Fox as "life on the assembly line."[61]

Shifting to corporate management strategies and assembly line production helped create a new set of power and social relations inside the studios. Buhl and Wagner reach a conclusion that at first comes as a surprise: they see the studio system of the early 1930s "as less like a ghetto sweatshop of family memory than a plantation in the California sun."[62] If one considers the full force of this characterization, it seems to be a major contradiction in terms. The plantation system has been posited by Eugene Genovese, Elizabeth Fox-Genovese, and Gavin Wright to represent an alternative economic system to industrial capitalism.[63] These two significantly differing economic structures are the dominant economic modes of nineteenth-century America, represented respectively by the South and the North. Significant continuity in labor and racial practices between the postbellum and the antebellum South lingered on for nearly a century after the civil war, maintaining the distinction in economic systems. The Southern system was marked by a dominant planter class; its wheels were oiled by a paternalistic relationship between that dominant class and its labor force. The North was characterized by its degree of industrialization. The studios, although not a Southern economic force, could operate paternalistically in the plantation style toward their labor force due to New Deal legislation, passed in 1933, entitled the National Industrial Recovery Act (NIRA). To save faltering industries, this legalized "certain monopoly practices." In the film industry, "collusion among the Big Eight to control the marketplace now had government sanction."[64] Studio producers then "attempted to impose salary ceilings, a limit to free agency . . . and, worst of all, a dictum that actors' (and writers') agents could not negotiate without being licensed by the producers themselves."[65] In a sense, the studios thus had something resembling the monopoly of the Southern planter class. They at least had the power of their convictions behind the advice the film offers Delilah.

Studio moguls reinforced control of their employees with assembly-line mass production strategies that broke down the division of labor in the studios, thereby limiting employee power by weakening any individual who might challenge the studio heads. This explains the professional decline of once powerful central producers such as Irving Thalberg and Darryl Zanuck. Schatz remarks, "the studios steadily phased out or downgraded the central producer's role, and developed management systems with a clearer hierarchy of authority and greater dispersion of creative control."[66] The studios' corporate strategies carried for studio moguls the added benefit of sending the message that studio employees were to stay in their respective places. The response of studio employees, however, was to fight such monopolistic control with union activity, also licensed by New Deal legislation.[67] Feeling the threat to their power posed by unions created anxiety at the top in studios to the extent that, though the studio had had ties to organized crime prior to the 1930s, "mob ties did not accelerate until the 1930s."[68] Organized crime infiltration of the studio unions was, in part, controlled by the studios through their organized crime connections.[69] African Americans, other than as performers in carefully defined roles, were virtually invisible in the internal studio hierarchy. As late as the 1940s black actors Ossie Davis and Ruby Dee reported of Hollywood, "we didn't see any black people working anywhere."[70]

At the bottom of the economic order going into the Depression, African Americans suffered more than other groups. Already victims of exclusionary hiring practices, black laborers were concentrated in unskilled labor positions. This led to a higher black unemployment rate than that of white workers. In Cleveland, more than half of all African American workers were out of work. One observer remarked, "the race is standing on a precipice of economic disaster."[71] The dire conditions of American workers led to some inclusion of African Americans in unions, notably in the United Mine Workers.[72] But given the twin hysteria capitalist leadership held for unions and communists, coupled with the 1935 Harlem race riot, black advancement repulsed most leaders of industry who wished instead to maintain the racial status quo.[73]

Eugene Genovese explains that Southern paternalism, with its roots in the slave South, made a space for African Americans by including them in the household "family." In thirties film, a servant can be sassy as long as s/he does not seek to overturn the overarching structure of the social establishment. Since *Imitation* contains a strong message for African Americans to stay in place in the socioeconomic hierarchy, the kind of allowance the film makes for subversive sass from the servants (here and in *Gone With the Wind*) fulfills the paternalistic relationships that Sundquist sees as having been carried from the South to the North while America "solved" its race problem. But a psychological danger existed for African American women who played the mammy role so effectively that they internalized the mammy identity: "The tension was inherent in the black situation: a need to role play — to use the stereotypes of the larger society to one's own advantage — and a need to make sure that role was not internalized, that the stereotype did not become real."[74]

The only significant challenge to the racial order of the film comes from Delilah's multiracial daughter, Peola. From an early age Peola learns she can pass for white. The film attempts to close off this threat. Facing a mirror at one point, she cries, "I want to be white, like I look. . . . Look at me. Am I not white? Isn't that a white girl there? . . . what is there for me, anyway?" Within the social dynamics of the Depression era, the film struggles to contain this outburst. Delilah explains that Peola's light-skinned father also protested the system: "He beat his fist against life all his days. Just eat him, through and through" (perhaps as a union agitator). She sees Peola's father's racial railing as pointless, a concept supporting the film's effort to reaffirm 1930s order. When Delilah calls herself Peola's "Mammy," Peola corrects her with the title, "Mother."

Bea recommends that the angry Peola be sent to a good "colored" college in the South, "where she won't have to be faced with the problem of white all the time." But specifying the South suggests containment. Why not take a shot at Barnard, where Zora Neale Hurston had already broken the color line in 1925? Given the quick resort to familial terms such as "Aunt," one suspects Peola's journey South (where Jim Crow codes were invented) to an all-black school might strike Depression-era audiences as an education in racial order. Soon Peola runs away from the "colored" college where Bea and Delilah have sent her.

Delilah dies of a broken heart, and Peola returns. Not in the church during the funeral, she rushes to the coffin, crying, "Can't you forgive me, mother?" I killed my mother!" Her guilt blunts her rebelliousness. At the film's end, Jesse tells Bea that Peola has gone back to college in the South, restoring racial hierarchy. One of the last images of the film is of Delilah's broadly smiling face on the sign that lights up the sky advertising Aunt Delilah's Pancake mix. The corporate world smiles down on a restored racial order, where everyone, now that Peola has behaved, is in her proper place.

4

U.S. Foreign Policy and Shifting Racial Identity

ASIAN AMERICA

Between 1925 and 1941, the cinematic racial identity of Asians underwent significant shifts. The Chinese screen image improved, moving from that of savage or hapless peon to rustic ideal or citizen, while that of the Japanese became ever more negative. These shifts bore the imprint of U.S. interests of the period, which contributed to revising racial presentations on American screens. From 1882 to 1924, laws restricting Chinese entry into the United States had been passed. They remained in force until Franklin Roosevelt began sponsoring a bill to lift restrictions on Chinese immigration; the bill passed in the midst of World War II in 1943. This change in immigration policy did not occur because the United States had undergone an introspective reconsideration of the meaning of Chinese racial attributes. What had changed were U.S. global interests. While in the early thirties hostility to Chinese Americans remained high, events abroad were beginning to shift U.S. foreign policy; this shift would impact Hollywood's willingness to openly portray the Chinese on screen in a negative manner. For precisely the same foreign policy reasons, the Japanese would wind up, by the end of the thirties, portrayed as vicious beasts.

The shift in official U.S. attitudes toward the Chinese began not with the Chinese but with the Japanese in Manchuria in 1931. Having both industrialized and militarized in the late nineteenth and early twentieth centuries, to avoid being humbled by Westerners as the Chinese had been in the Opium Wars (which forced trade agreements favorable to the West on the Chinese), the Japanese sought a colonial empire modeled on that of the British.[1] They believed an Asian colonial empire would make them secure in global relationships. Having obtained extraterritorial railroad rights in Manchuria at Versailles, without Chinese participation, the Japanese in 1931 sought to expand their influence there by provoking an incident which would give them an excuse to seize more territory.[2] Eyeing the riches and power they could derive by colonizing China, as the British had done in India, in 1931 in Manchuria they staged a dispute designed to initiate their takeover of China, along the lines of their earlier takeover of Korea. The United States objected to the acquisition of territory by force. As Japan expanded its influence in China to five northern provinces, the United States feared the Open Door policy would be abandoned, severely hampering American economic interests in the region. During the same period inside of Japan, military assassinations and a military rebellion moved that country into a more warlike stance. By 1936, Japan was withdrawing from United States-British–Japanese negotiations over the size of respective navies in the Pacific. Furthermore, the Japanese had flirted with allying themselves with Germany, and in 1936 signed a pact with the Germans. Early in the decade, the United States resisted giving aid to the Chinese for fear of further antagonizing Japan. But soon, the United States was aiding China and placing embargos on Japan. Thereafter Japan repudiated the Open Door policy and strengthened its ties to Germany. By the late thirties, Roosevelt and his advisers began lumping Japan in with Germany and Italy as a totalitarian threat to the democratic way of life.[3] As World War II broke out, Japanese Americans were interred in camps, while Chinese Americans wore badges and carried identity cards to keep them from being mistaken for the Japanese.[4] China had become an important piece in the Allies' desire to block the Japanese in Asia, and the Japanese had joined Germany and Italy as enemies.

In cinematic terms, one can get a glimpse of this trajectory in an odd and ongoing little conceptual thread that runs through the Charlie Chan movies of the thirties. The Chan films, through the mid-thirties, evince an underlying hysteria over the question of whether Chan, who lives in Hawaii—not yet a state—might actually have aspirations to remain in the United States. Though the Earl Der Biggers Chan novels and the Chan films offer a multidimensional account of the Chan family as assimilating into mainstream American life (with Chan's little exposed wife speaking a very mixed version of Chinese and English, Chan speaking a more accomplished English, and their teenage children, who eventually go to first-rate American universities, speaking almost exactly the jargon one hears from Mickey Rooney in the Andy Hardy films), Hollywood was sufficiently touchy about any suggestion of advocating Asian immigration that it went to great lengths to clarify that it was not advocating it in the Chan films of the early thirties.[5] By the thirties the open door of immigration policy had been closed. Asians had been targeted by exclusion acts. Though the Charlie Chan films present Chan in quite a favorable light, throughout most

Evidence that America was not merely a racist monolith in the thirties. Charlie Chan plays with a racially diverse group of children in *The Black Camel*, though Hollywood persisted in its unwillingness to cast Asian actors to play Asian leads (Fox, 1931).

of the decade the Chan writers make it a point to communicate to their audiences that Chan is a citizen of pre-statehood Hawaii and not the United States. In *Charlie Chan's Secret* (1936), for example, it is a Hawaiian murder case that draws Chan into the investigation and into coming to the United States mainland. The film takes pains to make clear to a U.S. populace opposed to Chinese immigration that Chan is returning to Honolulu. In *Charlie Chan at the Opera* (1936), Chan makes pointed references to his family back in Honolulu. At the film's end, when it appears he will miss his ship back to Honolulu, the police suddenly appear to offer a disproportionately enormous escort, traveling at breakneck speeds to get Chan to the docks, an assurance to American audiences that the authorities only allow Asian visitors so much leeway on United States soil, even if that visitor is a renowned detective. Only when World War II looms and China is on the verge of becoming a United States ally does Chan assertively inform a woman in *Charlie Chan in Rio* (1941) that like her he is a U.S. citizen.[6]

The Mask of Fu Manchu represents a quite different current of thought of the early decade, that of pop racial hysteria, a current that by decades end would be suppressed. Made in 1932, at a time when

Charlie Chan was not welcome to live in the United States, *Fu Manchu* seems to have anticipated the concept of political correctness and done all it could to violate it. Sax Rohmer's 1931 novel upon which the film is based operates as a colonialist's nightmare. Unlike the film, it involves a secret Middle Eastern society of Iranian, Afghani, and Egyptian fanatics (rather than the Chinese of the film) who threaten British colonial order. In the novel, Chinese Fu Manchu is exploiting the Arab society's belief in a ghost prophet who will return to lead them to victory over the colonialists. A Scotland Yard agent and a group of archeologists work to keep the prophet's relics out of the hands of Fu Manchu. The agent tells one of the archeologists, "The peace of the world, Greville, may rest upon your accuracy."[7] While there are clear racial undertones in Rohmer's novel, the logic of the film would satisfy a Ku Klux Klan wizard.

The film builds its plot out of fears of a Chinese assault on the white world and—specifically—on white women. Out to save the world, a group of British archeologists race to China to excavate Genghis Khan's tomb. Fu Manchu seeks relics from the tomb, specifically Khan's sword and death mask, which hold special powers. With them he intends to rule the world. The film admits no irony in the archeologists looting the grave of an indigenous Mongol ruler to keep relics away from the Chinese descendant of one of the Mongol Empire's subjects, the political logic of which is reinforced when we learn that the man behind the archeological expedition, Nayland Smith (Lewis Stone), is a member of the British Secret Service. Rather, the relics come to stand for the empowerment of a meaningful national tradition. To remove any ethical shades of gray from the struggle, the plot makes Fu Manchu's motivations all racist. He mixes his urges for conquest, sexual dominance of white women, and sadistic pleasure in torture.

First seen, Fu Manchu performs an experiment, his face near a mirror that distorts his appearance: in a private moment we can see Fu for the true monster he is; visually, the film argues, he's two-faced. The filmmakers make a point by casting Boris Karloff as Fu Manchu, just after he had made a huge splash playing Frankenstein's monster. Conversely one early scene featuring the archeologists is set against an enormous lighted map, evoking both the magnitude of British colonial power and the history of colonial incursion into foreign land—suggesting both its advertised redeeming idea (civilization) and its will to dominate. The light echoes Conrad's imperialists who "bring light to dark places on the map." Fu drinks the smoking liquid he has been making, one of several suggestions of the degenerate drug use he, his daughter, and his slavish followers rely on. His boast of receiving several doctoral degrees from U.S. universities suggests the danger of for-

THE SAILORS KEPT HER A SECRET . . .

323

Ursula in Tiffany Thayer's mass-market novel, *Thirteen Women*, filmed in a toned-down version in 1932 with Myrna Loy as Ursula. As extravagant in its racism as the *Fu Manchu* film, Thayer's novel equated mixed racial ancestry with sexual decadence. Here the Indonesian Ursula pays for her passage on an ocean liner by servicing the sailors.

eign immigration and reifies the logic of the Exclusion Acts and immigration restriction. Fu's men kidnap one of the archeologists, Barton, and try to persuade him to hand over Khan's relics. Depraved to the bone, Fu offers the archeologist sexual favors from his daughter, Fah Lo See (Myrna Loy), as an inducement.[8] When Barton refuses, he is elaborately tortured by being placed inside a large bell.

Fu captures and tortures Terry, an archeologist, while Fu's daughter exhorts black slaves to whip Terry faster, after which she climbs onto his unconscious body and fondles him. Fu remarks on her sexual appetites as she returns to her opium pipe. Scenes of opium use punctuate the film as part of larger assumptions favoring Western civilization against that of the depraved East. To gain control of Terry, Fu injects him with a mixture derived from scorpions and Fu's own blood, which is meant to render Terry a slave. The stakes of the struggle are racial dominance, illustrated by Nayland's demand of Fu as Fu injects Terry, "In the name of the British government, I demand the release of this boy." Fu responds, "British government! I'll wipe them and the whole accursed white race off the face of the earth!" When Terry, having been injected with Asian blood, returns to Sheila, Bartons daughter, she locks her door against him, suggesting that the drop of Asian blood in his veins can be sensed intuitively by a white woman. Once Fu gets possession of Sheila, she screams, "You hideous yellow monster!" Later he displays her to his stock fanatical followers, crying out to them, "Would you all have mates like this for your wives? Then conquer and breed. Kill the white man and take his women!"

By 1937, with the appearance of the film version of Pearl S. Buck's *The Good Earth*, a shift was occurring in onscreen representations of the Chinese. The appearance of the best-selling novels, *Thirteen Women, Northwest Passage,* and *Drums Along the Mohawk,* were all followed within about a year to a year and a half, and in some cases the same year, by cinematic adaptations. *The Good Earth,* written by an outsider daughter of missionaries who grew up in China, was published, with immediate best-seller status in 1931 (at a time when anti-Chinese sentiment was high and U.S. foreign policy demands were not yet the deciding factor they were about to become), but it was not filmed until 1937, at which point such a work could receive a more favorable reception. Presenting a roseate portrait of its peasant farmer subjects, *The Good Earth* gives its Chinese farmers a kind of Joad family status. While as peasants they are not threatening characters, they are not stereotypical coolies either.[9]

John Coltons 1926 play, *The Shanghai Gesture,* a critique of colonial racism in Shanghai, is so thoroughly whitewashed in the 1941 film version that taken together the two works offer a history lesson in shifting racial dynamics. As Japan invades China it becomes apparent that if a second world war breaks out China will be an ally against Japan, U.S. treatment of the Chinese changes. At the same time, films representing past Western wrongs to the Chinese become unwelcome. No need to rile up anyone of potential strategic value. Colton's acidic critique of colonial racial behavior falls into a category of American works which examine the constructedness of racial identity and which include as a precursor Mark Twain's *Pudd'nhead Wilson* and as a later entry William Faulkner's *Light in August,* both of which are preoccupied with what errors in racial identification reveal about racial suppositions.

The play operates on the memory of the past half century of racism directed at Asians. Throughout the nineteenth century Asians had been discriminated against in the United States by employers, labor unions, and laws which denied them property and rights accorded other immigrants.[10] Newspaper editor John Swinton summarized widespread views regarding Asian immigrants: "Mongolian blood is depraved and debased blood. The Mongolian type of humanity is an inferior type—inferior in organic structure, in vital force or physical energy, and in the constitutional conditions of development." In 1863, a law was passed forbidding Chinese from testifying in court against whites. The 1893 Geary Act prohibited Chinese immigration for ten years. In 1906, California passed an antimiscegenation law barring white and "Mongolian" marriage.

In the United States covering the period from 1870 to the release of the film, one historian notes, San Francisco's Chinatown functioned as a "ghetto prison."[11] In 1876, San Francisco Congressman Pixley argued that "the Chinese have no souls to save and if they have, they are not worth saving."[12] Historian Chalsa M. Loo notes that "Physicians in San Francisco testified that the Chinese had nerve endings farther from the surface of the skin than whites, thereby making them less sensitive to pain—a justification for why Chinese workers could labor under terrible circumstances without complaining." In 1882 the Chinese Exclusion Act was passed, then renewed in 1888 with even more restrictive rules. Chinese were prohibited from immigrating until 1943 (when China became a U.S. ally in World War II); in 1904 the Democratic Party in California had a "no Chinese" plank in its platform. Burned out in other areas of San Francisco, the Chinese were forced into slums in what became known as Chinatown. At one point the San Francisco Board of Supervisors passed a "queue ordinance that permitted officials to cut off a Chinaman's queue to one inch from the scalp." Only the Chinese carried their vegetables and clothes on poles. Soon a Pole Ordinance was passed "which prohibited persons from walking on sidewalks while using poles to carry goods."[13]

The city of Shanghai, described as "Shanghai and Gomorrah" by Omar (a character in the film but not in the play), became what it was through colonial exploitation. The film's opening words on the screen compare Shanghai to the Tower of Babel, conveying to the film's American audience they were about to be treated to non-Western decadence, emphasized visually by race mixing. Though by the late thirties Shanghai had for some years been a city marked by prostitution and illicit trading, history demonstrates that it became so through colonialist interference. By the mid-nineteenth century, the British were correcting an imbalance in their foreign trade by selling opium, received in another colony, India, in China (though initially it was sold under the table). When the Chinese government sought to end the trade, the British used force in the Opium Wars to reopen China to the opium trade.[14] Once the British had militarily achieved dominance in China, they turned Shanghai into a city of sections (recalling the logic of United States Chinatowns). The Chinese were only permitted to enter some European sections where they were servants. Joesph von Sternberg, the director of *The Shanghai Gesture* recalls seeing signs in a European sector which read, "No dogs or Chinese allowed."[15]

Notorious for its immorality, Shanghai, in the 1930s, had more women practicing prostitution in proportion to its population than any other metropolis in the world. The Chinese characters make the name Shanghai mean "above the sea."[16] But the word has come to mean to kidnap, usually to take someone out to sea by force, trickery, or with the "help of liquor or a drug."[17] Stella Dong points out that "It was a form of shanghaiing that created the modern city of Shanghai." The British invaded China in 1842 and forced one of "the harshest ever" treaties on a defeated people. They effectively took control of five Chinese ports, one of which was Shanghai; they shanghaied it. Like the railroads built with Chinese labor in California, Shanghai was a city "Occidentals designed but Oriental sweat and labor built." Though the city was tightly segregated along racist lines, it became common for British officials to take Chinese mistresses. For example, Sir Robert Hart, "the inspector general of the Imperial Maritime customs service, had fathered three children with a Chinese woman when he was stationed in Ningpo and Canton."[18] Perhaps one reason Christian missionaries found Shanghai a hard place to win converts was that Christian claims to morality were so subverted by the behavior of officials representing Christian countries.

In Colton's play a British aristocrat, Sir Guy Charteris, is a colonialist man on the make. He vows to marry the Pink Lady, a Manchu princess (who later becomes Mother God Damn), and borrows money from her to buy advancement in the carefully named China India company. When he has made his fortune, he finds a socially acceptable English wife who will fit into his ambitious plans and abandons Pink Lady. When she refuses to stop trying to see him, he conspires to sell her into prostitution. Before he succeeds, she manages to slip into his house and exchange their racially mixed child for Charteris's child by his English wife (exactly the move that the black Roxy makes in Twain's *Pudd'nhead Wilson*). That he never notices the difference challenges racist assumptions of the period; spotting a child with some Asian ancestry is a state of mind rather than a racial reality. Pink Lady places the English baby in the care of a wharf rat who keeps and abuses the child over the years that Pink Lady travels as a sex slave—until she eventually makes her way up in the Shanghai underworld to the position of madame of a brothel. Years later, she lures Charteris to the brothel in order to avenge herself on him by making him feel the pain she felt by sending his biological daughter into the white slave trade. She places his biological daughter in a cage and, as Charteris witnesses, offers the girl for sale to Chinese bidders. The intended horror of the scene depends on the racial dynamics of Charteris feeling revulsion at seeing not a woman being sold, but a white woman being offered to Asian men, an inversion of Charteris's selling Mother God Damn into prostitution.

When Poppy, the daughter Charteris raised, not knowing she was half Asian (whose name evokes the Opium Wars), shows up at Madame God Damns's brothel she is not looking for her father; she is slumming with a Japanese consort. Poppy tells Mother God Damn, "I don't mind in the least—mixing up—outside my color." The Japanese consort, Oshima, flatters himself that Poppy is a virgin, a condition of his having chosen her. She corrects this misimpression, however, taunting him, in effect, taking back ownership of her virginity as Caddy Compson does in Faulkner's *The Sound and the Fury:* "Had heaps of 'em—heaps of 'em! Ha, ha, ha! And after you—and when you go—they'll be lots more—didn't think you were the first, did you? Ha, ha, ha! Me! I am a nymphomaniac. . . . Never going to get married either . . . Yes, I'm a bad one! That's what I want to be!—Want to live my life like man! All most women get is the same four legs in a bed always—always!—That's marriage! Ugh!—Horrible! Low—I wouldn't stand it—not one minute!"[19]

From a philosophically opposed perspective to that of *Fu Manchu,* Colton's *Shanghai Gesture* addresses much of the racism that characterized the colonial enterprise in China. When Joseph von Sternberg set out to make a filmed version of the play, which would be released in 1941, the MPPDA, under the auspices of Will Hays, offered thirty-seven challenges to the adaptation.[20] In global terms, *Fu Manchu's* demonizing of the Chinese in the early thirties had been acceptable before events in Asia rearranged global strategy. Shifts in U.S. global goals had made *Shanghai Gesture*'s explicit racial exposures and its particular critique of colonial racism unacceptable. By the late thirties, global objectives determined what practices one could and could not put on the screen. Colton's play directly challenged British colonialisms racial dynamics. The finished film, stripped of this challenge, aesthetically and logically a mess, is nevertheless invaluable in offering insights into the underlying racial anxieties that materialized in the thirties.

The oddness of *Shanghai Gesture* results from the confluence of conflicting forces. Because U.S. global aims now included China, the film removes much of the harsh criticism of U.S. ally, Great Britain.[21] What is left is hardly anything. The absences in the film point backward to a history Hollywood felt it could no longer represent. The play's Mother God Damn is softened to the film's Madame Gin Sling (Ona Munson), the mention of alcohol apparently being rough enough for audiences. Absent is the shock of the caged Chinese slave prostitutes which had made the play sensational in the 1920s. Poppy (Gene Tierney) arrives at Mother Gin Sling's notorious establishment, now a gambling casino, no longer with a Japanese escort, but rather accompanied by a twitish Englishman. The film's music repeatedly accompanies any appearance of Mother Gin Sling with an increase in volume meant to signify evil, a meaningless substitute (if one doe not know the play) for the play's racial criticisms and explicit examples of sexual exploitation. The film's visual racial guide tells us the establishment is evil because sexual race mixing is going on; we see Omar, a poet, joined by two women of different races, reversing the play's critique entirely.

Charteris (Walter Huston) heads a company that means to shut down Mother Gin Sling's establishment to develop the land in her area. The film translates the colonialism of the play into a moral force; the depravity of the Chinese will be replaced by the sound banking practices of the British, which, racially speaking, will put an end to the immorality. Mother Gin Sling does plot to bring Charteris to dinner, but, in the film version, primarily to expose his having abandoned her after borrowing her money. Charteris, lecherously pursuing Mother God Damn in the play, in the film has no sexual interest in her and soon clears himself of all wrongdoing. In the film, he has repaid Mother Gin Sling's money, leaving it in a bank in her name. He has left with their daughter (there's only one daughter in the film) because he believed Pink Lady was dead. Thus the film replaces the play's tragic sense of history with a progressive history, one in which the colonialist acted fairly, his one mistake being diluting his blood with the depraved

Asian. His coming to China will rid it of depravity. The girls in cages briefly appear in the film, but Mother Gin Sling assures everyone that it's just a stunt to entertain foreigners. They are not really selling them.

The film represents a desire not to revisit the racist past, though, typically, the refusal to employ a Chinese actress to play a central role in the film represents an instance of the film's averting its eyes from past racist practices while participating in a history of unequal treatment, one which had denied fulfillment of a uniquely American promise to the huddled masses gathering at Ellis Island. Shortly after *The Shanghai Gesture* appeared in film form, *Little Tokyo, So Proudly We Hail, USA,* and *Air Force* were released. These films, all depicting the Japanese during World War II, often revert to characterizations of the Japanese as "slant-eyed," "apes," and "yellow monkeys." World events dictated that what was suppressed in *The Shanghai Gesture* would reemerge in films depicting the Japanese.

THE NEW SAVAGE OF THE LATE THIRTIES

As jobs became scarce in the thirties, people were discouraged from immigrating to the United States. Some who were here were encouraged or coerced to go back where they came from. At its nastiest, this practice meant that "Mexicans and their American born children were transported to the border and abandoned, often starving."[22] Illustrating the paradoxical form relations between film and society could sometimes take, on film Mexicans were presented in quite favorable light in such movies as *Viva Villa!* (1934) and *Juarez* (1939). As fascism made frightening headway in Europe, debate over superior forms of government raged. On screen, Mexicans are used as models of a people fighting for democracy to give commoners a voice and fairer treatment. In effect, foreign policy rather than national sentiment dictates screen representation in this case.

Native America would seem far removed from events in Mexico, China, or Japan. And in important ways it was. But its image on screen was nevertheless tied to global events of the thirties. By 1890, after the massacre at Wounded Knee, the Indian wars in the United States were over. But perceptions of Native Americans as savages who preyed on unoffending settlers had already been undergoing revision, with Helen Hunt Jackson's 1881 book, *A Century of Dishonor,* and her 1884 novel, *Ramona,* both exposing exploitive treatments of Native Americans. And miserable conditions persisted on reservations. Zane Grey's son, Loren, referring to the early decades of the century, argued that "missionaries who honestly attempted to help the Indians were driven away by others who were in league with the Federal Indian agents administering the reservations."[23] Expecting extinction for Indian America, public identity of Native Americans in popular cultural forms was gravitating to one of bittersweet nostalgia.

The 1906 Julie Opp Faversham novel and subsequent film versions of *Squaw Man* present Native America as part of American resources available to feed—colonial style—British needs.[24] In that novel a British aristocrat, having fled England under a false accusation, marries and has a child with an Indian woman. Once the cloud of disgrace is lifted he plans to send the boy to England to receive a British education. The sweetheart he left behind in England remains unavailable to him because he is married. His Indian wife helpfully commits suicide, sacrificing herself, enabling him to return to England and his old sweetheart with the child. As in Cooper's novels, the Indian in the novel and film versions of *Squaw Man* is sacrificed on behalf of white progress.

In Zane's Grey's 1925 novel, *The Vanishing American*, Indians are presented as spiritual: "The Indian's comprehension of religion is beyond the comprehension of most missionaries. He thinks in symbols. His God is Nature." The white reservation establishment, however, "is not honest or fair with the Indian. . . . Politics, money, and graft—these are the assets of the Indian Bureau." Nevertheless, Grey sees Indians as lower on the evolutionary scale than whites, possessed of "a thousand other manifestations of ignorance compared with whites . . . closer to the original animal progenitor of human beings." As many did in the early twentieth century, Grey believes Native Americans will pass away as a race, they will "inevitably be absorbed by the race that has destroyed [them]." As Walter Benn Michaels argues in his analysis of Greys novel, this leaves the fathering of children, racially speaking, to white America. Michaels argues, "Whether responding to racist demands or rejecting them, Grey made sure that the Indian vanished."[25]

In the 1925 film adaptation of Grey's novel, the notion of Indians vanishing as a race and their being lower on the evolutionary scale than whites are made central points. The film goes to great lengths to demonstrate the goodness of the reservation Indians and the crookedness of their Indian agent. But it finds a way out of the moral responsibility for this by quoting Herbert Spencer on the naturalness of "a ceaseless devouring of the weak by the strong." It then presents the coming and going of various tribes through the ages as a demonstration that the passing of a people is natural, "for races of men come—and go. But the mighty stage remains." By this logic white America cannot be responsible for the extinction to which it has contributed. The passing of Native America is a stage in a natural evolutionary progression.

Edna Ferber's 1930 novel, *Cimarron*, and its 1931 film adaptation
offer a much more radical vision of Native America. The novel is full
of speeches about how the United States mistreated Native Americans,
especially in its removal of the Five Civilized Tribes to Oklahoma,
where both the novel and its film adaptation are set. The novel
makes a more militant case for racial equality than one typically finds
in a period of Nativism and Jim Crow. Yancy Cravat (Richard Dix),
who takes his wife, Sabra (Irene Dunne), and son, Cimarron, to Osage,
Oklahoma, to start a newspaper may have Indian blood himself. He
befriends and defends a Jew who is the victim of anti-Semitism and
responds militantly to Sabra's objection when adult Cim intends to
marry an Indian woman. Interracial marriage, he argues, "is what I
wanted it to be when I came here twenty years ago."[26] In the film,
Sabra, a congresswoman in old age, more racially enlightened than she
is in the novel, introduces Cim, his Indian wife, and two interracial
children to a group of congressmen, in an image which works as a
glowing vision of a racially egalitarian America.

As the Depression worsens and Europe becomes increasingly
threatened by a resumption of war, the United States becomes ever
likelier itself to be drawn into war. Germany, Italy, Spain, and Japan
have evolved into militaristic totalitarian governments which threaten
the globe's democracies. Depression beset and now threatened by war,
one American woman captures one central current of the national
mood, when she remarks that "we had to circle the wagons," an us-
against-them image drawn from pioneer mythology. Traveling the
country to get a good look at the Depression, Lorena Hickok wrote
to Eleanor Roosevelt that blacks, Mexicans, and Indians were getting
too much of the scarce relief money. Whites, she wrote, "really have
to have it." To clinch her argument, she wrote that whites, as opposed
to Indians or Mexicans, "are our babies."[27]

Developments in the status of Indian reservations in the United
States, at the center of such films as *Vanishing American* and *Cimarron* by the mid-thirties, seem far removed from representations of
Indians on American screens. In the thirties, Native America resembles the Chinese circumstance of the past few decades. China was perceived as a weak country; and the United States had passed Chinese
Exclusion Acts with little regard for China as a nation or the Chinese
in the United States. But Japan had developed as a military and industrial power. To restrict Japanese immigration but avoid insulting a
powerful country, Theodore Roosevelt had worked out the Gentlemen's Agreement, according to which Japan did not send emigrants to
the United States so the United States would not have to reject them.
In turn the United States made a public show of not racially insulting

the Japanese.[28] In relations between the United States and the Indians in the thirties, Franklin Roosevelt had actually offered Native America a New Deal, "sometimes termed the New Deal for Indians," the primary component of which was increased tribal autonomy in governance.[29] But in the arena of internal U.S. power dynamics, Native America remained close to voiceless. Thus, Indians could be represented on screen in a negative light with relative impunity for filmmakers.[30] Put another way, racially the Japanese, Chinese, and Native Americans were regarded in a discriminatory light; but, of the three groups, the Japanese initially were too powerful to insult. When China evolved as a strategic global chip which could help block Japanese aggression, the Chinese became too valuable to insult, and the Japanese became enemies. Native America remained with little bargaining power and could be used to stand in for a force threatening American stability throughout the decade.

Increasingly, Indians could be employed as part of allegories of pioneer heroes beset by outside attack. Reservation circumstances and the actual history of the treatment of Indians less frequently become subjects for film treatment. Instead films featuring white-Indian war or violent engagements increasingly resemble the colonial and Foreign Legion films which proliferate in the mid to late thirties. The 1936 film *The Plainsman* is representative of this shift away from the world of *Cimarron*. The central strategy of *The Plainsman*, vis-à-vis the actual facts of American history, telegraphs its status as allegory of heroic Americans building and retaining their civilization while under attack. It puts Buffalo Bill Cody, Wild Bill Hickok, General Custer, and Calamity Jane into the same time period and makes them share the same events. The film matches its account of history to that of the Depression. Faced with likely unemployment after the Civil War, Lincoln wants to open up and settle the West. The Indians stand in the way of such development. Thus, the film makes the Indians an obstacle to full employment. Recalling the scandals following World War I over U.S. businesses accused by the Nye Commission of profiteering in munitions sales, a group of capitalists faced with an oversupply of weapons, having been churning them out for the Civil War, now plot to profit by secretly selling them to the Indians. Therefore, those perceived as the villains of World War I have their counterparts in the post–Civil War profiteers, with the Indians as the embodiment of the threat. In a strategy for representing Native Americans that becomes dominant by the end of the thirties, then persists into the 1960s, Hickok (Gary Cooper) responds to the explanation that Lincoln wanted to settle the West by describing the central problem: "You've never seen the Indian tribes at war. . . . You've never seen men killed and mutilated and bodies of women burned. And babies dragged from their mothers' arms and dashed." Soon the film implies that the Indians have raped Calamity Jane (Jean Arthur). Whereas in the early thirties wrongs done to Indians dominated films, or as in *Fighting Caravan* (1931), Indian violence was shown as the effect of white actions, by the mid-thirties Indian "savagery" is increasingly cut off from its history, from the explanation of the provocations of white expansion. The extensive explanations of white treatment of Indians found in *Cimarron* give way in *The Plainsman* to a single brief statement made by an Indian chief about whites taking land and breaking promises. Hickok has no answer, and the remark is soon buried in the Indian torture of Hickok. Soon the settlers are surrounded by overwhelming numbers, then saved by the cavalry, from the late thirties forward a staple of such films.

Two best-selling novels, both released a year later, and both translated into film at the end of the thirties, illustrate the transition that was occurring in popular representations of Native Americans. Walter Edmunds's novel *Drums Along the Mohawk* presents a young pioneer couple, Gilbert and Lana Martin, who move into the Mohawk Valley to farm a year before the outbreak of the Revolutionary War.[31] They are soon caught up in the battle with the British and their Indian allies. The book foregrounds atrocities committed on the whites by the Indians, and it operates by aligning its sentiments with the white settlers, but it does admit the violence the whites do the Indians. It offers an explicit description of Indians raping white women, while only hinting that the colonists probably also committed rapes. And like Grey's *Vanishing American,* it presents Indians as lower on the evolutionary scale. Kenneth Roberts's novel *Northwest Passage* serves as a paradigm text for the film treatments that will be accorded Native Americans from the late thirties forward, although it too is fairer than are most of the ensuing films.[32] It concerns Robert Rogers and his Rangers, a military unit allied with the British and their expeditions against the Indian allies of the French. It focuses on atrocities committed by the Abenaki Indians of upstate New York during the French and Indian Wars. Nevertheless it does include some positive Native American characters. It draws its narrative tension, however, by focusing on Indians as savages and the threat they pose to white settlers. The amount of ink devoted to Indians beheading whites and using their heads in games and other mutilations of whites dominates the book and allies the reader's sympathy with the Rangers.

The shift that occurs in the film adaptations of these two novels characterizes the overall shift in depictions of Native Americans. *Drums along the Mohawk* is a faithful cinematic adaptation of those parts of

Edmunds's novel which depict the Indians as savages. It leaves out the material that balanced the view of mutual atrocities. Viewed without a knowledge of the novel or history of the period, the Indians' hostilities appear as unprovoked. They descend upon the hardworking farm families and burn them out. They now are motiveless, historyless. As they assault a fort full of settlers near the film's end, we see a close-up on the face of an old woman, righteously rather than sadistically gleeful as she pours scalding water down from the wall of the fort onto the Indians below. By the film's lights, she is clearly giving them what the rest of the film has shown they deserve. *Northwest Passage,* released a year later, devotes long scenes to accounts of Indian mutilations of whites. The Rangers head up to St. Francis to avenge a long history of such savagery and to put a stop to it. Individual Rangers stand up and testify to Indian mutilations, beheadings, and eviscerations of innocent whites. The film offers no historical explanation for Indian motives. They are simply a threat to early Americans, their behavior barbaric.

The shorthanding of history represented by these films is summed up in *Stagecoach,* released in 1939. The long and disgraceful treatment of the Apache nation is entirely absent from the film. Apaches attack the hapless band of whites traveling by stagecoach, one of whom is a young pregnant woman. At one point the Ringo Kid (John Wayne) explains, "Geronimo has jumped the reservation again." No account of wrongs done to Apaches is forthcoming. Two years later in *They Died with Their Boots On* sentimentalized white characters are shown, one by one, dying at Little Big Horn, with no mention of wrongs done the Sioux or Cheyenne. When American film history reaches later John Wayne films, *Red River* (1948) and *The Searchers* (1956), unprovoked pestilential Indian attacks on unsinning white settlers have become a stock device. *Red River* presents an unjustified Indian attack on a wagon train; *The Searchers* opens with an unprovoked Indian attack on innocent settlers, and it makes a point of focusing on later Indian rapes and mutilations of white women. It tells its audience nothing about possible Indian motives or past wrongs done them. Its audience sees threatening savages and threatened whites, with whom the film creates emotional identification. As the thirties drew to a close, public cinematic identity for Native America had been rewritten.

5

Sexual Politics and the Depression

MEN LEANING ON WOMEN

THE PRIMAL SCENE OF THE GREAT DEPRESSION FOR FUTURE *NEW Yorker* writer John Cheever occurred at the level of family. In the late 1920s Cheever's father, like a generation of hopeful men, invested his money in stocks that quickly became worthless with the crash of 1929. Cheever's mother opened a small shop and, succeeding at that, opened a larger one, eventually adding a tearoom. Soon she was supporting the family. John Cheever's daughter Susan reports of his father, "My grandfather, once a dapper, literate businessman who read Shakespeare to his sons, became desperate and bitterly sorry for himself. In 1930 he was forced to begin borrowing from the Wollaston Cooperative Bank against the fine house at 123 Winthrop Avenue. (In 1933 the bank repossessed the house and tore it down.) The family's financial disaster became a personal disaster . . . [John Cheever's] mother expanded her business to a larger gift shop . . . Being supported by his wife was a humiliating experience for my grandfather . . . To him, his wife's competence was an emasculation."[1]

Emasculation may have been the point for Cheever's father, but the subtext of the account points to the way in which the woman of the family was enabled (or called upon) by financial disaster to occupy a new role, sometimes in the family, sometimes in the workplace, and sometimes in both, once the patriarch's position had been weakened. Florence Ellenwood Allen, who was called by the Federation of Business and Professional Women the "pre-eminent professional woman of the nation," said to that organizations convention, "I do not know what many a family would have done if it had not been for that refuge from their problems, the 'old maid . . . in the family. When married women were being turned out of their jobs because they were married, and when fathers and breadwinners lost their employment . . . it was the salary of the old maid in thousands of homes that kept them going."[2] She may have overstated the loss of jobs by married women, since clerical positions actually increased in the period, but her point about the rise in importance of female earning power is correct. For significant numbers, the Depression changed male and female power relations in the family. For many Depression-era women the Cheever family experience serves as a paradigm.

At the community level, similar things were happening. By 1932, the community of Beckerstown in Arlington County, Virginia, faced economic disaster. Bank failures and a drought had sent the town reeling, with the effect, a *Harper's* writer explains, that the disasters "unsettled all their fundamental beliefs." The writer describes the solution the town arrived at as though he expects it to come as a shock to the reader: "It was a woman to whom they turned." The woman was Mrs. Jane Kennedy Whitcomb, whose position in the town was steeped in patriarchal power. "A descendant of an old aristocratic family. . . . It was she whom her father had chosen, of all his gifted and intelligent children, to care for the family estate." Given the chance to occupy a major role in the town's future, "Mrs. Whitcomb dominated the [town's crisis] meeting."[3] Like John Cheever's mother, Mrs. Whitcomb, once provided with the opportunity, proved she could rise to the occasion.

An unlikely series of events conspired to generalize this paradigm nationally. In 1921 Franklin Roosevelt, who had just run for vice president, was struck with infantile paralysis, polio. Polio "was absolutely critical to Roosevelt's later relationship with victims of the Great Depression. . . . He was able to understand suffering in a way a country gentleman would not otherwise have been likely to."[4] The polio also changed the role of Eleanor Roosevelt as first lady. She was to be Franklin's legs. She would go where he couldn't go, see for herself what the Depression was doing to people, and report back to her husband. In June 1933 a contemporary magazine judged her the "busiest first lady" in U.S. history, with Dolly Madison coming in a distant second.[5] This role contributed to Eleanor's already growing understanding that she could be independent. About this time, she "realized henceforth that advancing her husband's career was a means to advancing her own." As a result, "it is almost certain that Franklin Roosevelt would not have become president without Eleanor's help; it is absolutely certain that if he had, he would not have been the same beloved, benevolent father figure that he became during the Depression."[6] If one considers American civil rights history, and American class history, in the context of Eleanor Roosevelt's liberalizing influence on these things, one can see that changed gender relations (however oddly they had evolved in this case) contributed to the American liberal tradition.[7] And the image of Eleanor at Franklin's side, often giving him physical support to help him stand, was one of the presiding images of the thirties.

Franklin and Eleanor. Franklin gains support from his cane with his right hand and from Eleanor with his left. Franklin D. Roosevelt Library.

Little more than a decade before Roosevelt assumed the office of president, women had won the vote in America. For the following decade they had been more visible as flappers than as the political activists some male doomsayers had predicted would seize the high offices of government for members of their own sex. With the social reforms provoked by the Depression, the opportunity for some upper-class women to open doors for other women increased. Susan Ware remarks that Eleanor Roosevelt was the foremost member of the women's network in the 1930s. Her institutional role as first lady, her willingness to use public position to push for public reform, and her ability to inspire loyalty in friends and colleagues placed her "at the center of this growing New Deal political sisterhood."[8] The result was rising prestige for women under the Roosevelt administration. "The network among women in politics and government in the 1930s became an important force in enlarging women's influence in the New Deal. Women in the New Deal network took an active interest in furthering the progress of their sex."[9]

Partly because men were weakened by the Depression, and partly because the traits valued by Herbert Hoover and others in the 1920s (rugged individualism, resistance to change, and resistance to government charity for individuals) gave way to a set of values associated with the feminine (cooperation, sensitivity to suffering), male-female dynamics were significantly altered.[10] On film, male-female bonds characterized by men dominating women gave way to greater equality in romantic relationships, a situation that would be significantly undone by another shift in gender dynamics at the outbreak of the Second World War. The changed sexual dynamics of the 1930s were worked out on screen, especially for the middle and upper classes. The decade saw the rise of some of the strongest female personalities in film history: Barbara Stanwyck, Rosalind Russell, Claudette Colbert, Ginger Rogers, Katherine Hepburn, Irene Dunne, Joan Blondell, Bette Davis, Carole Lombard, and Jean Harlow. Though looks were important, these women are mostly remembered for being the most verbally dexterous (and thus verbally powerful) group of actresses in screen history. The lack of assertive female roles often lamented in the decades following the Depression had not been felt in the 1930s. Molly Haskell writes that "women screenwriters . . . were more numerous in the thirties than during any other period." Unlike women on screen in the earlier twenties or later forties, Haskell argues, women on screen in the thirties "were always doing something, whether it was running a business or running just to keep from standing still." Writing in 1974, Haskell comes to the conclusion that if the Depression-era female screenwriters' "point of view was not particularly feminist, neither

was it slavishly submissive to a male ethic, as it is today."[11] Given
that Betty Friedan's *The Feminine Mystique* appeared in 1963, Kate
Millett's *Sexual Politics* appeared in 1970, and Germaine Greer's *The
Female Eunuch* appeared in the same year, Haskell draws a striking
comparison with her own period, giving the militant edge to 1930s
women over those of the revolutionary 1960s and early 1970s. Her
conclusion requires explanation in economic and political terms to comprehend fully the effects of the Depression on gender-based power
relationships.

A *Time* writer in 1933 provides a clue to the assertiveness of women
on screen in the 1930s, and to the rearrangement of male-female power
relations in film romance. Referring to Owen Young, whom Franklin
Roosevelt "had used" during the presidential campaign, though he had
since "passed [him] by as an advisor," the writer quotes Young on the
likely success of the New Deal in ending the Depression, Young makes
the odd point that the Depression would be hard to cure because of
"the immobility of men's minds." He associates this "immobility"
with "rugged individualism," a code term for Hoover values, and sets
the Hoover ethic in opposition to "politics as the lovely lady in the parlor, and economics as the kitchen maid who did the work." Recalling
Hoover's strong ties with the business establishment (he had often
repeated Coolidge's "the chief business of the American people is business"), Young remarks, "I see no escape from some direction and control by the lady in the parlor." Young associates two sets of values with
male and female principles. Business and individuality (male values)
are associated with the by then discredited values of the Hoover
administration. The Roosevelt New Deal embodies the "lady in the
parlor and the maid in the kitchen," who Young says represent a need
to "surrender . . . to the extent necessary to co-operate in a plan."[12]
Thus, cooperation replaces individual, profit-motivated values. Summarized, the economic trauma brought on by the Depression led to a
reconsideration of the perils of strict individualism and the advantages
of cooperation. Male values were not effaced by the times (they return
to dominance during and after the Second World War), but a readjustment in values had occurred by 1933. This readjustment was not absent
from movie screens, where new sexual politics were materializing as
new gender dynamics.

The gender imagery in thirties films was grounded in American
domestic and economic life of the Depression. If unemployment, or
anxiety over potential unemployment, had an effect on a shift in male
authority, researchers in the period were interested. Mirra Komarovsky,
a Barnard College sociologist, conducted a study throughout the mid-
thirties, which she published at decade's end. Komarovsky was espe-

cially curious about the ways in which gender identity was subject to economics. The Depression opened up the opportunity to question whether gender roles were "natural" or constructions with an economic foundation. She and her team of researchers interviewed family members to assess the effect the Depression was having on male self-worth, male authority, family power dynamics, and family respect for husbands and fathers. Komarovsky's team asked questions which focused on ties between economic power and the assumed essence of male identity: "What powers does the man have by virtue of being the provider? What effect does the economic dependence of the wife and the children have upon their attitudes towards the head of the family? ... What happens to the authority of the male head when he fails as a provider?"[13] Komarovsky noted that "In the traditional patriarchal view of the family, the husband is expected to support and protect his wife, and she, in turn ... to honor and obey him. A certain subordination to the authority of the husband is part of the woman's share in their reciprocal relations. In so far as the husband's claim to authority is based upon his supporting his wife, unemployment may tend to undermine it. . . . Unemployment does tend to lower the status of the husband." Even in cases where men had not lost their jobs, the research team found an "underlying" current of "deep anxiety of both husband and wife." In cases of the man's losing his job, "in some families the hitherto concealed contempt for the husband came into the open; in others unemployment has reversed the husband-wife relation, dominance of the husband having been changed to complete subordination; in still others the husband suffered a loss of respect, a change which is best described in the words of the wife: 'I still love him, but he doesn't seem as "big" a man.' " In other families, the economic upheaval of the Depression resulted in "more egalitarian relations in a family hitherto led by the husband."[14]

On screen the necessity for women to assume a new role when their men suffered financial failures worked its way into film scripts and cinema images. *Dinner at Eight* enacts this shifting paradigm. It offers a version in one of its images of James Thurber's observation, registered as a complaint, concerning radio soap operas originating in the thirties: "The man in the wheelchair has come to be the standard Soapland symbol of the American male's subordination to the female and his dependence on her greater strength." Burton Bernstein remarks that "The soap-opera male was really the Thurber male with a resonant voice—weak, confused, dominated, and even emasculated by a variation of the Thurber female." The famous Thurber male came into his own as a character, as did the female-dominated Laurel and Hardy husband personas, in the traumatized thirties.[15] *Dinner at Eight* captures

the moment of this shift in gender-rooted power. Economics had contributed to the materialistic gin swigging flapper identity of the twenties; and economics provoked a shift away from this identity in the
thirties. Oliver Jordan (Lionel Barrymore), a shipping magnate, finds
his family business failing. In a takeover attempt, someone is buying
up his stock behind his back. The sense of his being eaten alive by
forces beyond his control captures the creeping feeling of dread that
had infected the national consciousness by 1933, his plight a version of
the question of who was responsible for the trauma of the Depression,
which haunted its victims in the 1930s.[16] Oliver's engaged daughter has
begun an affair with a failed alcoholic actor (John Barrymore), who
eventually commits suicide. While father and daughter suffer, the
matriarch (Billie Burke) flits about, superciliously fussing over her
party, warding off her daughter's efforts to confide in her, and complaining about having to prepare for a party designed for social climb-
ing in the presence of an expected duke. She opens the film rushing into
a room and announcing, "Darling, I've got Lord and Lady Ferncliff!"
Tied to an old patriarchal set of class-based values that for the first part
of the film define her, she doesn't notice her husband cannot sleep at
night (though he has noticed his daughter's trouble sleeping). Nor, as
she prattles on about her shopping, does she notice her daughter's anxiety. When she asks her daughter a question and receives no reply, she
doesn't miss a beat in her phone conversation, not realizing her daughter has left the room. As Jordan humbles himself at his office, asking
the crude economic predator Packard (Wallace Beery) for a loan to see
his business through the Depression, his distraught wife calls Oliver to
announce she can't find an "extra man" to keep the male-female ratio
even at her party.

The social situation echoes the twenties as F. Scott Fitzgerald
described them: "All the catering to vice and waste was on an utterly
childish scale, and he suddenly realized the meaning of the word 'dissipate, . . . to dissipate into thin air; to make nothing out of something. . . . He remembered thousand-franc notes given to an orchestra
for playing a single number, hundred-franc notes tossed to a doorman
for calling a cab."[17] Millicent spends her time fussing over an ornate
lion, made of Jell-O, a table centerpiece offered in tribute to Lord and
Lady Ferncliff. At the film's end, she undergoes a transformation;
brought into the reality of the Depression, she proves that, given the
chance, she is up to it. She learns that Oliver is suffering from arterial
thrombosis, a life-threatening condition. His illness is one with his
Depression-provoked financial woes. He tells her that the worst part
of his physical condition is that he is losing the shipping business. She
replies, "I've always loved you, even though I've turned into a silly,

stupid, useless wife." She adds, "We'll economize." She cancels her box at the theater, her table at the Embassy club, and her hairdresser's appointment. She suggests they move to a smaller house. Millicent has been a holdover flapper, resisting adult responsibility. She holds on to a pre-Depression ethic for women, one which stressed entertainment rather than responsibility. As described by Jenna Weisman Joselit, she is the flapper mother of the previous decade: "Ten years ago women still had ages . . . Today mother and daughter may be found . . . supplementing their wardrobe from the same rack."[18] Frederick Lewis Allen remarks of the flapper, "women of this decade worshiped not merely youth, but unripened youth: they wanted to be—or thought men wanted them to be—men's casual and light-hearted companions; not broad-hipped mothers of the race." The flapper said to the shattered post–World War I man, "You are tired and disillusioned, you do not want the cares of a family or the companionship of mature wisdom, you want exciting play."[19] Millicent moves from the waste of the 1920s to the cooperative model of the 1930s in almost no time. In an image of a woman actually holding a man up (its dynamics echoing the FDR-Eleanor relationship and that of Thurber's Soapland man), she goes from lightweight cared-for social butterfly to physically supporting her shaky husband as they descend the stairs together.

Other films deepen the image of women rising to shoulder the problems of the Depression to ward off economic failure. By the late period of the Depression, films display them propping their men up Eleanor Roosevelt-like to ward off economic failure. By the late period of the Depression in which *Swing High, Swing Low* (1937) was made, audiences had come to understand the iconography of the Depression environment, politically, economically, and socially. The slight adjustments offered by Millicent in response to the economic disaster facing the Jordans seem inadequate by 1937. Americans had seen too much. The central character, Skid Johnson (as in skid row), is just finishing his stretch in the army. On his last day of guard duty at the Panama Canal Skid (Fred MacMurray) meets Maggie (Carole Lombard), a cosmetician on her way to the financial security of marrying a California millionaire. When Maggie asks Skid about his plans, he is uncertain what he will do next. Faced with the question, he repeatedly states, "I can always go back in the army," a remark, after the Bonus Army experience of the early thirties, which would have sounded pitifully optimistic.[20]

Skid has talent: he can play the trumpet. But he lacks the self-confidence to go after a job. Maggie moves in with him on a platonic basis. Falling for Skid, she gets him a job, helps write his songs, and holds him together. The film emphasizes that Skid needs Maggie. Her willpower enables him to take a job at a posh club in New York. He

A shaky Oliver Jordan, with one hand supported by the rail, the other by his wife (*Dinner at Eight*, MGM, 1933).

goes ahead and she is to follow, but without a strong woman to keep him going he falls apart and winds up living on the street, boozing himself into oblivion. Visually he is the replica image of the unshaven down-and-outer of the Depression. An old friend offers him a last chance for a comeback on a radio show. Maggie is on hand for the performance; when Skid cannot go it alone, she has him encircle her in his arms. Since Skid cannot stand on his own feet, professionally or physically, she literally holds him up, an image that a devastated nation, with many families experiencing the possibility of a shift from male to female providers, would have understood.[21]

For some men the shift in gender identity resulted in more than just a loyal wife coming to his aid. Marital power relations were more deeply altered than in just a moderate gain in female authority. In one case a Mrs. Adams found that her husband's pre-Depression tyranny and irresponsible behavior had, by his loss of power resulting from his loss of job, empowered her to the point that she "had become more secure than in any other period of her life." When the family went on relief, "she insisted on getting the relief check herself. She also controlled the money that was coming in from the boarders." Her husband remarked, "I relinquished power in the family." Of his new domestic situation, he commented "now I don't even try to be boss.

She controls all the money, and I never have a penny in my pocket but that I have to ask her for it."[22] A set of circumstances studied by Komarovsky's team suggest the extent of power reversals that sometimes occurred in thirties marital relations. Much could be learned in connection to family radio habits or to a husband's cigarette smoking. Attempting to get at shifts in male power, Komarovsky asked, "If members of a family want to listen to different programs," how is the conflict resolved? Does the father's choice take precedence "over that of the wife and children?" Or if in a marriage hard pressed by Depression unemployment, "smoking is practically the only personal expenditure of the unemployed man . . . it is often symbolic of marital conflicts. . . . In families with conflict, the wife says, 'smoking is not a necessity. There are things that the children and I need more.' " In one case it "was awful" for a Mr. Patterson, who was reduced to having to "ask his daughter for a little money for tobacco."[23] Men at the bottom, without savings or substantial property going into the Depression, were most vulnerable to such loss of authority. On screen, in Laurel and Hardy's *Blockheads* (1938), Hardy receives a daily allowance of seventy-five cents from his wife. He has to importune her for an extra quarter if he wants to buy something; and he has to ask permission to use the car. In *Sons of the Desert* (1933), when Laurel and Hardy lie to

Oliver Hardy being pummeled by his Thurberesque wife in *Sons of the Desert* (Hal Roach, 1934).

their wives about going to a convention, Laurel's wife brandishes a gun
and threatens what she will do if she ever catches Stanley lying to her.
To keep Laurel from confessing, Hardy threatens to tell Mrs. Laurel
that Stanley has disobeyed her by smoking. At the film's end, when
their wives learn the truth, Hardy's wife mercilessly beats him with
pots and pans. Laurel humbles himself and confesses to his wife, for
which she rewards him with a cigarette.

THE PERILS OF WORKING GIRLS

In a 1936 poem describing a woman of the working poor, Genevieve
Taggard highlights the double peril of the physical and economic vulnerability to which such women found themselves subject:

> Clearly it is best, mill-mother,
> Not to rebel or ask clear silly questions,
> Saying womb is sick of its work with death,
> Your body drugged with work and the repeated bitter
> Gall of your morning vomit. Never try
> Asking if we should blame you. Live in fear. And put
> Soap on the yellowed blankets. Rub them pure.[24]

   While a network of politically active upper-class women worked
with the Roosevelt White House to make changes in American life, the
class divide left most working poor women of the 1930s to fend for
themselves.[25] This division can be identified early in the twentieth century, when the Women's Trade Union League (WTUL) "was the only
national organization dedicated to the unionization of women workers."[26] The WTUL "pursued trade union organization as a primary
function," but "the organization also stressed political action." The
"dual emphasis reflected the membership of the WUTL, which was
composed equally of working women and wealthy women (called
'Allies . . .)." The class differences between the two groups emerged in
their goals. The working-class women wanted the WTUL to "concentrate its limited resources on union membership drives and support for
striking women." The wealthy Allies were more interested in legisla-
tive goals. "Since these women controlled most of the money for the
budget," the Allies won and their working-class sisters lost.[27] Working-class women found their situation further exacerbated in the 1930s
as the public perception that they took jobs away from men in traumatic times contributed to their difficulty in finding jobs outside
"women's work": nursing, teaching, domestic, and clerical work. Lois
Scharf documents the point that clerical work "increased 25 percent"

during the Depression, largely as a result of an army of hard-pressed women seeking work and being funneled into a limited (and limiting) number of professions. Ominously Scharf adds, "by the middle of the decade, students of occupational trends noted that employers placed greater emphasis on the type of woman, her personality and appearance, rather than on her abilities."[28] For women at the bottom hard times and gender bias left them susceptible to exploitation and harassment, a condition intensified by male attitudes towards women in the workplace.[29]

One film after another which treats the subject—suggestive of life in the workplace for working-class women of the 1930s—of women working in offices deals overtly with the potential for sexual exploitation, and, especially, with women who end their employment with the happy solution of marriage. Many such films contain a subtext of threat and sexual harassment, often with marriage as the lesser of competing evils. Commenting on the dangers of sexual harassment in offices for young women who contributed to the swell of women in the workplace in the early twentieth century, Janette Egmont remarked that when the working-class stenographer "goes into the office, she burns her bridges behind her. She must be a law unto herself. . . . male clerks will compare the blond with the brunette, and the discussion is apt to last a little too long."[30] Depression-era women who "sought reemployment after losing managerial positions were encouraged to display passive, compliant, 'feminine' . . . qualities. . . . Meridel LeSueur noted that younger, prettier girls could get jobs in stores or restaurants. Age was assuming great significance as women over thirty were refused jobs as waitresses, stenographers, or salesgirls."[31] So was sexual attractiveness, as a number of films about working-class women testify.

Ever Since Eve, with its ambiguous title suggesting that the harassment it is about to depict is natural (it has existed since the beginning of history), opens with a book crashing out of a skyscraper window. Secretary Marge Winton (Marion Davies) has thrown the book, not at the window, but at her boss Mr. Mason who, she explains to her roommate Sadie later, was sexually harassing her. She tells Sadie, "I don't want romance, I just want a job." In her next job, her new bosses, all men, vie to concoct ways to keep her after-hours. One man is shown preening before calling for her on the office intercom. Repelled by the unwanted sexual attention, she decides to quit. To make her point about the harassment, she finds a plain-looking secretary to sit at her desk and volunteer to do night work when the men arrive. The men lose interest in working late.

Marge pursues a new job-interview plan. She dresses dowdily, to remove her looks as a factor. When she comes home still wearing her plain disguise. Sadie's boyfriend Mike arrives, with a friend, Al, who is hoping for a date with the attractive girl Jake's been describing. When McCoy sees Marge in her dowdy outfit, he leaves. Marge explains to her roommate that she was nice to McCoy, but in this film being nice cannot be just hospitality; it must entail looks. When Marge applies for a job the next day, she gets lucky. Her employment agency sends her to a publishing company where the boss is a straitlaced assertive woman, Abigail Beldon. Beldon is having trouble with one of her writers, Freddie (Robert Montgomery). Immediately Freddie begins to complain about Marge's looks: he wants her to take her glasses off. But Beldon has chosen Marge for her plainness to keep Freddie's mind on work. Eventually Marge has to bail Freddie out and finish his book for him. When she falls for Freddie, Sadie asks her, "Hasn't he any idea that you are you?" Identity, such a question implies, depends on looks. Working-class feminine professional identity and sexual identity are in tension: attractive girls get harassed; competent but plain girls can't get men.[32] Freddie describes his ideal woman in physical terms, "five feet three, one hundred and twelve pounds." He only reciprocates Marge's affection when she takes off her drab disguise. She is then "rescued" from the workplace by marriage.

The notion that an influx of women into the workplace during the First World War altered female work experience has been demonstrated by William Henry Chafe to have been a myth. Chafe quotes Harriet Stanton Blatel, who advised women that "service to the country in the crisis may lead women to that economic freedom which will change a political possession into a political power."[33] But, Chafe notes, "The facts did not support such an optimistic interpretation. . . . Contrary to popular opinion only 5 per cent of the women war workers joined the labor force for the first time in the war years. The rest had transferred from lower paying jobs and were expected to return to them when the emergency had passed."[34] Constance Green concurred: "The brief interlude . . . which some enthusiasts heralded as launching a new era for women in industry came and went with astonishingly little permanent effect upon women's opportunities."[35] At the war's end, the Central Federated Union of New York advised, "the same patriotism which induced women to enter industry during the war should induce them to vacate their positions after the war."[36] When women objected to the blatant prejudice of such a position, refusing to leave positions to make room for men, they suffered discrimination: "Male workers went on strike in Cleveland in order to force women streetcar conductors out of work . . . in Detroit female conductors were dismissed despite a National Labor Board decision in their favor."[37]

Films of the 1930s reflect the curious situation of women clerical workers during the Depression. Male attitudes towards women in the workplace are touched by bias and insecurity. Such feelings are captured by a term that became common during the period, "office wife," which conveys mixed notions of work, domesticity, and sexual promise. From the perspective of the wife at home, it also embodies a threat. Several films of the period capture the transitional moment in American employment history embedded in this term, among them the 1930 film, *The Office Wife,* and an especially sinister mixture of work and sexuality which emerges in the 1933 Loretta Young film, *She Had To Say Yes.*

The Office Wife makes a point typical of several thirties films: a woman who wants equality with men in the workplace is probably a lesbian. Early in the film a mannish female writer (short hair, man's suit, cigar) named Kate Halsey (Blanche Frederici) complains to her publisher, Lawrence Fellows (Lewis Stone), that she wants to write like Hemingway, rather than be restricted to the romance subjects she is given. Fellows refuses, instead assigning her to explore the phenomenon of the office wife. He tells her that most men choose their secretaries more carefully than they choose their wives (a point that conflates the two roles). The film demonstrates how convenient a stenographer who carries wife potential can be for a man in the workplace, especially since she can be studied for domestic suitability. About to be married, Fellows gives Miss Andrews, his secretary, the news and she faints: she had her own romantic designs. Miss Andrews resigns and is replaced by Anne (Dorothy Mackaill), an attractive blonde from the secretarial pool. An undercurrent of sexual innuendo accompanies Anne's promotion. Her previous male boss tells her, "You got this on your own," as though she needs reassurance that she wasn't chosen for her looks. Back at her apartment Anne, who rooms with her sister Katherine (Joan Blondell), gives a little speech on merit in the workplace. Katherine cynically responds that she got the position of lead model in the dress shop where she works because she allows the manager to kiss her ear now and then.

The blurred boundaries of Anne's role as secretary, potential sex object, and possible wife all play a part in her initiation into her new job. Mr. McGowan, Anne's previous boss, assures her that Mr. Fellows's wife is pretty enough not to have to worry about competition from Anne. He supports his assertion by adding that Mrs. Fellows's knees are magnificent. In spite of her own remarks about merit in the workplace, Anne practices pulling her skirt up to expose her legs, while she pretends to talk to the absent Mr. Fellows, imagining as she does his gaze on her body. In the midst of her reverie, McGowan interrupts with the words, "He wants you," suggesting a sexual response to Anne's exposing her legs. As though he has read her mind, McGowan adds, "for dictation purposes." Once she is in Fellows's office the pressure of potential expectations on Anne emerges; motivated by fears she might not meet them, she slides her dress up to expose more skin for Fellows. As a piece of history, the scene suggests the ambiguity of a working woman's plight at this transition point in feminine work history.

The film interrupts the scenes between Anne and Fellows with Kate writing about office wives. Kate concludes that the secretary evolves into a wife figure and gains an iron hand over her boss, who becomes psychologically dependent on her. So natural is the notion of the woman serving a male boss that he comes to need it too much. The film means to use the interruptions from Kate as a witty sort of introduction to the two main characters, Fellows and Anne, who are meant to exemplify her theory. But these interruptions also suggest the film's own uncertainty over the role of the woman in the workplace. The filmmakers cannot seem to believe in the businesslike intentions of such women; they must really be fishing for husbands, and this is presented as natural. The film establishes its beliefs on this point in two ways.

First, Fellows gives Anne a little test, to determine her worthiness as woman and wife. He takes her down to a beach to work, a place packed with children. As the children race by, Fellows asks, "Do you like children?" Anne responds, revealing her genuine feminine nature, "Who wouldn't?" Fellows replies, "Oh, I don't know. I thought they were becoming less popular." Just ten years after the introduction of women's suffrage, his remark suggests that he finds changes in female roles threatening. Second, Anne quickly falls in love with Fellows, just as Miss Andrews did. The film asserts that a natural woman, a woman unlike lesbian Kate, cannot be around a man in a professional environment without giving in to her desires. A working woman is unnatural; a profession doesn't lead to children. The film dispenses with the problem of Fellows's wife by showing her cheating on Fellows. After Fellows and Anne decide to get married, which ends her career-woman days, she says to him, "Let me pick out your next secretary."

An exposé of much nastier treatment of female sexuality in the workplace can be found in *She Had to Say Yes*, a film treating a male wet dream over the sexual possibilities of male authority over working-class women at work. During the period, one Fessendon Chase put together a pamphlet, which conveys what is apparently his own wishful thinking, concerning the vogue of female office workers. Setting out to prove "many business offices were no better than brothels and many stenographers no better than prostitutes," Chase asserted, "we cannot escape the fact that the 'private-office . . . girl is generally quite willing to kiss and be kissed, in order to secure special favors and perhaps an increase in her salary from her susceptible employer."[38] In *She Had to Say Yes*, when a company's executives complain of poor business, they ascribe it neither to the Depression nor to their product; instead they conclude that slow business results from the hardened look of their "customer girls," a group of women whose job it is to entertain buyers after hours. The film barely resists calling the girls prostitutes, though events show they must be. Unhappy that the customer girls aren't virginal looking enough, one executive, Tommy Nelson, suggests that the stenographers ought to have to entertain customers. A co-ed workplace might mean female employees can be flesh to be exchanged for business. If men have charge of women at work, the men reason, why can't they use them for sexual purposes? Lisa Fine points out that "some contemporary commentators believed that a large number of stenographers were venturesome butterflies masquerading as stenographers."[39]

Initially, Tommy doesn't want his stenographer girlfriend Flo (Loretta Young) entertaining any customers. But faced with a big sale, he presses her to go out with Danny Drew, a client. Danny takes Flo to a hotel room where he makes crude advances. In language revealing of the customer girls' real task, she tells him, "You do feel cheated. I'm just not a good sport." Danny repeats Tommy's actions. He maneuvers Flo into going out with another lascivious customer, Mr. Haynes, whom Flo only escapes by tricking Haynes's wife into arriving. Later Haynes complains about Flo, lying about what she did sexually: in this film, when a man gets beaten he cries "whore." Feeling if Flo has given in to Haynes, then he should be able to use her sexually, Danny assaults her, stopping just short of rape when he realizes that Flo is a "good girl." Tommy (who earlier took a shot at raping Flo) arrives just after the assault and offers her further sexual insults. Having tested her resistance to rape, Danny now decides Flo is good enough to marry. She agrees, remarking: "I suppose it's just a matter of choosing the lesser of two evils." Her remark clarifies the ugliness of the film's title. The only way to escape rape or prostitution in the workplace is to marry a rapist or a pimp.

The Limits of Thirties Feminism

The vast majority of women in the 1930s who were active in social affairs did not set out to repudiate the roles of wife and mother. Eleanor

Roosevelt remarked, "When all is said and done, women *are* different from men. They are equals in many ways, but they cannot refuse to acknowledge the differences."[40] She envisioned a social order built not only "by the ability and brains of our men," but also with "the understanding heart of the women."[41] Her distinction illustrates an unwillingness to entirely abandon traditional gender roles. The majority of women who held significant roles in national affairs during the Depression, called the "network" by Susan Ware, did not support an equal rights amendment. And most either shied away from or repudiated the term "feminism."[42] The unwillingness of women's networks of the 1930s to go all the way in their treatment of women's liberation is embedded in the plot resolutions of several films. The logical foundation for many films that broach the subject of gender power relations is identical. Some man has committed a moral wrong towards a woman, with the result that the woman in the film responds by asserting herself and breaking with accepted social gender practices.

Let Us Be Gay, based on a play written by a woman, Rachel Crothers, opens by piling one mawkish domestic action upon another. Kitty (Norma Shearer), married to Bob and mother of two children, brings Bob his breakfast in bed. Her clothing is frumpy, and we learn she dresses this way to save on the household budget. As she carries out one household task after another, she sings, "I love you." Her domestic bliss is shattered by the appearance of a woman whose looks sum up the era's notions of a sexy and dangerous woman: she is a dolled-up platinum blonde. Kitty sees that Bob has been cheating and the marriage collapses. The film then cuts to a few years later. Next seen Kitty is smartly dressed and verbally dexterous at flirting. At the home of Bootsie (Marie Dressier), a rich dowager who has opened her country house for guests, Kitty has dropped Bob's last name and taken her maiden name. The plot suggests Bob won't know she is present until he runs into her. Bob's first meeting with Kitty shakes him, while she remains nonplussed, reversing their earlier positions emotionally. When Bob approaches her, Kitty stops him with the film's title, "Let us be gay," meaning adult, but also meaning moving beyond traditional patriarchal values. She says she knows what it's "like to be a man," a remark that suggests she has been active sexually, a concept Bob finds shocking.

Though Kitty talks as though she's been playing the field sexually, the film takes pains to preserve acceptable morality by showing its audience how, when one of the male guests comes to Kitty's room at night, she fends him off. Her verbal worldliness has been all talk, all anger and sarcasm over Bob's infidelities. Dressed for the final scene of the film in a man's tie and coat, Kitty delivers speeches on her new-found freedom. She announces she's not ready to sit by the domestic fire. At the moment when it appears that she really means it, she breaks down in tears and takes Bob back, sobbing, "I'm so lonely." The effect of the breakdown is to convey the film's sense of the unnaturalness of divorce, an unnaturalness given visual expression by her male clothing. This film winds up arguing that a woman may stretch the boundaries of traditional gender definitions, but given the chance she will flee back into traditional domesticity.

In spite of its worldly espousals and feminist elements, *Let Us Be Gay* reverts to reinforcing the domestic dynamics of its early scenes. Consistent with the leading women activists of the period, its intent is not to reject romance, motherhood, or marriage. Rather, it cloaks a conventional message about the costs of adultery and the male double standard in feminist trappings. The sentimental core of the film is the parent-child relationship, given visual expression near the film's end when Bob is surprised by the appearance of his children, whom he has not seen in three years. Bob is emotionally overcome. Unintentionally, the film becomes a kind of rebuke to women who lose themselves in domesticity and fail to keep themselves sexually attractive for their husbands. It is the new, sharply dressed, carefully made-up Kitty who regains Bob. Her tears at the end emphasize the penalty for severing the marriage bonds and undermine the force of her feminist language. Nevertheless, something more subtle than this does occur, merely as a result of the presence of the assertive logic Kitty mouths. The film at least puts into public play ideas with the power to subvert traditional notions of gender power relationships.

Female (which featured Kathryn Scola as one of its writers) commences at what was, in terms of sexual politics, the halfway point for *Let Us Be Gay.* Alison Drake (Ruth Chatterton), president of a car-manufacturing company, runs the company with assurance, bossing around several male executives at a board meeting. While at work she is visited by an old friend, Harriet Brown. Harriet is a model of domesticity, discussing all of her husband's activities but none of her own. Alison, however, is so busy running her company, she can barely converse with Harriet, as she is repeatedly interrupted by business concerns. She tells Harriet that "a woman in love is a pathetic spectacle" and asserts, "I decided to travel the same open road that men travel." When Kitty in *Let Us Be Gay* makes an almost identical claim, she's only bluffing; in *Female*, Alison means it. In practice, she has captured some of the obnoxiousness of powerful men who ogle subordinate women, as she openly leers at young men she employs. She invites male employees to her house, seduces them, then, if they try to pursue the relationship, transfers them to another location.

She eventually pursues Thorne, a man who views her as unnatural, telling her he prefers to do his own "hunting." Soon Thorne launches into a class-based attack on Allison, calling her undemocratic and snobbish. But by his doing so the film averts the issue of gender power, evading the issue of female asertiveness in favor of the class issue. In this way like *Let Us be Gay*, *Female* averts its eyes from the issues it has advertised itself as confronting. Instead, after intial sympathy, both films find ways to view assertive women as unnatural.

Somewhat surprisingly, Thorne says he wants to marry Alison. When she resists this idea, he criticizes her with the words, "You and your new freedom." Referring back to their first meeting he casts a sexual slur, calling her a "pick-up." Having for a moment held the high ground on the question of class snobbery, Thorne loses it by resorting to chauvinistic name-calling. He leaves her, and back at the office she is suddenly faced with a crisis in the form of a challenge from a competitor. With her all male executive staff awaiting her plan of action, she suddenly breaks down, sobbing, "This is no place for a woman." Her male assistant comforts her with the words, "You're just a woman." This aspersion irritates and toughens her up and she takes charge of the company again, but soon leaves in pursuit of Thorne, finding him at a democratic carnival, a point the film telegraphs by making sure its audience sees some African Americans milling around. By the film's hazy "semio-system'" we are supposed to see that Alison has learned a lesson in democratic behavior. Though she has shown traces of class snobbery, the film illogically conflates its class rebukes with her needing a lesson in natural womanhood. When she confronts Thorne and he can see that she is now properly submissive, the film makes a gesture towards its earlier feminism: Thorne tells her that she should continue to run the company. But, overcome by hormones, Alison responds that he should run the company and she will stay home and have "nine children." She has become a "natural" woman. As in *Let Us Be Gay*, in *Female* feminism is an aberration provoked by male mistreatment.

THE NEW EQUILIBRIUM

Nevertheless, on film, approved heterosexual male and female romantic equality becomes a more desired ideal than it had been at any earlier period in the twentieth century. Weakened male authority does not result in a complete abandonment of romance. Instead, in an economic period when positing an alternative ideal in place of the perceived failed dynamics of the individualistic and male-dominated Hoover era was

Something approaching equality in a marriage (*The Thin Man*, MGM, 1934).

bankable with mass audiences, a new romantic equilibrium materialized on screen.[43] In *The Thin Man* when Nora Charles (Myrna Loy) enters the nightclub where her husband Nick (William Powell) has been drinking all evening, she asks him how many martinis he's had. He tells her six, and, since she already has one in her hand, she orders five more. In all things she pushes for balance. Verbally, the two spend most of the film trading quips. When he pulls a prank on her, she pulls one on him in return. In *Nothing Sacred*, reporter Wally Cook (Fredric March) falls in love with Hazel Flagg (Carole Lombard), who's feigning a terminal illness to get a free tour of New York. Learning that they are in danger of being discovered, Wally wants to make Hazel appear truly sick to fool a doctor. Among other tactics, he slugs her, temporarily knocking her out. When she comes to, she returns the favor, socking him on the jaw and thereby restoring a level of equality to their relationship. Therefore it makes sense that immediately after hitting him, she gushes with love.

The condition of equality which materializes as a desirable end for middle-class heterosexual romance in the 1930s is often the condition that drives a film's plot, making it the goal of the plot complications and problems the characters face. But achieving equality inside an approved heterosexual relationship often necessitates remaking traditional male or female qualities in order to match one's love; that is, remaking them in accordance with Depression-era values. Two films, *Bringing Up Baby* and *His Girl Friday,* exemplify this point. In *Bringing Up Baby,* the male lead, David Huxley (Gary Grant), a paleontologist, must be feminized before he can meet his soul mate, Susan Vance (Katherine Hepburn), on common ground. The film becomes a process of removing or adjusting masculine qualities that serve as obstacles to his matching up with Susan. *Bringing Up Baby* also illustrates how screwball, as a comic style, served the end of feminizing comedy. Its logic challenges male rationality and patriarchal power structures.[44] David Huxley, whose last name evokes a scientific history and matching mind-set, begins the film with a mannishly dressed masculinized fiancée, also a scientist. She tells David that there will be no sex in their marriage; the dinosaur they are working on will, she says, "be our child." Ultra masculinity bereft of romance, this film suggests, is not a desired goal. Instead the film seeks the middle ground of equilibrium. David soon meets the more feminine and intuitive Susan and tells her, "You look at everything upside down." She informs her aunt at one point, "I'm going to marry [David]. He doesn't know it, but I am." Her feminine intuition proves superior to his rationality, since she is proven right. She explains her apparent irrationality to him by saying, "All that happened happened because I was trying to keep you near me and I just did whatever came into my head." At the film's end, when she knocks over his assembled dinosaur, which represents years of work, she divines his feelings. She asks him a quick-fire series of questions, but intuits and answers them all herself. She cries, "David, can you ever forgive me? You can. And you still love me? You do."

For this last point to be true, David first has to be feminized. This occurs by Susan's repeatedly subverting his masculine dignity and disregarding male property values (the latter a particularly appealing concept in Depression America). At a golf course, Susan takes David's car, possibly thinking it her own, and promptly damages it, dismissing his protests with upside-down logic. Tricking David into accompanying her on a trip to deliver a leopard, she gets them into an accident that messes up David's clothes. They arrive at her aunt's and she persuades him to take a shower. While he's in the shower, she takes his clothes and sends them out, while she wears his hat, a visual reversal of gender. Without his suit, he's powerless to leave. The only available outfit is a negligee. Wearing this accelerates David's immersion into feminine values. When Susan's aunt appears at the door, she asks David—still in the negligee—who he is, twice, emphasizing the instability of his identity. He replies, "I'm not myself today. I just went gay all of a sudden." The animal world, representing "natural" beings, cooperates with Susan. Baby, the leopard, keeps David in Susan's company. And George,

A visual of David's feminization (*Bringing Up Baby*, RKO, 1938).

Susan's dog, suggestively steals David's bone, the last needed to complete the dinosaur. Repeated references to David's loss of "his bone," and Susan renaming David "Mr. Bone" to keep his identity from her aunt, contribute to a feminizing of David's masculine self. When he has been properly feminized, he and Susan can be a match; they have become equal enough.

In *His Girl Friday* it is the woman, reporter Hildy Johnson (Rosalind Russell), who needs to be masculinized in order to achieve the desired equilibrium with her male match, Walter Burns (Gary Grant). Hildy has divorced Burns and left her profession as a reporter. She tells Burns she is remarrying, with the identity-related explanation, "I want to go someplace where I can be a woman." Burns, believing she still loves him, reveals that he is possessed of superior intuition (a feminine trait) by asking, "Been seeing me in your dreams?" The man she intends to marry, Bruce Baldwin (Ralph Bellamy), sells life insurance, here conflated with domesticity as a job which smothers masculinity. The male workplace of the newspaper represents spontaneity and challenge. Life insurance insures against surprise. And Bruce is feminized by being dominated by his mother who, it is revealed, will live with the couple once they are married.

Walter spends the film playing tricks to get Bruce arrested and keep Hildy exposed to her old job, to lure her back to him and to her profession. The more Hildy works on her story about a convicted murderer, the more she returns to being a journalist and the more masculinized she becomes. In her interplay with other reporters the traditional domestic value assigned to the wife erodes. When one reporter asks her if they're invited to the wedding, she reverses his gender and says, "I might use you for a bridesmaid." Soon she joins the reporters in ridiculing Bruce and domestic life. In her absence a reporter remarks, "I give the marriage six months." When another asks why, he responds, "Because she won't be able to stay away from the paper any longer than that." Seeing her excitement at a fire alarm (with its potential for a story), a reporter remarks to the all-male group, "She's just like us." Walter destabilizes gender when he tells Bruce, speaking of Hildy, "you're getting a great newspaperman." Using the term "lady" in a derogatory fashion, Hildy reverses the reporters' gender, telling them that it is "getting so a girl can't leave the room without being discussed by a bunch of old ladies." When the murderer escapes, Hildy hikes up her skirts, pursues the fleeing warden and, manlike, tackles him. By the film's end, Hildy has accepted Walter's regendering of her. Bruce charges, "You're just like him." She responds, "I'm not a suburban bridge player. I'm a newspaperman." *His Girl Friday,* by rewriting a role originally intended for a man, also adjusts the definition of feminine gender to include assertiveness and workplace professionalism. Walter and Hildy become a match only after she has been properly masculinized.

MONEY, ROMANCE, AND IDENTITY

In 1964 John Cheever, child of the Great Depression, published one of his best short stories, "The Swimmer." The central character, Neddy Merrill, approximately Cheever's age, would also have been young in the 1930s. Unlike Cheever, Neddy has not yet learned the harsh Depression lesson that money can create identity. A New England aristocrat from the sort of family that came over on the *Mayflower,* Neddy regards his social standing, from which he derives his identity, as part of the natural order. On the day of the story, he gets the idea that he will swim across country from the party he's attending to his home, by way of a series of mostly private swimming pools. He encounters a procession of people from his past as he swims their pools en route home. In the process, democratic and undemocratic things happen. To complete his trek he has to swim across a public pool, something he has never done. Facing the pool teeming with commoners he thinks that he might "contaminate himself, damage his own prosperousness and charm, by swimming in this murk."[45] Encountering a crass couple, the Biswangers, at their pool, he recalls how they had invited him and his wife to their parties and he always declined: "They did not belong to Neddy's set" because "they were the sort of people who discussed the price of things."[46] At the story's end, it becomes clear that Neddy has suffered some sort of nervous breakdown. Arriving at his old house, "He shouted, pounded at the door, tried to force it with his shoulder, and then, looking in at the window saw that the place was empty."[47] He has lost it to business failure. Neddy has been awakened to a fact that is at times suppressed in glamorous films of the 1930s (*Top Hat*, for example). Beneath the glamour, the glow of romance, often happiness itself, lies the necessity for the enabling power of money. Definitions of gender identity, as well as romance itself, are exposed as subject to economic forces. The severity of the Depression lays bare this point. Romantic films of the Depression era convey that gender identity cannot be separated from prevailing economics.

Women, even feminists of the 1930s, continued to speak of women as occupying a dual role, in the workplace and as wives and mothers. For women, the stakes in 1930s romances are high, since a good or bad marriage is invested with almost spiritual meaning, and it also determines how one will live. Given the stakes, romance is often treated as though it exists in a vacuum, as a transcendent verity. For women it is often presented as a solution to life's worries.

Nevertheless, several films on which Busby Berkeley worked, like Cheever's story "The Swimmer," recognize that identity and romance have economic underpinnings, especially in an era beset by economic trauma. *Gold Diggers of 1935* brings together idealized male-female romantic identities and offers a sharp exposé of how money enables them. The plot itself has been contrived to call Hollywood romantic conventions into question. A wealthy young woman, Ann Prentiss, staying at a posh hotel with her family, and smothered by her tight-fisted, controlling mother, needs only her romantic match for fulfillment. A young man, Dick Curtis (Dick Powell), has come to work at the hotel to earn money for medical school, and he meets Ann. It's clear from the outset, as it would be in any number of lesser musical romances, that Ann will marry Dick. But as the film's director, Busby Berkeley is interested in exposing the relationships between identity, romantic fulfillment, and money. Beneath the plot question of whether Ann will find fulfillment lies the desperation of most of the film's characters to get money. Money is connected to issues of unemployment and the stock market, making the Depression a force in creating or destroying romances, as opposed to their being achieved through sheer magic.

The film works hard to demonstrate that virtually every character at the hotel is an economic predator. Early images in the film are of smiling, dancing hotel employees, but these are soon undermined when we see that employees who are paid in tips are coerced by their supervisors into handing over a percentage. Ann's wealthy mother, Mrs. Prentiss, ever-worried about the stock market, is sharkishly trying to marry Ann off to a rich older man, Mosley Thorpe, referred to in economic terms as the "snuff box king." Romantically he is unattractive, but financially he represents power and security. Dick and Ann don't meet Romeo-and-Juliet style, with a sudden burst of connecting magic; rather, he's hired by her mother to take her shopping. In a seeming rejection of her mother's materialism, Ann goes on an obscene spending spree, while the song "I'm Going Shopping" plays maniacally in the background. A Mr. Lampson manipulates and exploits a desperate out-of-work director into putting on the show Mrs. Prentiss pays for each year. We soon learn she does so not out of an interest in the arts, but because there is a tax deduction for it. Scenes of Mosley and his private secretary, Betty Hawes (Glenda Farrell), reveal that she is working him for glasses of champagne. Eventually she tricks Mosley into autographing a love song for her and then gets a lawyer to sue him for alienation of affections, framing the love song lyrics as a promise to marry her. Mrs. Prentiss eventually agrees to Dick's marrying her daughter, but only because it will be financially advantageous.

The show that is put on at the hotel becomes a subversive commentary on the connection between the glamour of romance and the necessity for money to make it possible. The main number, "Lullaby of Broadway," juxtaposes images of romance, glamour, work, money, and prostitution.[48] The whole piece draws its visual images from strategies that can be traced back to German expressionism and modernism, using narrative gaps and psychological perspective to convey its destabilizing meaning.[49] The film uses camera angle and voice to emphasize humans as disembodied parts available for commercial use. We first hear only the voice of the lead woman, Wini Shaw, a minor character, seemingly peripheral to the main plot (a cigarette girl), because the camera is so far from her disembodied face (the rest of her body is entirely blacked out). We then see, close up, her whitened head severed from her body by blackness. In a sense we've been prepared for the subject matter of this number by the predatory money-grabbing tactics of the film's secondary characters, but the visual techniques are so different, so purely modernist, that the whole number has a disorienting effect. It achieves what Picasso and modernist poets often sought: by abandoning the narrative conventions of film romance it jars us into rethinking the whole film, especially the idealized romance at its center. Instead of connecting directly to the male-female romance, it connects more directly to issues of money, labor, and gender identity. As the camera closes in on the face of the singing woman, we learn that the "Lullaby of Broadway" isn't the romance the film has set us up to expect; it is the sounds of economic industry on Broadway, the "rumble of the subway train, the rattle of the taxi, the dancing girls who entertain." Pairing the entertainers with other mundane vehicles of profit exposes their shared function, which in turn dehumanizes them, the same effect Berkeley gets in numerous dance numbers where he emphasizes the chorines, or even just parts of their bodies, as parts of a dance line, cogs in the economic musical machine.

As Wini finishes the first run through of the title song, the camera circles her head and slowly it becomes the city of New York: she has merged with the industry she's been singing about. The camera closes in on the milkman's work, then on intimate items of women's apparel, a silk stocking being rolled up a woman's leg, a woman struggling with her bra: it is all economically grounded. Newspapers are delivered; people rush to work and pay to get on the subway. We see them gulping their food, like Chaplin in *Modern Times*, eating against the clock, a point emphasized by the immediate close-up on a blaring factory whistle. A pencil sharpener is juxtaposed with a man's hand turning the hand of a barrel organ. Music, we are reminded, is part of an economic enterprise.

While everyone else rushes to work, Wini, the "baby" of the song, arrives at her apartment escorted by a society swell, Dick Powell, here no longer occupying his original role as romantic lead in the main plot. But his appearance in the hotel's show visually connects the film and the show and casts the film's romance into a relief composed of the show's images. Wini's going to bed as others go to work initially seems romantic. But outside her window we see a giant clock, part of a sign for Credit Jewelers, a reminder of inescapable connections between economics and romance. Night falls and we see Wini depart with the swell. They enter a posh nightclub and we see a show, now a show inside a show that is already inside a show. A couple performs an Astaire-Rogers sort of dance, all costume and style. Soon they are replaced by enormous dance lines of men and women; the men's apparel resembles the hotel's bellboy costumes, another reminder of the economic aspect of performance. Much has been made of the crass dance marathons of the Depression era, preying as they did on the desperation of the unemployed.[50] Here the hard-hitting emphasis on the precision of the dance lines, with camera angles emphasizing the effort of each move (down to a glass floor so that we can see dance steps from below — there is no privacy for the individual here), recalls the financial importance, or dance marathon-like desperation, of making it in show business in perilous times. Smiling, Wini looks down at the dancers, who beckon her to "come and dance." She answers, "Why don't you come and get me?" The dancers pursuit of her becomes a press and they force her onto a window ledge. They move in and she falls. Their horrified screams precede the camera's following her dizzying fall to reveal that she lands on the clock of the Credit Jewelers sign. We see her now-empty flat, with her newspaper and milk bottle untouched outside her door. Her night work, with its more than hint of prostitution, is now over, but she seems to have been impaled on time and the reminder that romance is purchased on credit. The camera returns to its long shot of the city, which is Wini's head: she is the vocalist again. Her head, visually the number's nexus, organizes the jumble of images, connecting romance, sex, and financial pressure.

Like Cheever, Berkeley has worked to expose the hard economic foundation that enables what is perceived as romantic identity. The movie concept that romance in itself represents fulfillment for women, or that romance somehow exists outside of the economic system, is exploded by the subversive reminder that romance is enabled by cash. Put another way, the Ginger Rogers–Fred Astaire-style romance, and the male-female identities at its center, either on screen or in the bonds of holy matrimony, are enabled by money, a point for which the Depression served as a penultimate lesson.

6

The Arc of National Confidence
and the Birth of Film Noir, 1929–41

Fragile Certitude, 1929–36

In the thirties, art and confidence were closely entwined. Looking back at the Depression decade in 1939, Malcolm Cowley, writing for *Harper's*, lamented that for the American art community the thirties closed "with a sense of defeat and disillusionment, when [artists] saw the world falling into the hands of their other enemies, the generals and power politicians."[1] The combination of the Depression and the attendant rise of fascism provoked significant shifts in the art community. Ezra Pound responded to the convulsions of suffering democratic countries by going over to the fascists. Tyrus Miller describes Henry Miller in the late thirties as one of the many writers of late modernism who had become "bereft of . . . any calling in which they might believe." Miller explains that "modernist fiction . . . is predominantly epistemological: it seeks, despite the confusing webs . . . to *disclose* a coherent knowable world." In the late thirties, "modernist poetics begins to hemorrhage, to leak away." This occurs because of a failure of faith; and modernism's "desire to restore significance to a broken world [is] abandoned."[2]

When one recognizes the stakes in Fredric Jameson's describing film noir, which materialized near the end of the thirties, as a modernist art form, one begins to see the implications of the modernist phenomenon Tyrus Miller describes and how they illuminate the genesis of film noir, especially considering the phenomenon of the emergence of noir coinciding with a modernist crisis of confidence. Jameson discusses one of the central characteristics of both literary and cinematic noir when he takes up the issue of uncertainty in Raymond Chandler's work: "Inveterate readers of Chandler know that it is no longer for the solution to the mystery that they reread him, if indeed the solutions ever solved anything in the first place." His remark captures the loss of certitude that is at the heart of noir. He illustrates his point about uncertainty by describing an argument John Huston and Humphrey Bogart had one night over *The Big Sleep.* To settle things, "they finally phone Chandler himself," with the problem result that "he can't remember."[3] The problem of failed certainty, of not being able "to disclose a coherent knowable world," and the anxiety that attends the problem, serves as a defining noir element.

The issue of when noir emerges on film is complicated by one of its oddities, its roots in the German Expressionist period, the high period of which ran from roughly 1919 into the early years of the international Depression (ending with the ascent of Hitler in 1933). This was an extremely anxious period for the Weimar Republic, one marked by runaway inflation, street warfare, depression, and, eventually, the impending threat of Nazism. American film noir shares its emphasis on subjective psychological states and its paranoia over authority as corrupt as the criminal world with German Expressionism.[4] Two of the most important Expressionist films, *Caligari* and *Mabuse,* illustrate both of these points. In both films a psychiatrist may or may not be a psychotic criminal. In Expressionist film, states of mind cohere with sets and camera techniques. Certainty is elusive. But American film noir (unlike pop fiction noir) does not emerge until the late thirties. To understand why it does not emerge earlier and why it emerges when it does, one must first track developments during the decade in American national confidence; for film, throughout the Depression decade, participates in and thereby exemplifies America's touch-and-go communal confidence. On this point it is important to recognize that the mass audience for film, marked as it was by immigrants, minorities, and the poor, roughly corresponds to a significant portion of the New Deal voting alliance, an alliance whose confidence would be shaken, after some roller coaster surges in confidence, from about 1937 forward.

In the twenties, American confidence outpaced that of the Weimar Republic. Until the end of the twenties, Germany continued to strain under the debt of World War I reparations that were, as John Maynard Keynes, who was at Versailles, points out, stupidly and self-servingly engineered by the French and the English, mostly by the French. Keynes predicted, accurately, that in the wake of World War I the Germans would suffer economic and political upheaval. Soon after Versailles, the Weimar Republic suffered runaway inflation, French occupation of the Ruhr, and persistent harassment from secret, mostly right-wing organizations. When Wall Street crashed Germany suffered more than any other Depression-stricken country, primarily because its economy had been propped up by credit from U.S. banks who were after 1929 themselves in a crisis; its economic crisis led directly to Nazi ascendance. At his inauguration in March of 1929, Herbert Hoover had told the assemblage, "I have no fears for the future of our country. It is bright with hope."[5] As late as December 1929, two months after the market crash, Charles Schwab, Chairman of the Board of Bethlehem Steel, remarked, "Never before has American business been as firmly implanted as it is today."[6] Shortly thereafter such confidence would be viewed with acidic irony. Paul Johnson recalls the anger the public directed at Hoover as it was embedded in popular jokes: "What was a 'Hoover blanket'? It was an old newspaper used to keep warm a man forced to sleep in the open. And a 'Hoover flag?' An empty pocket turned inside out as a sign of destitution. . . . In the autumn of 1932 hitchhikers displayed signs reading, 'Give me a ride—or I'll vote for Hoover.' "[7]

A year earlier, Gerald W. Johnson had remarked on the "fathomless pessimism" that had overtaken the American people: "The energy of the country has suffered a strange paralysis. . . . We are in the doldrums, waiting not even hopefully for the wind which never comes."[8] As early as 1930, people had begun hitting the relief roles, but at that time these were local relief organizations and they soon began to crack under the strain. And out of money and out of work, "unemployed men and their entire families began to build shacks . . . in the city dumps there appeared towns of tarpaper and tin, old packing boxes and old car bodies."[9] Many began to feel that America and even Western civilization had played out. In the spring of 1931, Africans in Cameroon sent New York $3.77 to relieve starving. Later that year one hundred thousand Americans applied for jobs in Soviet Russia. A few days before he died in 1933, Calvin Coolidge remarked, "In other periods of depression it has always been possible to see some things which were solid and upon which you could base hope, but as I look about, I see nothing to give ground for hope." As William Leuchtenburg remarked, "Society seemed to be disintegrating."[10]

In two significant ways Americans of the thirties experienced some fundamental shifts in how they perceived their nation. First, there was a political shift away from conservative traditional values. But in some ways this was of the surface. And developments in the late thirties would expose the whiplash effect on people who had been moved away from the traditional political right by the force of economic trauma, with an attendant—and nasty—response from those who had stayed on the right and waited for their time to come around once more (which, in the late thirties, it would). Secondly, there was an anger-provoking re-conceiving of society's leaders, especially those in business. And this contributed to a new cynical view of national leadership which scoured recent history for villains all the way back to World War I. This para-noiac element, as a sourness set into the national bloodstream late in the decade, would materialize in a new and dark form in popular film.

The first of these cases materializes at all levels of American life in the early decade. At the primal level of family, in Pennsylvania a father wrote to Governor Pinchot, "I don't want to steal . . . but I won't let my wife and boy cry for something to eat." This also occurred at the class level. Speaking to the Senate Agriculture Committee in 1932, A. N. Young, President of the Wisconsin Farmers' Union, asserted, "The farmer is naturally a conservative individual, but you cannot find a conservative farmer today. . . . I am as conservative as any man could be, but any economic system that has the power to set me and my wife on the streets, at my age—what else could I see but red." Young warned the Committee that if the farmers could "buy airplanes, they would come down here to Washington to blow you fellows up."[11] Oklahoma ranchers would have seemed the least likely group to talk about revolution, but in the early thirties they embodied explosive anger. One told a congressman, "We have got to have a revolution here like they had in Russia . . . I just want to tell you that I am going to be one of them, and I am going to do my share in it." He then proceeded to outline a plan to capture a fort, seize its munitions, and cut the West off from the hated Northeast.[12]

At the level of state politics, talk of revolution came from the least likely places. Governor Theodore Bilbo, the sort of Southern governor one would expect to be leading communist witch hunts, told an interviewer, "Right here in Mississippi people are about ready to lead a mob. In fact, I'm getting a little pink myself."[13] Yet these remarks do not mean exactly what they seem to suggest, that a communist revolution was a likelihood. Rather, as Leuchtenburg notes, "There was less an active demand for change than disillusionment with parliamentary politics, so often the prelude to totalitarianism in Europe. . . . Many Americans came to despair of the whole political process, a contempt for Congress, for parties, for democratic institutions."[14]

On the second point, that of a new disgust for leadership, it was business leaders, and especially the bankers and stock speculators, a group notable for their conservatism, who early in the thirties caught the main force of the nation's ire. The economic crisis provoked a close examination of financial practices and then a new anger toward leaders of finance. Calvin Coolidge had unwittingly participated in setting the nation up for an abrupt and painful loss of faith. He had remarked, "The chief business of the American people is business." And he had virtually sanctified business leaders: "The man who builds a factory builds a temple . . . The man who works there worships there." William

Allen White saw Coolidge "as persuaded of the divine character of wealth as Lincoln had been of the divine character of man, 'crazy about it, sincerely, genuinely, terribly crazy.' "[15] Coolidge's remarks are just pieces of evidence supporting the oft-repeated assertion that the banker and stock investor had been the heroes of the twenties. With the crash, all eyes were on them. Soon the investigations that followed undermined the mythology that had grown in the twenties. A 1932 Senate investigation into Wall Street practices "revealed that the most respected men on Wall Street had rigged pools, had profited by pegging bonds artificially high, and had lined their pockets with artificial bonuses."[16] The once-confident Charles Schwab was soon revealing a distressing uncertainty, which he connected to the way the economic crisis undermined American values: "I'm afraid, every man is afraid. I don't know, we don't know, whether the values we have are going to be real next month or not." When in 1932 "one of the supposed miracle workers of international industry and finance," Ivar Kreuger, shot himself, it slowly became apparent that "Kreuger's operations had been fraudulent, and that he had readily deceived with false figures and airy lies one of the most esteemed American financial houses."[17] Intensifying the collapse of prosperity was the sense that the reputations of society's pillars had been illusory; intensifying the dissolution of respected reputations was a fear that fundamental American values had themselves been an illusion. At a sudden confidence-deflating moment, the criminal and the paragon, what was admirable and what was repulsive, were indistinguishable.

The sense that somehow accepted values and respected personages had all been a mirage made its way into the American mind. In John Dos Passos's *U.S.A.*, Woodrow Wilson becomes Satan. The character Savage describes him as "A terrifying face, I swear it's a reptile's face, not warm-blooded."[18] Attacking Wilson, Senator Gerald Nye's committee investigating arms profiteering during World War I charged "Wilson had 'falsified' when he had denied knowledge of the secret treaties" between American businessmen and European war allies.[19] The vitriolic language of the committee, which operated in the mid-thirties, illustrated the deep distrust of formerly respected leaders that had materialized in the first half of the thirties. It also revealed the effect the Depression was having on something like national paranoia. Conservative Paul Johnson describes the congressional investigations into Wall Street that took place in 1932 as a "witch hunt." But even the more liberal David Kennedy characterizes Nye investigation's indictment as "grossly overdrawn."[20] The search for someone to hold accountable, to punish, the party or parties responsible for the Depression, was creating a culture with a concrete inquisition element, an element that would crystallize as inquiry in the HUAC investigations which began in the late thirties and which would ironically turn the focus of hostility away from the captains of capitalism and back onto the liberals.

The complexities of communal confidence in the thirties find their center in Franklin Roosevelt. To understand Roosevelt's place in the bumpy history of national confidence, one must start with his being stricken by polio in 1920. Robert McElvaine remarks, "In searching for the basis of Roosevelt's compassion and his rapport with the down-trodden, the importance of this dream-shattering disease deserves heavy emphasis. . . . This was absolutely critical to Roosevelt's later relationship with victims of the Great Depression."[21] As a victim of polio, New England aristocrat Franklin Roosevelt got a severe dose of what it was like to be an outsider. He acquired a new insight into what it meant to suffer, suffering being typically foreign to his class. When he later talked about suffering he did so with the legitimacy of one who had experience in the matter. This acquired empathy gave him a status with commoners that set him apart from the bankers and investors, and it served him in good stead as he embarked on social welfare reforms.

The final months of Hoover's time in office, prior to Roosevelt assuming the presidency, represented a low point in American spirits during the Depression. Leuchtenburg remarks that "In Hoover's last days the old order tottered on the brink of disaster." Roosevelt wondered if the country would make it to inauguration day.[22] In his inauguration speech Roosevelt largely reiterated what Hoover had been saying for the past three years. Nevertheless, by one historian's account, "Roosevelt had made his single greatest contribution to the politics of the 1930s: the instillation of hope . . . in the people. . . . He had made an impression . . . of a man who . . . had faith in the future." Faced with a bank crisis, which was at heart a crisis of investor confidence, Roosevelt declared a bank "holiday," convened a special session of Congress, and set forth an emergency banking measures that "with a unanimous shout" the House passed "sight unseen." The bill, in fact, was as conservative as had been Hoover's proposals; the difference was in the new confidence FDR inspired. The success of the bank measures is reflected in the banks having been closed to stave off bank runs and massive withdrawals; after they reopened, "Nothing so much indicated the sharp shift in public sentiment as the fact that people were now more eager to deposit cash than to withdraw it." Raymond Moley expansively announced, "Capitalism was saved in eight days." Just "two weeks after Roosevelt took office the country seemed a changed place." Confidence had been, if not fully restored, at least reintroduced into the national bloodstream.

What is notable about the early, jubilant period of the New Deal is how often in the early days of Roosevelt's presidency conservative politicians voted against their own political values, an action they repeated many times out of a sense that the country was in a warlike crisis and they had to back the president. This meant the rash of programs passed during the first New Deal were rife with internal friction in the body politic. The models used by New Dealers for how they wished to proceed and what they wished to achieve came from a business-government cooperation plan that had been used during World War I and from Progressive theory. But this did not mean that conservatives had been converted to a liberal position. They simply choked back their feelings. Illustrating the paradox in New Deal strategy, FDR would call bankers the "money changers" who had been "driven from the temple" in his inaugural address, then as his first act pass a banking act that should have made even conservative bankers happy. Thus his first term was marked by the contradictory realities that he 1) refused to give up the concept of working with business on a managed economy rather than treating business as an opponent, and 2) he could not shake his politically conditioned suspicion that the monopolists were responsible for the economic crisis. When the tide, and the Supreme Court, turned against a New Deal centerpiece—the National Recovery Act—internal dissonance became more pronounced, and external attack became more likely.

International events were aggravating what was already an anxious national mind-set. Back in 1931 Japan had invaded Manchuria, and even at that early point some in the State Department believed war with Japan was inevitable. Almost at the moment of Roosevelt's first inauguration, Hitler first secured the German chancellorship, then began using secret police to expunge his enemies. By 1934, Germany was a totalitarian police state. Soon the Germans and Italians were aiding Franco in Spain. In Germany, Jewish civil rights were being disregarded, and the Jews' property confiscated. In 1936, Hitler abandoned the terms of Versailles and remilitarized the Rhineland. Meanwhile Italy invaded Ethiopia. Frederick Lewis Allen characterizes the effect on the American sense of certainty: "Truly it was a new world upon which Americans were looking in 1936: a world full of the wreckage of the verities not merely of 1929 but even of 1932."[23]

FALLEN WOMEN AND GANGSTER FILMS, 1930–37

True film noir does not emerge until late in the thirties, although one can spot noir moments in films throughout the early part of the decade.

What defines the difference, however, is pretty clear. In true noir two core elements must be present: moral certainty must be somehow obscure (a pillar of society turns out to be a criminal; a detective is nearly as much a part of the underworld as he is a part of enforcing the law, etc.), and certainty itself must be thrown into question (voice-over narrators speak with confidence only to wind up telling us a story of how wrong they were all along, as in *Dead Reckoning*). But films from 1929 to the late thirties participate in a concerted national effort not to give up faith in "the old verities," even though such faith is sorely tested by the ongoing economic crisis. To the extent that this giving up of old verities happens in film noir, it happens nationally, and more and more recognizably, after 1937. One can support this assertion by examining some films in genres recognized as those from which noir emerges, the genres being those of the fallen woman and gangster movies.[24]

If one considers the ways in which liberalism grows out of progressivism, the reason for the popularity of the notion that such things as poverty, immorality, and crime are sociological phenomena in the early thirties comes into focus. Sociology as a discipline was still relatively new in the early twentieth century; it was still in the process of being introduced by Durkheim and Weber. By the thirties, social science had acquired a confidence that social problems could be "managed" once they were understood. The political manifestation of such logic was that they could be managed by government. What had up until the nineteenth century been treated as natural conditions, such as ghettos and poverty, were by the late twenties being viewed by liberals as solvable problems. Paradoxically illustrating this point, since it is neoconservative Paul Johnson speaking, Hoover (whom he calls derisively "the Great Engineer") is criticized for being too liberal, for not sticking to strict laissez-faire logic, instead giving in to a belief that government can "manage" its populace: "The new fashion of social engineering—the notion that action from above could determine the shape of society and that human beings could be manhandled and manipulated like earth and concrete—had come into its own in World War One." For this way of regarding government's relationship to the governed, Johnson blames the pernicious influence of social theorist and economist Thorstein Veblen.[25]

In spite of the oppressive conditions of the Depression, films of the early thirties continued to share a logic with prevalent sociological theory of the first three decades of the twentieth century. Politically such faith was enabled by the injection of hope that Roosevelt had supplied. Therefore such figures as the noir femme fatale and the detective with one foot in the underworld are staved off by popular film for much of the thirties. Part of the reason for this has to do with the ways film differed from theater and print fiction during the period. The same interests that engineered a degree of censorship in film feared the potential effect film might have in stirring up immigrants and the working class (and the latter was already making gains through new union legislation, as soon demonstrated by the Wagner Act). Thus, ideas and characters that were appearing in other art forms were partially staved off by the censorship forces. This occurred because it was believed that ideas critical of mainstream America might incite resentment and worse—action—from the lower denizens. This had implications for film noir. With the implementation of the censorship code in March 1933, a number of film projects were rejected, including an adaptation of James M. Cain's noir novel, *The Postman Always Rings Twice* (though when American ideological dynamics changed, it was made in the forties).[26] And the thoroughly noir novel *The Maltese Falcon* was filmed twice (in 1931 and 1936, each time with distinctly non-noir endings) before it finally became a film noir in 1941.

But the primary interest of the fallen woman film, unlike the fatal woman of noir film, was in a sociological rescue of the woman. The continuity of a logic with roots in the literary version of the social engineering that Paul Johnson finds objectionable (that is, naturalism) shows up in a 1921 Eugene O'Neill play, *Anna Christie*, which is filmed in 1931 and which illustrates a confidence in identifying moral issues that might make a woman appear to be immoral, which evaporates in the later noir films. *Anna Christie* and many subsequent films like it are purely sociological in their inquiries into right and wrong. They demonstrate a confidence that the causes of poverty and moral behavior can still be uncovered and that individual responsibility must be considered within social and economic environments. Clearly such logic touches a communal nerve during the Depression. In the film, we first see Anna (Greta Garbo) as a worldly wise barfly, who encounters Marthy, a drunk in a bar, and who answers the remark about having Anna's number "the minute [Anna] stepped in the door" by responding, "You're me forty years from now." Starting with this image of Anna, the film peels away the layers of Anna's history to revise the concept of her tragedy as resulting from either choice or the natural immorality of the underclass. Anna had been shunted off on relatives by her father at a young age and raped by a relative. She was unsuccessful in her effort to escape from sexual abuse. She has been a prostitute, but the film makes clear its view she had no choice. This is a liberal rather than conservative interpretation of individual responsibility. One can see its attractiveness to audiences who were themselves trapped or threatened with being trapped by traumatic economic circumstances. What the film resists is any failure of certainty

After first presenting Mary as a hardened criminal, *Midnight Mary* makes the sociological move of taking us back into her childhood so we can see how she came to be the person we first encounter (MGM, 1933).

concerning its ability to explain Anna. Unlike later noir treatments of women in similar circumstances it exhibits a sociologist's confidence that it can delve into environment and explain economic and class-related phenomena. In pre-noir circumstances, people are often excused of immorality by our understanding the responsibility their environments bear in making them.

Perhaps the quintessential exhibition of sociological confidence in the fallen woman film occurs in *Midnight Mary* (1933). It opens by showing us a criminal woman, Mary (Loretta Young), who is sitting in court awaiting sentencing. Soon she begins explaining her life, and, through a series of flashbacks, we see the environmental forces that have made Mary. Our first impression of Mary as criminal slowly gives way to a redefinition of her moral character. We see she began life in a slum. Her mother died when she was nine. When a girl steals then drops a stolen pencil in a store, Mary picks it up and is falsely accused of theft. Typical of the harsh criminal justice system presented in films of the early thirties (*I am a Fugitive from a Chain Gang, Paid, Hell's Highway*, etc.), which is disinterested in the causes of human behavior, she is given a sentence of three years in reform school.

When Mary is seventeen, she and a girlfriend are out riding in a car with two boys who tell them to wait in the car while they go into a store. Without the girls' knowledge of their intentions, they rob the store. When one of the boys forces fifty dollars of stolen money onto Mary she gives it to the Salvation Army. Without money herself, she is soon evicted from her home. The camera follows her as she walks the streets searching for work. In one employment line a girl faints. Businesses feature signs that read "No Help Wanted."

Driven by desperation Mary looks up her old friends, who operate as a gang. Its leader, Leo (Ricardo Cortez), tells her she belongs to him. When the gang holds up a club at which Mary works as a hatcheck girl and serves as a lookout for the gang, she meets a wealthy man, Tom (Franchot Tone), and leaves the gang for him. She starts secretarial school in an effort to escape her old life. When her past threatens to disgrace her new boyfriend she goes to the police and turns herself in to protect him. Once Mary is released, Leo tries to regain control of her and threatens to kill Tom. As Temple does in the film version of Faulkner's *Sanctuary, The Story of Temple Drake* (1933), Mary attempts to seduce Leo to keep him from going off to murder Tom. Both films seek to make the point that true morality is more complex than society makes it out to be. When the film finally returns its audience to the point at which it opened—Mary's trial—Tom now has allied himself with her and the film ends with his assuring her that they will win. By this point the film has completely constructed an argument that Mary's environment has led to society's falsely labeling her as immoral and criminal. We have been shown that repeatedly she does the moral thing, even when society fails to correctly define her actions that way, a point that would have been popular with the heavily represented working class and immigrant audiences of the thirties, who saw these films under the shadow of economic crisis. Nevertheless, the progressive-liberal faith that the environment can be overcome survives to the end of the film, but just barely.

The gangster films present a slightly different aspect of the same issue. But they present a more persistent threat to faith in authority. They often make the same claims the fallen woman films make concerning the relationship of environment and character, but in the process they threaten to make the criminal so attractive he could become a role model, especially in a country which has suffered a major blow to its confidence in leaders of industry and government. In his study of gangster films, Jonathan Munby points out the gangster films were so popular with the public that they "had a profound influence on 1930s fashion codes. . . . Showcases for imitators of Cagney and Robinson were held before screenings as part of publicity campaigns for their movies." Munby concludes, "we don't get a criminal as such, but a new hero whose way of life corresponds more accurately to the problems of modern urban-American everyday life."[27]

Like the fallen woman, this new hero could gain sympathy by a thirties audience seeing the unfair environmental circumstances from which he emerged. This may explain why the gangster films do not go as far as the fallen woman films in assigning antisocial behavior to environment. In *The Public Enemy* (1931), slum children Tom Powers and Matt Doyle steal watches to gain the approval of a neighborhood thug. But the film stops short of making environment responsible for Tom Powers's (James Cagney) gangsterism. Tom has a brother who goes to night school and holds a job. The film argues that Tom's criminality results from choices. He is not the victim of an environment that cannot be overcome; if his brother can do it he can do it. Typical of the gangsters, he chooses his behavior. In *The Doorway to Hell* (1930), gangster Louis Ricarno (Lew Ayres) tells a girl he was born in a slum, and his brother and sister died of typhoid from bad milk sold to poor children. But like Powers, Ricarno has a brother who has gone straight; he is in a military academy, again insisting that life offers choices. As will happen in *Little Caesar* and *Scarface*, *Doorway to Hell* settles on a psychiatric explanation of Ricarno, who, like Rico in *Caesar* (1931) and Tony in *Scarface* (1932), suffers from a Napolean complex. Lest we miss this point, the film offers a picture of Napoleon on the wall of the room where Ricarno makes his last stand before he is killed.

The aversion in the gangster films, even in those that feature slums, to offering the sort of complete sociological explanation offered in fallen woman films like *Midnight Mary* arises from a fear of the effect of an antisocial hero who lashes out at society or who takes from capitalists when he may be otherwise blocked from responding to society's prompts to acquire, a fear that he may become too much of a role model, especially given the film gangster's frequent ethnic proximity to immigrants. A starting place for understanding the core difference between the gangster films and film noir comes from an unexpected characterization of the James Cagney gangster persona by film critic Richard Schickel many years ago. Schickel called Cagney's gangster "the first existential antihero of the American films."[28] What makes Schickel's language of interest is that it matches that of two influential theorists of noir, Raymond Durgnat and Robert Porfirio. Durgnat sees "nihilism" as noir's defining characteristic, and Porfirio sees "existentialism" as its defining characteristic.[29] One might then think that *Public Enemy* must be an early example of film noir. And it certainly has some noir features: notably it demonstrates identifiable connections to German Expressionism in its imagery. At the film's end when Tom Powers is delivered back to his family by rival gangsters, he is wrapped up mummy-style, placed in the door frame, and allowed to fall on his face. The image, with his terrified eyes just peeking out through the hospital bandages, captures his psychological state, and the bandages, which prevent all movement, capture his real and psychological circumstance: he is powerless in all ways, a tremendous irony since he got into this fix as a result of his hunger for power.

But no one thinks *Public Enemy* is an example of film noir. Schickel's revealing language, however, demonstrates the connections between gangster films and noir, even as it also demonstrates that gangster films are not noir. What separates *Public Enemy* from noir is a matter of significant degree. If Schickel is right that Cagney's Tom Powers is an existential antihero, he is one, nevertheless, in a clearly defined moral universe. He does not have one foot in the moral world and one in the criminal world (which is one of the defining characteristics assigned by Raymond Borde and Etienne Chaumeton in the first significant effort to explain and name the cultural cinematic phenomenon of film noir). They found that the detective of film noir was partly of the world of established morality and partly of the criminal underworld; from this point of departure one finds that noir itself is characterized by the evaporation of a clear line marking decency and criminality. One could say that line, given the characteristic imagery of noir, gets lost in the fog (as in *While the City Sleeps* [1956], in which the newspaper executives and their women are morally indistinguishable from the serial rapist-murderer they cover in their morning editions).

The censorship codes of the period speak directly to this point, and they do so as a form of participation in a larger American communal resistance to collapsing the distinction between established morality and that of the underworld that later in the decade would begin to materialize in film noir and separate it from its cinematic ancestors. In other words, for most of the thirties Hollywood resisted the sort of assault on confidence in traditional verities that would later emerge in film noir. In 1921, A. T. Poffenberger, a Columbia University professor, made the argument that movies possessed the power to create role models that could influence children and categorical morons in a negative manner, especially if crime was modeled on the screen. His core argument emerged periodically during the twenties and thirties. In one entry in a series of codes designed to regulate what appeared on the screen, in 1927 the Motion Picture Producers and Distributors declared that films should avoid any appearance of offering "sympathy for criminals." Echoing this point, The Motion Picture Production Code of 1930 stated, "The treatment of crimes against the law must not . . . make criminals seem heroic and justified." Lest the distinction between accepted morality and criminality be confused, *Public Enemy* opens with a written prologue which informs its audience that the film does not glorify hoodlums. It ends with a written epilogue which reminds its audience that hoodlums are a social problem. *Little Caesar* offers a similar disclaimer in its written prologue, and *Scarface,* which was subtitled "The Shame of a Nation," in its prologue blamed the government for a "callous indifference" to gangsterism and claimed the purpose of the film was to "demand of the government . . . what are you going to do about it?" Motivated in large part by a desire to escape government regulation which was being called for by religious organizations and others, Hollywood set out to regulate itself. The external pressures on the movie industry explicitly condemned presenting a dark world that denied the certainty of traditional moral distinctions. This would change late in the decade when the culmination of cynicism afflicting national confidence and deepening skepticism about the morality of established power would meet in film noir.

A political manifestation of the connection between Hollywood resistance to representing an existential universe and an unwillingness in the movies to give up traditional certitude, or national confidence in traditional verities, materialized early in the New Deal era. In spite of a mind-set that was hostile to anything resembling a monopoly, the Roosevelt administration made an exception for the movie industry. As Thomas Schatz points out, "Hollywood was a Depression-era success story, and it owed its resurgence largely to Roosevelt's economic recovery measures. . . . The NIRA strategy . . . was to promote recovery by sanctioning certain monopoly practices among major U.S. industries." One of these industries was the film establishment. In 1933, the NIRA atypically sanctioned "collusion among the big eight [studios] to control the marketplace . . . committing to paper such unwritten laws as blind and block booking, whereby the nonaffiliated theaters were forced to take the studios output, sight unseen."[30] In other words, New Deal confidence in Hollywood as an enterprise in bleak times converged with New Deal confidence in being able to solve the Depression and, more generally, in widespread public confidence in Roosevelt. Less obviously, the censorship codes, which represented an effort by the studios to control their own destiny, rather than leaving their fate in the hands of various straitlaced morality groups, participated in a concretely defined national confidence in the Roosevelt administration to alleviate the economic crisis.

FRANKLIN ROOSEVELT'S DARK PERIOD

Two works (one a three-volume set) by major twentieth-century historian Arthur Schlesinger Jr., illustrate the abrupt shift in national confidence that occurs in the late thirties, especially from 1937 forward. Schlesinger's short nostalgic essay on movies of the thirties, written from the vantage point of 1963, comments on the crisis of national confidence experienced by Americans in the thirties, but Schlesinger reaches the conclusion that national confidence followed an upward trajectory until the end of the thirties when the crisis was over. But contemporary historians do not agree with him. Rather they see a political crisis for liberals emerge in 1937, which translates to a new crisis of confidence. Schlesinger's own three-volume work, *The Age of Roosevelt*, unwittingly explains all of this. Temporally speaking, *The Age of Roosevelt* starts with the stock market crash, but oddly enough, the third volume ends with Roosevelt's reelection in 1936 and assumption of office in 1937. One might think the third volume would end with either the end of the Depression in 1941 or with Roosevelt's death near the end of World War II. Since the focus of the three volumes is the Depression, 1937 does not really mark the end of anything, unless one wants to make Roosevelt the unequivocal hero of the narrative. This is Schlesinger's goal. The year 1937 marks Roosevelt's triumphant reelection and an apparent indemnification of New Deal policies. One thing one learns from Schlesinger's otherwise penetrating study of the period is that the years from 1937 to 1941 present a complication if one's goal is to make Roosevelt the hero of a thirties narrative. The nature of this problem is closely entwined with jolts to national confidence that begin in 1937 and a loss of stature for liberals.

Nevertheless, for the Roosevelt people, 1937 began very auspiciously. Going into the 1936 election, "there was a heady sense of a nation once more in the money. Not only had gains been made, but Roosevelt's measures had the curious effect of driving poverty out of sight. The applesellers disappeared from the streets, the breadlines from the cities." Roosevelt campaigner Jim Farley predicted Roosevelt would carry every state but two, and he did. FDR was reelected "by the most sweeping electoral margin of any candidate since James Monroe. The staunchly Republican state of Pennsylvania had gone democratic for the first time since Buchanan's triumph in 1856." But Alan Brinkley points out that the optimism prevalent at the time of Roosevelt's inaugural address "was difficult to sustain even a few months later." "By the end of the year liberals were expressing bafflement at the New Deal's rapid demise."[31] Brinkley explains this political nosedive as resulting from too successful a reelection. Southern Democrats had originally supported Roosevelt because they believed he was an establishment man who would not rock the boat, which in the South meant the racial boat. They became alarmed after the election at what appeared to be a mandate for liberal reform. Several shifts in the demographics of who Democratic voters were contributed to this alarm. Because New Deal work and social programs were more color-blind than previous government programs, African Americans, who had voted for the party of Lincoln in 1932, shifted to Roosevelt in 1936. They had also been migrating out of the South during and after World War I; as a result they began to have new voting clout in Northern cities. Responding to union-friendly legislation, labor also supported Roosevelt. And "newer ethnic groups in the cities swung to Roosevelt, mostly out of gratitude for New Deal welfare measures." Finally, ominously, given what was soon to follow, "a mass exodus of Socialists from the garment unions" also went to FDR. In sum, "at the 1936 convention, northern cities demonstrated their new power in the party when delegates wiped out the century-old two-thirds rule, long one of the chief defenses of Southern Democrats."[32]

This latter point is of considerable importance in understanding the shift in cinema to the mood of film noir, for the aesthetic rupture results from a larger political rupture. By 1937 Roosevelt recognized that he needed more than the traditional Democratic Party unity to rewrite America as a social democracy. He needed a liberal coalition that would work for social change. He had been facing opposition in the Supreme Court to earlier New Deal initiatives (the NRA, for example), and he faced trouble in his own party due to its dependence on Southern Democrats from a solid South (called by Dewey Grantham "the one-party system") that remained solid out of antipathy for Lincoln.[33] He attempted to beat the judiciary by "packing the Supreme Court" and he attempted to weed out Southern Democrats in the Senate and Congress who were increasingly forming a "conservative coalition" with Republicans by taking a step that would seem unthinkable today: he went into the South and campaigned against powerful incumbents in his own party. He failed with both the Court and the Southern Democrats. The glum mood in the Roosevelt White House became the glum mood of the New Deal coalition of blacks, labor, liberals, and women—and, in class terms, of the down-and-out.

Brinkley traces the vitriolic atmosphere of conservative disdain for liberalism in the wake of Roosevelt's late thirties defeats: "The assault continued over the next several years. Conservatives in congress worked to frustrate what remained of the President's domestic agenda and even to dismantle earlier achievements. . . . many were astonished by the intensity and bitterness of the opposition." A new House Special Committee to Investigate Un-American Activities (later known as HUAC) chaired by Southern Democrat Martin Dies "was launching a series of investigations of liberals and reformers in an effort to discredit the New Deal by tying it to radicals and communists." Dies made an effort to charge New Dealers Harold Ickes, Frances Perkins, and Harry Hopkins with being communists and to dismiss "dozens of federal employees."[34] One of the committee's first acts was to attack artists by closing down the Federal Theatre Project, in part because earlier in the thirties black participants had made common cause with communists on civil rights issues. Fears in the South, in rural areas, and in conservative quarters now matched and surpassed the investigations of banking and Wall Street that had occurred earlier in the decade. Now the investigators sought to ferret out imagined reds who were out to upend the established order.

International events contributed to a deepening national gloom. War in Europe became increasingly certain as the thirties drew to a close. And a distrust of leadership resurfaced in connection with World War I, as Americans suspected the United States might join the European conflict. A substantial number of Americans had come to believe that the same business leaders who had gotten the United States into the Depression had had profiteering motives in getting the United States into World War I. A 1937 poll asked if it had been a mistake for the United States to enter World War I, and "70 percent . . . answered 'yes.' "[35] During the period Senator Nye's Congressional Committee charged major U.S. companies with profiteering during the war. In 1935, 1936, and 1937 Congress "passed three successive Neutrality Acts aimed at preventing the United States from selling arms or munitions to any warring powers."[36] While the nation slowly grasped the inevitability of a new war, an undercurrent of resentment that had not been present at the outset of World War I could be glimpsed at the moment the United States entered the war. In 1940, even as Britain was in danger of falling to the Nazis, both Roosevelt and Wendell Willkie promised in the election of that year, to keep the United States out of World War II.[37] After the election, when the United States did enter the war, Frederick Lewis Allen pointed out the suppressed mood of residual anger over World War I. Explaining the differing moods of the United States going into World War I and Americans going into World War II, Allen writes,

This new war was astonishingly like that of 1917–1918, in Europe at least; and despite the obvious differences and the hard logic of circumstances, something remained in the subconscious of millions of people to rise and accuse them whenever they heard a patriotic peroration. They didn't want to be victims of "hysteria." They felt uncomfortable about flag waving. They preferred to be matter-of-fact about the job ahead. Morale officers reported an astonishing indifference to instruction on American war aims; the chief war aim in most soldiers' minds appeared to be to get back home.... Few bands played, few trumpets blew, there were no parades, and people who became demonstrative about America's war ideals sensed a coolness in the air about them.[38]

The Birth of Noir

Allen's remarks concerning Americans entering the Second World War point to the historical connectedness of American memory, the threat of a resumption of World War I which existed throughout the thirties, and the sourness that materialized in the thirties toward earlier United States involvement in World War I: as a result, the attitude toward World War II is formed by a lingering attitude toward World War I, one which was shaped by charges and counter charges that took place over the preceding decade. This connection illustrates the importance of comprehending noir as a phenomenon that is part of a larger historical fabric that materialized in the thirties. In trying to explain the sudden emergence of film noir in the late thrities, Raymond Chandler, for example, remarked, "the Hays Office has become more liberal . . . I think they're okaying treatments now which they would have turned down ten years ago, probably because they feel people can take the hard-boiled stuff nowadays."[39] Attempting to answer a similar question, but as applied to the crisis of confidence he sees among modernists in the mid-thirties, Tyrus Miller sees this crisis as having its "generative matrix in the years of war [World War I]." He correctly sees the period between the world wars as "one long bout of war neurosis, in which the effects of trauma have proliferated in a general contagion."[40] More directly addressing the same question to the appearance of film noir, but from a quite different angle, Phil Hardy cites sociologists Edhol, Harris, and Young, who suggest "that the emerging contradiction between the sex/gender and the sexual division of labor [as World War II loomed] 'provided a potential for struggle and questioning, for sexual hostility and antagonism,' " which they were arguing accounted for the appearance of the fatal woman of film noir.[41]

None of these theories is incorrect, but they need to be considered in relation to one another, and to be read against a more intimate account of the period. On the issue of the emergence of the fatal noir woman, in her study of the fallen woman genre Lea Jacobs notes that by 1938 (with specific reference to *Marked Woman*) films treating women were doing so with "an atmosphere of pessimism and angst characteristic of film noir" (though generally *Marked Woman* is not considered film noir).[42] Nevertheless, she is right that well before the outbreak of World War II, shifts were occurring in screen representations of women. And even truer noir women—Brigid O'Shaughnessy in *The Maltese Falcon* and Velma Baughmam in *High Sierra*—appear in films released before December 7, 1941. Much of the decade on-screen had been marked by women possessed of verbal dexterity and an assertiveness that would remain unmatched until the 1970s.[43] But a number of small shifts occur. Jacobs notes that the entrepreneurial gold digger of the early thirties (*Gold Diggers of 1933, We're in the Money*, 1935), in concert with toughening of Hays Office censorship, gives way to women who are punished for using sexual attractiveness to climb the social ladder (*Stella Dallas*, 1937, and *Kitty Foyle*, 1940, for example). And in *The Women* (1939) a good many of the most assertive actresses of the thirties (Rosalind Russell, Joan Crawford) play strong women whose assertiveness is treated as nasty predation and is contrasted with Norma Shearer's long-suffering and loyal wife who forgets about her husband's infidelities and takes him back. It would be fairly easy to construct an argument that *The Women* is an extended punishment lesson for women who reject traditional female dependency—as Scarlett is punished for rejecting Rhett's dominance (and accepted Southern tradition) in *Gone with the Wind* (1939). Women are further redomesticated at the end of the decade by turning them into mothers, as happens to the woman in the closest thing to an equal male-female on-screen partnership when Nora Charles has a baby in *Another Thin Man* (1939). Since this shift occurs before the outbreak of World War II, the period typically assigned by noir analysts as accounting for a new hostility to women, what accounts for it?

At the family level, thirties sociologist Mira Komarovsky concluded in a study of Depression effects on gender roles in the early part of the decade, "Unemployment does tend to lower the status of the husband." She added, "In some families the hitherto concealed contempt for the husband came into the open; in others unemployment has reversed the husband-wife relation—dominance of the husband having been changed to his complete subordination." And in some cases, "the husband suffered a loss of respect."[44] This loss of male power, accompanied by a gain in female power, caused resentment in conservatives who were inclined to resist any change in traditional roles.

In the political sphere, it is worth noting that by the late thirties Eleanor Roosevelt had her share of people who thoroughly hated her. And she was at the center of a group of powerful women, "the women's network," who were politically active.[45] Further, the Roosevelt coalition of minorities, labor, the poor, and immigrants included a strong contingent of women. Notably a shift in attitudes toward women occurs just as the New Deal begins to suffer inertia. This shift to hostility against strong women works as part of a larger dynamic that was at work at the outset of the decade and returned with the resurgence of conservative power from 1937 forward. The trajectory of American thought from the early thirties forward had been toward a feminine principle of cooperation and away from a masculine principle of rugged individualism.[46] In 1937, after the bitter battle over Roosevelt's Supreme Court-stacking plan, David Kennedy remarks, "the struggle had inflicted such grievous wounds on the president that the New Deal's political momentum was exhausted by 1937. . . . The way was open, but Roosevelt lacked the means to go forward."[47] Given Roosevelt's new weakness, conservative resentment of the feminine principle resurfaced. One way this manifested itself was in a more assertive hostility to liberals; another was in a rejection of the feminine principle and in a resurgent resentment of women who acted on their own desires rather than subordinating those desires to men. The fatal woman of noir does this.[48]

One can see a fault line in cinema treatments of women late in the decade, as good women, those who subordinate themselves to their men, are separated from those who act on their own desires. Hitchcock's *Rebecca* (1940), a film with a few of its own noirish scenes, and one which shares a view of domesticity with *The Women,* exemplifies this point. *Rebecca* dichotomizes women into two categories, women who desire things for themselves, and women whose desires are to satisfy their men. Rebecca and Mrs. Danvers (the housekeeper who loved her), fall into the first category, and the narrator (Joan Fontaine), whose own desires are so invisible that she is never given any name other than "the second Mrs. de Winter," falls into the second. Rebecca desires lots of men, including her cousin (in Daphne Du Maurier's 1938 novel he is her brother, so her desires are made incestuous and forbidden). Mrs. Danvers desires proximity to Rebecca, even after Rebecca is dead. The narrator, presented as the good woman in both novel and film, is entirely at the mercy of economics. She is first a traveling companion to a selfish dowager, another woman with desires; hence the dowager is presented as repulsive. Then the narrator marries Max de Winter (Laurence Olivier), and she obsesses over trying to please him. In the film, at the beach Max refers to his second wife as a child. In the novel he tells her, "just be yourself and look decorative."[49] The film ends with Rebecca the memory and Mrs. Danvers, the apparent lesbian, being immolated in a kind of mansion funeral pyre, which is the

same way the movies destroy the Frankenstein monster. *Rebecca*'s separation of desire from wife, or from wife's desire, converges with the
motherhood of Nora Charles in *Another Thin Man* (1939) and the
bitchifying of the desiring women in *The Women* (1939).

The two fatal women who follow, in films released just months after
Rebecca (Velma in *High Sierra* and Brigid O'Shaughnessy in the *Maltese Falcon*), are descendants of Rebecca. They desire and the movies
make them pay for it. Velma, the clubfoot of *High Sierra,* starts out
resembling the narrator in Rebecca. She's sweet and accessible, and best
of all, she seems to have no desires of her own: she's there for the taking. In *High Sierra,* a hybrid which connects the gangster films to film
noir, Roy Earle (Humphrey Bogart) wants Velma, so much that he
pays for an operation to fix her foot. Once Velma is empowered by
having the detraction removed from her sensual self, she evolves from
the dependent potential wife into a shallow, calculating, and desiring
nightmare. Her choice in men is repulsive. Unlike the fallen women
from earlier in the decade, she has no redeeming heart of gold. She can't
see Roy because of her ego. In the *Maltese Falcon,* Brigid comes as a
fully developed noir woman. She desires the falcon, which represents
empowerment and money. She wants to be Rebecca—assured, bank-
rolled, and free. Soon we see that women with that goal must be liars
and murderers. In *The Maltese Falcon,* Brigid is as bad as the queer, Joel
Cairo, and the potential queer, Wilmer. For that she has to pay.

Once one sees the economic and political underpinnings of the shift
to a new hostility toward women late in the decade, one begins to see
how the emergence of the fatal noir woman is part of a larger constellation of events that converge in the late thirties. Nearing decade's end,
while the country was trying to choke back nausea over a likely second world war, conservatives started to get in their innings in the area
of inquisitional congressional hearings. In 1937, Roosevelt Brain Trust
man Adolf Berle remarked, "practically no business group in the country has escaped investigation or other attack . . . The result has been
shattered morale."[50] The conservative-business coalition was able to
start to regain its morale when the Roosevelt loss in the Supreme Court
battle "destroyed the image of invulnerability that had been among the
President's greatest political strengths."[51] What goes unnoticed is the
effect of such inquisition tactics and shifts in authority on the con-
stituency shared by the politicians and the movie industry—the masses
—those who voted and bought movie tickets.

For the masses, respectable leadership in the thirties must at times
have appeared to be a function of a magician's trick: now you see it,
now you don't. The stability of reputations worthy of respect became
unreliable. Richard Whitney, Samuel Insull, Ivar Kreuger, and F. Don-

ald Coster were all major names in American finance, heroes of the twenties. Whitney entered the Depression as the savior during the stock market panic, when he represented bankers who temporarily halted the slide. But by the end of the thirties he was on his way to Sing Sing for fraud. Kreuger committed suicide because his massive international business was built on a house of cards and shifty tactics. Insull, head of a "lofty pyramid of public-utility holding companies," was pursued by the law throughout the thirties, but after being the subject of scandal for the decade, evaded penalty. Coster, "head of the reputable drug house of McKesson & Robbins," not only kept fraudulent books, but turned out to be an ex-convict whose real name was Philip Musica; he had altered his appearance and carried out an extended identity fraud.[52]

Of the mood of anxiety that came out of economic and international conditions in the thirties, one man interviewed in a bar remarked, "If someone came along with a line of stuff in which I could really believe, I'd follow him pretty nearly anywhere." Though his remark sounds religious, Frederick Lewis Allen explains he was speaking of "economic and political and social policy."[53] In the early thirties, when the Depression was at its darkest, any number of people had mistaken Soviet success for a concrete answer to the Depression. At that time, it was not yet known that the Soviets were misrepresenting the effects of their five-year plans. Interest in such alternatives would come back to haunt people when conservatives, energized by Roosevelt failures over the Supreme Court and Southern Democrats, would launch their own inquisition in the form of HUAC. Suddenly interest in communist economic solutions to the Depression was represented as traitorous behavior. As, in Allen's words, the "old verities" were crumbling in the face of developments in Europe, conservatives were raising questions about who was a loyal American. You thought you could rely on American capitalism, then you couldn't. You thought American business icons were reliable, then they weren't. You thought you were a patriot, then you weren't. Moral boundaries blurred. And HUAC took on a tone of anti-Semitism as well. So the Jewish producers, who had created "an empire of their own" in Hollywood, suddenly had reason for new anxiety, especially in the shadow of German developments.[54] Little wonder that a cinema phenomenon marked by uncertainty over moral boundaries should emerge.

This is not to say that noir moments had not crept into film off and on during the thirties. They just did not become a dominant stream in American filmmaking until decade's end. As early as 1931, Rouben Mamoulian's City Streets offered several noir elements. A young woman stands up for her crooked father, only to learn he's used her and she winds up in prison. Once there, Mamoulian uses Expressionistic techniques to demonstrate her psychological stress, e.g., when she lies on her cot and hears a myriad of voices from the past, a scene resembling the knife murderess in Hitchcock's *Blackmail* hearing echoes of the word "knife" at the family dinner table. And Mamoulian's *Dr. Jekyll and Mr. Hyde*, released the same year, contains an Expressionistic treatment in its exploration of the much-discussed noir interest in split personality, as do *Frankenstein, Dracula* (both 1931), and *Stranger on the Third Floor* (1940). *Fog over Frisco* (1934) offers an early glimpse of the fatal noir woman, in the form of Bette Davis's Arlene Bradford, who unlike Davis's *Marked Woman* character and the women of many early thirties fallen women films, has no heart of gold. And both *Heroes for Sale* (1933) and *Meet John Doe* (1941) contain quite noirish nightmare scenes.

If one goes back to the early Borde and Chaumeton effort to define noir, one can see how much a crisis of national confidence has played into noir's development. They sum up noir as a result of "moral ambivalence . . . contradictory complexity of the situations and motives [which give] the public a shared feeling of anguish or insecurity."[55] Discussing the crisis of modernism in the late thirties, Tyrus Miller remarks that the late modernist text abandons modernism's "desire to restore significance to a broken world." Brian McHale asserts that when late modernist "poetics begins to *hemmorhage* . . . it is still (barely) possible to recuperate these contradictions by invoking the model of the 'unreliable narrator.' "[56] This is why film noir so often relies on an unreliable narrator in the form of voice-over, or more generally why it ironizes subjective certainty. In an unstable universe, we can see characters who feel certainty discover their subjective error as they discover the ambivalent universe. Noir characters start out certain—a subjective mistake. Then events overtake them.

The shift from a universe with its moral lights in place to one characterized by ambivalence materializes in the 1937 film *You Only Live Once*. In film noir, the much discussed voice-over is part of a broader shift to ironizing subjective certainty. And this film does that by confining its audience to the perspective of ex-con Eddie Taylor (Henry Fonda). Borde and Chaumeton saw the result of presenting the noir universe as "the state of tension created in the spectators." This seems to be the central goal of *You Only Live Once*. Because the Depression had moved into its later stages, early noir films—or films with strong noir elements—focus on people who have been assigned an identity that they do not accept, as the economic crisis had rewritten identity for many Americans. By the latter part of the decade, many had moved past fighting the effort to reidentify them and into a mind-set of living with the irony. Eddie is identified as a criminal, but until the end of the film, we don't see that he is one. Nor is it ever clear why he was in prison in the first place. Furthermore the priest he meets in prison takes the position that the prison authorities are wrong in their treatment of the men. Eddie spends most of the film trying to fulfill the American dream of marrying his soul mate and holding a job, while trying to get past the irony of his identity as criminal other. The moral ambiguity spreads when his wife (Sylvia Sidney), the ideal spouse and mother, chooses to join him as he is on the run from the law. When they are both gunned down at the film's end the universe seems empty and the audience, having identified with the young couple, is suddenly alienated. Apparently this ending was too hard-core for the early noir period, and Expressionist director Fritz Lang tacked on a few seconds of film in which the pair are called to heaven (thereby contradicting the film's title). But the few seconds of running time the tack-on takes cannot counter all of what has preceded it.

This shift to an uncertain universe can be further illustrated by noting the way noir treated the modern city. One of the most discussed elements in film noir, and in the thirties, is the new urban world.[57] Louis Brandeis, T. S. Eliot, and Franklin Roosevelt all felt that one problem of modernity was the new industrial city.[58] One difference between the earlier detective of crime films and the later detective of noir is in his relationship to the modern urban world. One of the identifying features of this new urban center was its living quarters—the apartment. When apartment building hit Chicago in the late nineteenth century, William Dean Howells complained that an elevator flat provided "no room . . . where the family can all come together and feel the sweetness of being a family." In New York, *The Architectural Record* warned of the threat that ethnic mixing in apartment buildings represented: "Some day there will elude the vigilance of the janitor or the real estate agent a hook-nosed tenant."[59] These anxieties aside, apartments, along with skyscrapers, took over urban America. They characterize the city. The traditional detective can master this city; the detective of noir finds in it a revelation of his own inability to know.

This point is illustrated by William Powell's Philo Vance in *The Kennel Murder Case* (1933). Vance is presented with an apartment house-murder that the police have ruled a suicide. To support his belief that it was murder, Vance constructs a model of the apartment building. The screen image presents Vance looming as master over the doll-house-size model apartment as he deftly shows the police why they are wrong. In 1933 the film detective can still "own" the city. When the noir detective exhibits such confidence regarding the city, he usually finds himself brutally beaten in a dark alley somewhere.

The pre-noir detective demonstrates his mastery of the city with this model of an apartment building, which he takes apart for the benefit of the police. (*The Kennel Murder Case*, Warner, 1933).

In several ways, the apartment of noir is quite a different place. It is the heart of the new urban anonymity and disconnectedness from tradition. In it traditional gender lines are uncertain, friends are bought and sold, romance is abandoned, and apparently knowable value is destabilized. This is what happens in the noir apartment in *The Maltese Falcon* where Sam Spade, Brigid O'Shaughnessy, Kasper Gutman, Joel Cairo, and Wilmer Cook wait together through the night for the arrival of the priceless falcon. Gutman describes Wilmer as being like his own son, then sells him out as the fall guy for earlier murders, Cairo's homosexuality is foregrounded (which is regarded as sexual decadence in 1941; if you were in the government, you could get blackmailed for it) and he demonstrates an interest in Wilmer. Spade offers to sell out his romantic soul mate, Brigid, who has lied nonstop throughout the film. And the falcon, upon which they all place their certain hopes for wealth, turns out to be a mirage. When Spade attempts to explain to Brigid why he "sends her over" at the film's end, he has to finally revert to something like primal urges. He tells her he won't lie for her, remarking, "I won't because all of me wants to." All certainties with which the film started are abandoned in the apartment of *Maltese Falcon*. Unlike the detective of *The Kennel Murder Case*, Spade

The apartment of *The Maltese Falcon* and of noir in general is not the manageable place of the classic detective film. Here it is a place of sexual dysfunction and betrayal (Warner, 1941).

cannot even explain himself, let alone the city, with certainty. And no other character has been entirely right about anything.

The outbreak of World War II would follow on the heels of the release of *The Maltese Falcon*. The new demons of blurred morality released in *You Only Live Once, Rebecca, Stranger on the Third Floor, High Sierra,* and *The Maltese Falcon* would soon meet the world of Bergen-Belsen and all of the early anxiety would explode in a world that could no longer be depended upon.

7

Escaping the Thirties

THE PARISH AND THE PRIMITIVE
COME TO THE MOVIES

IN THOMAS MORE'S SOCIETY OF LATE FIFTEENTH- AND EARLY SIX-
teenth-century England, one could lose one's head for disagreeing with
those in power. This happened to More, the author of *Utopia*, in 1535
for his reluctance to approve of Henry VIII's split from Catholicism.
Given his fate in his own society, one can see why More might have
been imagining some sort of escape to some sort of utopia. In fact, a
principle arises from More's own situation: suffering breeds dreams of
escape. In his analysis of More's *Utopia,* Louis Marin sees the "utopian
drive" as "a desire for an elsewhere that nevertheless would be realized
here and now: a representation within which, around which, desires,
wishes, hopes, and expectations are longing for blissful achievement."
Marin quotes Ernst Bloch on necessary elements of utopias, with
Bloch remarking that in utopia "we are entering into the possible, the
unfated [or] at least into a fate that can be modified." Marin remarks,
"in Utopia we can see the unfigurable figure of Infinite Liberty."[1] In a
totalitarian society in which beheading lingered just around the corner,
freedom of choice appealed to More. The desire for "a fate that can be
modified" exposes the connection between escapism and utopia, as
well as the need for understanding the circumstances of the escapist. In
his study of the concept of escapism, Yi-Fu Tuan asserts that "it means
. . . steps taken to change or mask an unsatisfactory condition."[2] To
understand escapist films of the thirties means to understand the particular social environment—the "unsatisfactory condition"—which
provokes the desire to escape, as well as seeing what in the environment might promise a better "elsewhere." Changes occurring in the
early part of the twentieth century suggest an explanation for the pre-
occupations of escapist films.

In the thirties, T. S. Eliot made his case for the parish as the ideal
social unit, which he opposed to the city as the problem social unit. He
characterizes the parish as "a small and mostly self-contained group

163

attached to the soil and having its interests centred in a particular place, with a kind of unity which may be designed, but which also has to grow through generations. It is the idea, or ideal, of a community small enough to consist of a nexus of direct personal relationships." He connects the parish to a primitive ideal: "That is a state of affairs which is no longer wholly realized except in very primitive tribes indeed."[3] Eliot's view, expressed in 1939, emerges in different forms in differing ideological environments during the same period. Raymond Moley, a member of Franklin Roosevelt's Brain Trust, criticized Louis Brandeis's notion of an idealized American life (see note 58, chap. 6 of this book)." David Kennedy remarks, "The Brain Trusters regarded Louis Brandeis as Woodrow Wilson's 'dark angel,' the man whose trust-busting advice, [Rexford] Tugwell thought, had mischievously derailed the early twentieth-century reform movement and stalled the development of appropriate industrial policies for nearly two decades."[4] The conservative Southerners who in 1930 issued their agrarian manifesto, *I'll Take My Stand,* in words derived from the Southern anthem, "Dixie," agreed with Eliot about smallness and social relations based on a connection to the land, but they put the concept in terms of a nostalgia for the plantation South, though they carefully substituted "agrarian" for "plantation" to avoid the slave connotations the plantation South also represented. Nevertheless, in his contribution to the collection, after blasting the city, industrialization, communism (or the social welfare that FDR would decide upon), Lyle Lanier makes clear the nature of the agrarian dream he argues for in a reference to the Confederate South: "Unless steps are taken toward the restoration of the balance of economic forces in America, which was destroyed in 1865, we cannot hope to avoid the unsavory sequel of industrialism outlined above." Lanier pits the city and Depression unemployment against what he terms "the old individualism" of agrarianism.[5] Associating notions of the genuine self and social relations based on a small and land-connected community were not new to America or to Western thought, though the Depression provoked an outpouring of arguments for alternatives to what some regarded as failed urban based, industrial capitalism.

The connection between small communities, the primitive, and the genuine appears in an early twentieth-century aesthetic philosophy which made its way into the popular marketplace of ideas. At least from Gauguin forward, various schools of artists had been expressing an interest in primitive art. Wassily Kandinsky saw the primitive past as unencumbered by artificial aesthetic rules, which had been piled on top of what was "authentic" in art over centuries of civilization, with the effect that art itself had become artificial: "Indeed, the further we look into the past, the fewer imitations, sham works we find. They have mysteriously disappeared. Only the genuine art objects remain."[6] Expressing a widely held logic, Franz Marc connected the natural and the primitive as desired ends: "Natural law has been the vehicle of art. Today we are replacing this law with the problem of religiosity. The art of our epic will undoubtedly show profound analogues with the arts of long past, primitive times."[7] Expressionist theories of the artist connected the true twentieth-century artist to the primitive artist, because each relied on the natural intuitive self rather than on conditioned conceptions. Oscar Kokoschka remarked, "Thus in everything imagination is simply that which is natural. It is nature, vision, life."[8] The artist's motive was to recuperate the natural perception senses, to free them of civilized education. In their 1935 study of primitivism, Arthur Lovejoy and George Boas explained the impulse toward the primitive in the context of responses to Western civilization, remarking on "the discontent of the civilized with civilization, or with some conspicuous and characteristic feature of it. It is the belief of men living in a highly evolved and complex cultural condition that a life far simpler and less sophisticated in some or all respects is a more desirable life.[9] Commenting on the primitive decorations in the studios of the Expressionist Brücke artists, Colin Rhodes remarks, "the primitive studios-cum-living spaces represented precisely their day-to-day working and social environments. In this way, the decorated studios should not be read as essays in escapism, but, rather as an effective and convenient means of situating the artists outside (or at least on the periphery of) bourgeois society."[10] Rhodes asserts that the search for the genuine was not solely centered on Rousseau's "noble savage." In national terms, artists explored national peasant traditions, often moving into less populated rural communities to immerse themselves in the authentic "uncorrupted" rustics. Rhodes notes, "The ideologies that underpinned the artists' community at Worpswede in Germany, established in the 1890s, were characterized by the rejection of cosmopolitanism and the espousal of Romantic beliefs that spiritual integrity and national purity were to be found only in the countryside and among its inhabitants."[11] This notion of small community relations as somehow genuine and those of the big city as artificial became especially attractive in the thirties when the country was in the throes of an unprecedented capitalist trauma.

No Escape

A July 10, 1933 *Time* article, ironically entitled "fiscal: New Year" (considering what follows) opens with four paragraphs of violent deaths. For "fiscal" reasons, "a 30 year-old married woman" who had "lost her job with the Interstate Commerce Commission . . . went home in despair, turned on the gas, died." A war veteran who was "removed from the pension rolls" and "ushered out of the National Military Home," sought out the home's medical officer and "shot him dead." A clerk who lost his job, "took poison, cut his throat." An "ex-Army captain wrote to President Roosevelt: 'Suicide is the only way I can provide for those dependent on me, by making available to them the miserable balance due on my adjusted compensation certificate.' "[12] Roosevelt had been president just a few months at the time of these events, and the deepening shock of the Depression made economic reality nearly unbearable for many. As the article illustrates, it was entirely unbearable for some.

At the time of Roosevelt's inauguration, there was a crisis of confidence over core capitalist practices, evidenced in the inaugural address in which the president-elect argued, "Practices of the unscrupulous money changers stand indicted in the court of public opinion. . . . there must be an end to a conduct in banking and in business which too often has given to a sacred trust the likeness of callous and selfish wrongdoing. Small wonder that confidence languishes."[13] The economic crisis of the thirties led to a reorganization of the U.S. economy. The intertwined emotional upset caused by the threatened collapse of the economy and the subsequent government intervention had repercussions for art and for popular cinema. If one takes the force of Fredric Jameson's point that a society's means of production exists in an intimate relationship with its form of aesthetic expression and that history reveals a series of ruptures in forms of production (slave, feudal, capitalist), one would expect the economic ruptures of the thirties to have repercussions for cinematic representation. And this happens.

One can see it happening in the least likely of places in the thirties: in fantasy, screwball, and historical films — in other words, in films described as escapist that advertise interests directly opposed to a confrontation with the Depression.[14] In 1934, documentarian Pare Lorentz complained that he would make documentaries because Hollywood studios "ground out the same old escape stuff."[15] More recently, the text *Who Built America?* characterized films of the thirties as escapist and, surprisingly, cited *Gold Diggers of 1933,* a film that directly confronts Depression issues, as an example. Throughout the even more recent documentary, *The Great Depression,* film-going in the thirties was categorized as an escapist enterprise. While some films seem to advertise an escape from their audience's present, the economic disruptions of the period contributed a "political unconscious" that illustrated that the dynamics of the period made a kind of running evaluation of Depression alternatives inescapable, even in films that struggled to avoid confrontation with economic trauma, that is, films that seemed most escapist.

DREAMS OF ELSEWHERE

If for the modernists interest in the primitive was motivated by a desire to attach themselves to a standard apart from traditional European civilization, engagements with the primitive during the Depression more pointedly involved a nostalgia for alternatives to a misfunctioning capitalist economy. *Mutiny on the Bounty* (1935) exemplifies the exploration of possibilities other than the capital-centered civilization of the Depression. It recalls alternatives to capitalism and looks wistfully to models outside of Western tradition. It is one of several films to offer comparisons of Western capitalism and alternative civilizations.

A comparison of the 1935 version of *Mutiny* with the two other most notable filmings of the story (in 1962 and 1984) demonstrates that the 1935 version is more interested in exploring the meaning of money than are the other two. The 1962 version, with Marlon Brando as Fletcher Christian, exploits Brando's on-screen angry young man persona to interpret the story as a generation-gap war in which Bligh (Trevor Howard) comes across as an authoritarian cold warrior. As would be true of the generational war (soon to be tabbed the generation gap) in the ensuing years of the sixties, the 1962 version pits Bligh's repressed sexuality against Christian's plunge into sex. In the 1935 version, Roger, a young officer is punished for fighting with another officer by being made to climb the mast and stay there through a storm. The 1962 version revises this incident so that an officer is punished for making fun of Bligh. The 1984 version, made during Reagan's conservative rollback of the liberal gains of the previous two decades, treats Christian as irresponsible and dissolute; he appears to be on drugs while he immerses himself in sex in Tahiti.

In the 1935 version Roger Byam refers to the Tahitians as "perfect primitives," and Christian adds, "What a contrast to the ship." Bligh (Charles Laughton) pointedly explains himself to Christian as a self-made man, like Hoover embodying the characteristics of rugged individualism. He is obsessed with profit, making the men eat maggoty food and forcing Christian to sign for food the men have not received. The sexual liberation of the 1962 version is less a factor in 1935. The emphasis is more on Tahiti as an alternative civilization to British capitalism. Byam is assigned to record the Tahitian language. In a segment missing from the 1962 and 1984 versions, Byam soon learns the chief,

Punishment on the *Bounty* (*Mutiny on the Bounty,* MGM, 1935).

Hiti Hiti, does not know the meaning of money. Once Byam explains how money works, Hiti Hiti responds that he dislikes the concept. In contrast to Bligh's driving and torturing the sailors to labor on the ship, on Tahiti, Christian lies in the grass, picking bananas while the women swim nearby. Though Gauguin had dreamed of a Tahiti where capitalist-driven labor would be unnecessary, he soon learned that hard work was required to succeed on the island, remarking, "one has to climb a high tree, to go up to the mountains and come back laden with heavy burdens; to be able to catch fish [or] dive and tear from the sea-bottom the shells firmly attached to the rocks."[16] Nevertheless, in the thirties Christian is imagined as being relatively free of the labor that characterizes a capitalist society while he is on the island, as well as being free of the harsh shipboard methods needed to acquire and bring back the breadfruit (which will function to maximize profits from slave plantations in the New World).

Mutiny on the Bounty typifies thirties films that demonstrate that far from being removed from the tensions of the Depression crisis, movies built themselves out of the anxieties of the period. Films that present some escape from an individual's worrying about a job lost at a bank or a failing farm nevertheless appealed to their audiences by offering indirect ruminations on central aspects of the Depression. One element in many films is criticism of a capitalism that functions successfully when profits are made rather than being generated to serve the good of the people. In *Tarzan the Ape Man* (1932), upon first arriving in Africa Jane (Maureen O'Sullivan) remarks, "From now on, I'm through with civilization. I'm going to be a savage." That she regards such a choice as specifically an alternative to capitalist values crystallizes when she criticizes her father, who runs a trading post, for too successfully maximizing his profits at the expense of the Africans, "Father, you've done far too well out of one small store. I don't think it's quite right." In *Tarzan and His Mate* (1934), capitalist profit is made an issue in a running comparison to primitive life in the jungle. Two capitalist traders, Harry and Martin Arlington, arrive in Africa, and one remarks that he is out of money but when he gets some he will sit on it with a gun in hand. Harry once had a romantic interest in Jane, which he hopes to pursue. Arlington tells him that if you have money, women aren't hard to get. Harry attempts to use merchandise from back home to lure Jane away from Tarzan. He showers her with gowns, lipstick, and stockings. When Arlington tells Jane that all his and Harry's money is tied up in their safari, Jane makes a virtually identical statement to Byam's characterization of Tahitian chief Hiti Hiti, telling Arlington, "Tarzan knows nothing of money." Like Christian in *Mutiny on the Bounty,* Tarzan does little working or hunting for food. Instead, away from the safari and its European capitalists, he and Jane play in the jungle. When Tarzan goes to the river for a fish, he reaches in, pulls one out, sees it is too small, and throws it back for another. He pulls bananas off a tree, and what work he does is finished. What is at stake in the exchanges with the Europeans is Jane herself, or who will father children by her and what values that father will pass on to the next generation. The *Tarzan* films offer a dream solution to the economic crisis of the thirties, associating freedom from anxiety with abandoning capitalist civilization.

Gone with the Wind draws from more than a century of Southern claims about the South's economy, which was in the twentieth century explained (first by Ulrich Phillips, then by Eugene Genovese) as a hybrid economy with intermingled capitalist and feudalist features. Southern apologists both before and after the Civil War argued for a civilization that did not maximize profit. In 1856 George Fitzhugh attacked Northern labor practices, calling white labor in the North the "White Slave Trade." Fitzhugh put his finger on the Southern perspective of the difference between free labor in the North and slave labor in the South: "The White Slave Trade . . . is far more cruel than the Black slave Trade, because it exacts more of its slaves, and neither protects nor governs them. We boast that it exacts more when we say, 'that the profits made from employing free labor are greater than those

Utopia in *Tarzan*, where Tarzan does not understand the concept of money (MGM, 1932).

from slave labor.' "[17] Fitzhugh's remarks summarize two central Southern claims in favor of Southern civilization: First, feudal style, Southern masters protected their slaves; and, second, Southerners were not maximizing profits, as were the Yankees. After the war is lost, when Scarlett sets out to participate in the notorious convict lease system, Ashley Wilkes objects, saying it is inhumane. When Scarlett replies that Southerners owned slaves, Ashley repeats Fitzhugh's argument, that masters protected and cared for their slaves. This small point summarizes the film's own summa of more than a century of Southern ideology over slavery and Southern civilization. *Gone with the Wind* offers a moral lesson in the relationship between capitalism and decent behavior, one conceived in longtime Southern ideology. When Frederick Lewis Allen writes, "There was for example the desire to escape the here and now of Depression and anxiety. . . . Surely . . . the superlative success of *Gone with the Wind* . . . was the greater because [it] offered an escape into history," the escape Allen sees shares a logic with *Mutiny on the Bounty* and other escape films of the period. It is an example of Marin's "representation within which, around which, desires, wishes, hopes, and expectations are longing for blissful achievement."[18] Another way of putting this is to say that *Gone with the Wind* expresses for a popular audience what *I'll Take My Stand* was expressing for the intelligentsia.

It does so, however, in a quite a backhanded way, by punishing Scarlett for departing from the old-time religion of Southern civilization. If, as Elizabeth Fox-Genovese has argued, the South was a household economy (meaning, in a slave society, with the house at the center of economic activity) boundaries between the domestic and economic spheres blurred in a way they did not in the industrializing Northeast (where, for example, the factory was quite separate from the domestic sphere), Scarlett, in various ways, consistently disrespects both spheres throughout the film.[19] Her confidence in doing so leads to her misery at the film's end, which in turn demonstrates the value of the old South's civilization. It is offered as a utopia that America foolishly turned away from in favor of urban capitalism, which, as the writers of *I'll Take My Stand* point out in a myriad of ways, seemed to be failing in the thirties. Scarlett disregards the engagement of Melanie and Ashley, then she disregards their marriage in her continued pursuit of Ashley.[20] On a whim, she marries Charles, for whom she cares nothing—though she lucks out when he dies of pneumonia. Later, Scarlett betrays her sister by marrying her beau, Frank Kennedy, not because she loves him but because he owns a store and has the money to pay the taxes on Tara, the O'Harra family plantation. Having disrespected the domestic household, Scarlett abandons Southern economic values. She uses Frank's capital to open a lumber mill and, refusing to hire free black workers, contracts for convict labor. This separates her from her laborers in a way that departs from all Southern claims to superiority over Yankee capitalists. The paternalism claimed for the master-slave relationship is absent. Instead Scarlett announces she will make friends of carpetbaggers and outdo them at their economic practices. With this, she has abandoned all claims to the plantation household, as either domestic or economic unit. Her appropriate role was on the feudal pedestal claimed for the Southern lady, a point illustrated by Rhett telling her that he would pet and spoil their daughter, Bonnie, as he had wanted to pet and spoil Scarlett. Instead Rhett's position is given moral force by his announcing that he is going back to Charleston in an effort to recover something of the "charm and grace" of life. Scarlett is left to suffer in the knowledge that she has made all the wrong choices. Her new knowledge turns her back to Tara, back to the land, which exemplifies the central value argued for by the Southern agrarians in *I'll Take my Stand*.

Part of the dream solution to the capitalist crisis in films involves separation from established society, getting away from power bases to clear one's head, to consider alternative ways to live. In *The Adventures of Robin Hood* (1938), the outlaws establish a society in the forest away from court power. There they practice a democracy, with the film stressing one point of the legend in particular—their robbing from the rich to give to the poor, unmistakably like Depression-era proposals to increase taxes on the rich to alleviate suffering at the bottom. Anachronistic though their democratic society is, they take in the wretched of society and treat them as equals. When Robin brings Marion into the outlaw community, he shows her the victims of the king and the sheriff. Seeing them standing in a line, we recognize the miserable poor have been made to resemble the Depression poor standing in a soup line. Robin offers relief; the sheriff oppression. The film tells us this is how one should treat people.

A year later another film addressed the question of a small society established away from capitalism. In *Five Came Back,* a group of twelve people on a plane en route to Panama crash in a South American jungle near the Amazon. Notably their plane is flying over Mexico, which for a thirties audience would have been ripe for visions of utopia, since Stuart Chase and others had touted it as a small agrarian paradise free of capitalism.[21] Blasting capitalist America, Chase extolled the primitive cooperative society he imagined the Mexican village to be, referring to its "handicraft economy functioning much as it did in the middle ages": "You ought to know by now that business leadership is bankrupt . . . and that mechanical civilization can never give you what you want. . . . In a genuine civilization there is room for mass production, for small-scale production, for handicrafts. . . . Mexico takes no back talk from clocks. It is an art which you too some day must learn; for it is the art of living."[22] Along with two pilots and a steward (who is killed as the plane descends), there's the stock bad girl (Lucille Ball), a gangster caring for his boss's son, a spoiled millionaire and his fiancée, an old couple, and a bounty hunter and his anarchist-murderer prisoner. As in *Stagecoach* (made the same year), it is the financier capitalist, rather than the gangster or the whore, who is rotten. So is the bounty hunter, another representative of societal power. Once in the jungle, the survivors have to establish a temporary community. The old couple, a professor and his wife, rediscover each other. The bad girl turns out to be a decent sort with a maternal streak. The anarchist has integrity, and the gangster eventually dies caring for the boy. Soon they are all working cooperatively, sharing rather than hoarding their possessions. The millionaire and the bounty hunter get into a knife fight over the millionaire's stash of liquor. When the boy discovers a monkey at a stream, flute music plays in the background, telling us this is a pastoral paradise. The anarchist points out there are "no classes" in the camp. Everyone operates out of "mutual respect." He argues that modern living is wrapped up in nonessentials and calls their little group "an ideal community." The crash exposes the millionaire's true worth as he won't work, drinks himself stupid, and abuses everyone else. Only massive profits back in capitalistic society give him superior identity. Stripped of money, he is a nasty but ineffectual character. Conversely, the old couple express happiness that the plane has crashed since, away from civilization, the natural environment has allowed them to recover their values.

In his analysis of the concept of utopia, Louis Marin remarks that "utopias tend to begin with a travel, a departure and a journey . . . most of the time interrupted by a storm, a catastrophe that is the sublime way to open a neutral space . . . a cosmic accident that eliminates all beacons and markers in order to make the seashore appear at dawn, to welcome the human castaway." Marin sees crisis as a motivating circumstance in the creation of utopias, "precisely at this moment it is worthwhile to recall the fiction of an island appearing at the dawn of a period for which the present time would be the twilight."[23] His theory accords with Depression circumstances and the particular content of utopian films during the thirties, which involve a rethinking of capitalist values, none more obviously than *Lost Horizon.*

The film version of James Hilton's 1933 novel, *Lost Horizon,* makes a concerted attack on Western civilization of the thirties. Its central character, Robert Conway (Ronald Colman), a powerful diplomat, has written about better civilizations, and he is receptive to encountering one. One of five people whose plane is hijacked by an unknown pilot, he is flown to Shangri-La, somewhere in Tibet, where he enters a utopian society, which serves as an alternative to capitalist society. Chang (H. B. Warner), their host in Shangri-La, explains there is no avariciousness in Shangri-La society because they have a sufficiency of everything. Consistent with other thirties utopian films, he tells Conway and the others there is no money there as they know it. In a reversal of the colonial process in which Europeans often brought diseases to native people, Gloria Stone, the stock floozyish blond (who replaces the novel's missionary), suffers from some sort of sickness, which steadily improves in the healthy Shangri-La atmosphere. Given thirties films' sociological interest in the fallen woman, the film's rehabilitation of Gloria seems a philosophical move: in this case, she's been made what she is by an unhealthy capitalism of the sort that throws Blondie Johnson's mother out into the street in *Blondie Johnson* and makes a prostitute out of decent Anna in *Anna Christie.* Shangri-La does not abuse and discard such people; it recognizes they are products of an unfair society, then enfolds and heals them. In a criticism not in the novel, the film adds a gay character, Alexander Lovett (Edward Everett Horton), whom Henry Barnard, the crooked stock market manipulator of the book and apparently a public utilities crook of the

Samuel Insull sort in the film, ridicules mercilessly, calling him alternately "brother" and "sister." Later, Barnard calls him "Toots" and suggests Lovett play "honeymoon bridge." But the environment of Shangri-La removes the poison from Barnard's system and the film finds a place in Shangri-La for Lovett—and for Barnard, who initially plots to take gold from the rich vein that supports the community. Instead he turns to the practical alternative of devising a plumbing system for the community. By the logic of utopia, even Barnard is forgiven, since he is a product of a predatory capitalist system he did not create.

The kidnapping, it turns out, was aimed at bringing Robert to Shangri-La to succeed Father Pello, the community's spiritual leader. Robert meets Sondra, whom he tells that he keeps feeling he has been in Shangri-La before. In a remark of a piece with modernist theory about human instinct, she tells him he has always been part of Shangri-La. "Everyone has Shangri-La in their hearts." In other words, his instincts—rather than his artificial civilization—have been telling him what is genuine and unwittingly that is what he has been wanting. Father Pello summarizes the point of Shangri-La when he tells Robert the world is in the throes of "an orgy of greed." He believes nations will destroy each other in a coming war, and Shangri-La will be there when the world looks for a "new model," having preserved genuine culture and values. In cinema's look to Tahiti, the African jungle, the old South, Sherwood Forest, and Shangri-La, one can read the anxieties of the Depression thirties.

SCREWBALL

At first sight, perhaps no thirties film comes across as more purely escapist than *Topper* (1937). The fantasy plot can be summarized in a sentence: a stuffy upper-class man is set upon by a pair of nonstop-drinking lascivious social gadfly ghosts, who set out to have fun at his expense and to loosen him up. Nevertheless, the fingerprints of the thirties appear on the film version of Thorne Smith's 1926 novel, which itself offers a utopian alternative to the age of twenties Coolidge materialism. As the film also offers a corrective utopia, but one correcting Depression-era ills rather than those of the twenties, it is instructive to examine first Smith's *Topper*. The novel's Topper remarks at one point, "I've passed up all the good things of life."[24] Like Eliot's *Wasteland* clerk, Topper lives in a world of suffocating routine. His position at the bank, domestic convention, and public reputation have shut his brain and his senses down. When he meets the deceased Kirbys, now transformed to ghosts, Marion Kirby tells him, "The world does wicked things to us with its success and routine and morality" (59). Initiating small rebellions against convention, Topper is drawn to the ghosts, who introduce him to a world outside that of business. Soon "industrial bonds no longer inspired him with a feeling of solid security" (40). As an immersion in nature and violation of conventions begins to soak in on Topper, he realizes "his whole past life had been modeled on false standards which would have to be adjusted at once." As Topper begins to feel things around him, "He became quite elated about his brain. It was like a new toy to him. He had always believed that it had been providentially arranged for the purpose of making money, acquiring possessions and paying for legs of lamb. He found that his brain was quite playful, that it broke rules and was indifferent" (96). Smith's novel makes it apparent that its utopia is a summa of decades of modernist theory about the primitive, the genuine, and Western civilization's mechanical nature. In his glowing description of natives of Brazil, entitled "On Cannibals," Michel Montaigne once remarked there are "only leisurely occupations . . . no clothes."[25] Soon Smith describes Topper with the imagery of the "noble savage": He is "a skeptical cannibal" (17). "The Primitivist attraction to childhood . . . is an important factor in much modern painting and sculpture . . . [children] seemed to them to represent . . . a 'survival' of this more primitive historical past."[26] When Topper remarks that his eyes have "looked too long on desk tops and plumbing," Marion replies, "Only savages and children do proper honor to the sun" (59). Not surprisingly, Topper recovers himself through an immersion in nature. Topper decides he must leave the city for a time to sort things out. He leaves the "funeral atmosphere" of his home (116). He decides he must go away from the city and out into the country to clear his head. Unknown to Topper, Marion Kerby sneaks along, since she can be invisible if she wishes. Once she has revealed her presence, she suggests she and Topper go off to a "lost lake" she knows of, having gone there at times to get away from George. In the late nineteenth century, as Primitivism was gaining favor amongst artists as an alternative to Western civilization, concepts of savage life and immersion into nature sometimes took the form of an impulse to literally shed the raiments of civilization in the form of nudist colonies. "A number of . . . artists sought out remote European locations . . . often partly inspired by a desire to practice nudism away from the watchful eye of authorities."[27] At the lake, "Mr. Topper thought it would be a delightful sensation to strip himself naked and go running through the trees, to feel the night on his body and to meet like a free, unabashed creature of the earth" (142). Later Topper announces to Marion, "I cast decency to the winds. Let's strip ourselves naked and run around screaming" (168).

In this pristine pastoral environment, Marion becomes "the spirit of the lake, the priestess of the woods" (158). She tells Topper, "I'm Eveish all over" (153). The lake has the expected effect on Topper and Marion: "They sang and danced . . . and pursued each other across the meadows . . . Nature became intensely beautiful and their bodies madly alive" (173). The effect on Topper of all this is that "His body had grown lean and alert, ready to run at a moment's notice . . . And strangely enough, Mr. Topper, in spite of his disorderly life, or rather, because of it, had become a better member of society; more self-reliant, more capable and far more interesting" (177). In short, Topper becomes an example of the successful effect of an immersion in the primitive.

The 1937 film adaptation of Smith's novel alters the role of the ghostly Kerbys. Their Jazz Age wildness is not treated as quite as attractively as it had been before the stockmarket crash of 1929. The film starts with scenes of the Kerbys before their auto accident, scenes absent from the novel. Though in the novel Topper had once seen Marion Kerby while she was alive, he had had practically no exposure to her during her life. In the film George Kerby (Cary Grant) is the largest stockholder on the board of Topper's bank (in the film Topper is the bank president; in the novel he is a bank officer). Topper (Roland Young) knows George's careless ways quite well. There is a pointed remark at the film's outset about the Kerbys going to Wall Street to see Topper in the morning. The night before, they nightclub hop and drink themselves into a stupor. They arrive at the bank early in the morning and pass out in their convertible there. In the morning people en route to work gather around and gawk and laugh at the two. Once inside at the meeting George pays little attention, playing games on his tablet and singing to himself. Such dissolute behavior on the part of a stockholder, sitting as he is on Wall Street, echoes the low place such speculators occupied throughout the thirties, when many of them were being hauled into court or raked through the papers in ethics scandals. After the meeting George drives the car madly across the countryside, and they crash. In the novel Topper comes across the two ghosts as a result of his suffering a midlife crisis that provokes him into buying their car. His rebellion is all but absent from the film. He does come across the two in their car, which he has initially been about to sell as the executor of their will. Mrs. Topper (Billie Burke) has objected to his sitting in the car and in a small rebellion he has taken it for a drive. He comes across the Kerbys at the spot of their accident. In the novel they take up with him for fun. In the film, they are being punished for their careless ways by being kept on earth, rather than admitted to heaven. They have to do a good deed to be free; so they decide to make

Topper their good deed by making his marriage better. Though George lectures Mrs. Topper about her puritanical ways, in the film she is as much motivated by her desire to get into high society as she is by George's lecture. She finds that the old-money people she envies admire Topper once he has been in trouble. They find him imaginative. The film makes the dull banker better for his showing some imagination, something Herbert Hoover, for example, had become unpopular for lacking, and the Kerbys are wealthy stock investors who have to atone for their profligate ways before they can get into heaven. Gone is the lake, the Marion who was "priestess of the woods," the appeals to savagery and cannibals, Topper's wish to throw off his clothes, and the kissing between Topper and Marion. What is left is something tamer and unmarked by any claim for a primitive utopia. A bit more like Shangri-La, this *Topper* argues for universal moderation in its mild utopia: less jazz age carelessness, less Depression-era unimaginativeness, and a more balanced marriage.

Topper illustrates a departure for one current of American film which moves away from straight satire toward a new phenomena of the period, screwball. Screwball emerges in the same decade as does film noir, though earlier. A filmed version of a play written in the twenties but filmed in the thirties, *Holiday* (1938), for example, retains the logic of its period of composition. *Holiday*, like Thorne Smith's novel, satirizes the "business-of-America-is-business" ethic of the prosperous twenties. The capitalist system had not yet faltered in a way that destabilized American bearings the way the Depression would do. Unlike screwball, satire embodies a confidence in its ability to diagnose, know, and expose its subjects' weaknesses. Screwball is intimately connected with its social environment, but it is truly a phenomenon provoked by a deep sense of uncertainty. In American history, there had never been a depression as severe as that of the thirties.[28] And screwball functions in central ways through a strenuous non sequitur logic which reflects the loss of moorings that afflicted the nation. A recurring logic in screwball comedies of the period concerns imagining alternatives to the source of the decade's anxieties, the afflicted capitalist system. Whereas the bank in Smith's novel remains the one fortress impregnable to public opinion when Topper's drunken scandals make the newspapers, in the film the bank is the scene of the Kerbys' early moments of dissipation. They bring the instability of the speculation that helped bring the economy down directly into the bank, and we see how intimately their recklessness might be tied up with the failure of the market. For this, the film tells us, they need to do penance. Screwball embodies the terms of the characteristic escapist impulse of the thirties, since it enacts the contradiction between the effort to move away from the logic of the period while almost sub-consciously working out alternatives to the central trauma of the period. Being mad, a nut, crazy are all synonymous conditions in the thirties to being a screwball, which is used in the period as either a noun or an adjective. Screwball equals irrational. At its core, screwball comedy acts irrationally to make an escape from the present that is not rationally possible. It is escapist in its impulses but societal, economic, and political in its reality.

One can see both its roots in twenties satire and its degree of differ-ence from pure satire by comparing *Holiday* to the early and late screwball comedies, *Three Cornered Moon* (1933) and *You Can't Take it with You* (1938).[29] Early screwball is more identifiably connected to twenties satire than are such screwball films as *Bringing Up Baby* (1938), The *Awful Truth* (1937), or *My Favorite Wife* (1940), the latter two of which demonstrate how the irrationality of screwball could include other issues, domestic mores, for example, once screwball as a gesture toward escape had been discovered as a response to economic upset. A satire on the hollowness of business success, *Holiday* was written as a play in 1928 (by Philip Barry) at the height of twenties prosperity, then first made as a film in 1930 and remade, more famously, in 1938. In a carefully laid-out internal geography, it opposes art, play, and love, on the one hand, to business on the other. *Holiday* differs by degree from *Three Cornered Moon* and other screwball comedies in that it does not feature the irrational as the solution to the problem it poses. Its central character, Johnny Case (Cary Grant), is about to be married to the daughter of a rich stockholder. Johnny dislikes business and plans to make one stock market killing, then use the money to quit business (for ten years). Johnny remarks, "I ask myself what General Motors would do, and then I do the opposite." The household of Johnny's fiancée's father is divided into two realms. The fiancée, Julia, is too much like her father for Johnny's tastes. She and her father occupy the respectable business realm; Linda occupies the world of play, and their alcoholic brother, Edward, who wanted to be an artist, is caught in the middle. Too weak to stand up to his father, but dislik-ing the world of business, Edward survives by drinking himself into a stupor. Julia reveals herself with the remark, "There's no such thrill in the world as making money." Her sister, Linda (Katharine Hepburn), disdaining business, turns out to be Johnny's soul mate. As her mother did, Linda spends most of her time in her old playroom, which Linda informs Johnny "was mother's idea. She thought there ought to be one room in the house where people could come to have some fun. She used to be up here as much as we were before she died." Johnny makes

his killing and the film ends when he and Linda leave together, pre-
sumably to spend ten years having fun.

Three Cornered Moon departs from the certainty of *Holiday*. First
written as a play by Gertrude Tonkonogy it concerns a family, the
Rimpelgars, whose individual members are locked in their own subjective realities; a condition which makes them appear screwy, screw-
balls. Screwball as a cultural phenomenon suggests that filmgoers of the
thirties were fixated on the gap between subjective reality and larger
events which might overwhelm or contradict that reality. The audience
was positioned, as film characters were not, to see the difference. A rich
vein of audience sympathy existed in the context of a Depression environment for staying inside one's subjective mind-set, even in the face of
contradictory fact. Such a position was recognizable to the extent that
it got sympathetic laughs. Of the bedrock beliefs that Americans had
held, then saw smashed the Depression, Frederick Lewis Allen
remarks, "so many people had based upon one or more of them their
personal conceptions of their status and function in society that the
shock of seeing them go to smash was terrific. . . . to the men and women
of all stations of life who had believed that if you were virtuous and
industrious you would of course be rewarded with plenty—and who
were now driven to the wall. On what could they rely? In what could
they now believe?" Allen adds, "The problems were so bewildering, so
huge. The unsettlement of ideas had been so shaking. . . . This plan . . .
looked all right today—but would it hold tomorrow?"[30]

The Rimpelgar wealth derives from the stock market, especially
from their Three Cornered Moon stock. Unlike the wealthy of *Holiday*, the family's matriarch has no clue about how to survive in business, and when the market crashes she is at the mercy of conditions she
does not understand. This circumstance embodies the predicament of
the Depression, and it identifies the differing economic environments
from which the satire *Holiday* and the screwball sensibility of *Three
Cornered Moon* emerge. In screwball, characters have less control over
their circumstances; they respond by turning inward, locking themselves, or escaping, into subjective realities. The dark side of the shift
to screwball shows up a year after *Three Cornered Moon* with the
appearance of *The Merry Frinks*. The Frinks are a family of ne'er-do-
wells who all exploit their mother, who waits on them while they abuse
her and each other. Like the Rimpelgars they are locked in their own
subjective realities, but this occurs with a hint of their escape being
consciously achieved at the expense of their mother. The same year, *It
Happened One Night* demonstrated the difficulties of going back to
the satire of *Holiday*. As is *Holiday*, *It Happened One Night* is an alle-

gory of escape. A rich man's daughter wants to get out from under his thumb. Like the Frinks, she is selfish and spoiled. Her escape, unlike that of the characters in *Holiday,* is modified by her need to understand American economics of the thirties. Out on the road she hooks up with a reporter (Clark Gable). Together they encounter democratic America, especially in the form of popular music on a bus ride. Whereas a quick stock killing enables an escape in *Holiday,* recent stock market history of the period makes such a resort untenable; money as a pressure remains a persistent presence in *It Happened One Night.* This is characteristic of the shift that occurs in the thirties.

In some respects, in *Three Cornered Moon* Mrs. Rimpelgar is the most screwball character in the film, since she responds to catastrophe with non sequitur logic and nearly completely escapes into her own subjectivity. In that respect she embodies the screwball ethos. At the disastrous news that her stock is worthless and her bank account empty, she comes home and has her hair washed. When her son announces he has passed the bar, she asks him if her hat makes her look tall. In conversations the family members speak in emotional terms, but almost as though talking to themselves, since no one else listens. One running joke is built around the Polish maid, Jenny, and her not speaking English. They tell her they have no money to pay her, but she goes on working, obliviously. When Jenny seems to inquire about a bouquet of flowers the family daughter, Elizabeth Rimpelgar (Claudette Colbert), tells her the bouquet is George, a name Jenny repeats at the later sight of flowers. That the basis for the family's hopes has shifted from the mind-set of *Holiday* materializes when they are faced with starvation (one brother faints for lack of food). A practical doctor who has a crush on Elizabeth tells them all they have to stop being babies and face reality. Elizabeth's brother, Kenneth, who is studying law, calls out for his Lewis, a reference to the author of a legal text. When he finds Sinclair Lewis's *Main Street,* a satire on practical small-town business, he tosses it aside in disgust. Now the family has to be practical.

The certainty of satire isn't a reasonable alternative. When Elizabeth's fiancé, Ronald, who has moved in with the Rimpelgars after having been dispossessed for not paying his rent, refuses to take a job, Elizabeth screams at him that artists are "useless." She remarks that she is tired of discussions of "trees, sunsets, and souls." She no longer wants to shiver at the sight of a flower. She tells him now she has discovered she loves steak sandwiches.

In a sense the very screwiness of the Rimpelgars and their being forced to accept a new reality, as evidenced by Elizabeth moving from a twenties worship of iconoclastic art (the values of both Eugene

O'Neill and Sinclair Lewis are specifically satirized) to a new belief in practical solutions to problems, serves as an allegory of the Depression's power to change one's values, one's sense of verities. In this respect, the Depression triggers a new kind of humor, one related to the satire of *Holiday*, but lacking its certainty and ironizing its—and the twenties generation's—false confidence. In that respect screwball laughs at the very unstable subjective certainty it exemplifies. Once the Depression itself has exposed and foregrounded the instability of subjective certainty, initially on economic grounds, subjective error can be funny in a whole set of different environments (romantic—*It Happened One Night, The Awful Truth, My Favorite Wife*, or theatrical—*Twentieth Century*). This phenomenon of eroding certainty does not occur in an aesthetic vacuum. Both Tyrus Miller and Brian McHale argue that modernism suffered a crisis of confidence, of "certitude," in the thirties, and, as a result began to give way to post-modernism. McHale, remarking on forces that work to "destabilize the projected world, and consequently to foreground its ontological structure," concludes, "modernist poetics begins to hemorrhage, to leak away—though not fatally, since it is (barely) possible to recuperate these internal contradictions by invoking the model of the 'unreliable narrator,' thus destabilizing the projected world and reasserting the epistemological dominant of the text."[31] One version of this phenomenon in film is the emergence near the end of the thirties of film noir, characterized as it is by unreliable voice-over narrators; another is the emergence of screwball comedy, which attempts to ironize the problem, foregrounding unreliable character subjectivity while retaining an overriding plot that seeks to resolve the abyss of instability the characters' irrational perspectives have exposed.

As screwball comic logic exposes subjective error, the plots of screwball films, in a somewhat contradictory fashion, work toward either reintroducing old verities or gravitate to offering a tentative new political awareness. One can overstate this point slightly to at least illustrate it: The values of Hooverism can be exposed as having been subjective and false verities, while those of a more cooperative political logic, New Dealism, can be introduced as possible successors. To put this into the terms McHale uses, the plots, through conceding subjectivity by ironizing it, then attempt to recover some of the certainty lost by the characters' subjective irrationality through their resolutions.

No film illustrates this point better than *You Can't Take it with You*. Like *Topper, You Can't Take it with You* is divided into two spheres, the world of the bank; associated with business, routine, authority, and predatory behavior; and the world of the Vanderhof family, associated with instinct, sensual pleasure, freedom of choice, in sum, with escape from the world of the bank. More thoroughly than in *Topper*, these spheres are examined within the context of central issues of the thirties. The film opens with an introduction to the world of the bank and its president, Anthony Kirby (Edward Arnold). Kirby and his associates worry about monopoly busters. They are planning a monopoly on munitions production, and they discuss making bullets, guns, and cannons. They make clear they are not averse to getting what they want through force. They refer to a competitor named Ramsey, whom they are seeking to ruin, and to Martine Vanderhof, a homeowner who, by refusing to sell his house, is blocking their efforts to acquire a twelve-block area for their munitions operation. The subject matter of their plotting would have been common knowledge in 1938, having been drawn from central developments in the period. New Deal Brain Truster Raymond Moley, noted that FDR had vacillated between excoriating business and wanting to work cooperatively with it. But by the mid-thirties, "the President acquiesced in a campaign . . . blaming the depression on business. Jackson and Ickes at once began an oratorical 'trust busting' offensive—a series of bitter speeches."[32] Munitions makers had, by the mid-thirties, also come in for special widespread public distrust. In 1934 *Fortune* magazine charged that during World War I munitions makers had sought to prolong the war and thereby profit. A committee under Senator Gerald Nye investigated, and Nye acerbically charged, "When Americans went into the fray, they little thought that they were . . . fighting to save the skins of American bankers who had bet too boldly on the war."[33] Bank president Kirby's unnaturalness is telegraphed by his having to drink medicine for his indigestion to get through the day.

The Vanderhof household represents complete escape from the world of the bank. Alice Vanderhof (Jean Arthur) recalls her grandfather, Martin, had once been successful in business, but one day he walked away from his job because it made him unhappy. The extended family in the home makes choices instinctively rather than in accord with convention. Martin collects stamps and plays the harmonica; his daughter, Alice's mother, writes plays because someone mistakenly delivered a typewriter to their house years back; Alice's father makes fireworks in the basement; her sister, Essie, dances, often in a tutu; Essie's husband plays the xylophone. Alice is the only family member who works, and she works in Martin Kirby's bank, where she has been proposed to by Kirby's son, Tony (James Stewart).

The film goes out of its way to demonstrate the Vanderhof family behaving instinctively, acting as they feel rather than conforming to convention. This point reveals the film's philosophical connections to such seemingly different movies as the Tarzan films and *Mutiny on the*

Bounty. The motive for the escape in *You Can't Take it with You* conceptually descends from the logic of attraction to primitivism, from the belief that modernity has buried the true instinctive self. For this reason the film shows the family deriving pleasure from sensual things, appealing to taste, smell, sound, and sight: Essie makes candy and passes it around; they all make music; Penny paints. One can see the film's logic in a scene between Martin and Alice in Martin's bedroom when Alice confesses to him that she is in love with Tony. Martin asks Alice if she is in love. She stammers and he looks into her eyes, immediately remarking, "Oh yes." He has seen it, rather than her needing to articulate it. He asks, "Do you have fun together." She answers with an affirmative monosyllable. He replies, "You can't even talk about him, can you?" To which she remarks, "Not rationally." He adds, "Well, who's asking you to be rational?" This, of course, summarizes the central point of the film and points to the central benefit of screwball. One can reach a more satisfying plane by not being rational; or one can at least believe this to be true as a method of escape. Referring to his dead wife, he remarks on the fragrance in the room, saying that was his wife's fragrance. She is still present; in other words you can still know her through your senses.

This faith in intuition is repeated throughout the film. The rational is pitted against the irrational. At the bank Martin Vanderhof encounters Mr. Poppins, an accountant. He asks Poppins if he is happy. Poppins confesses he is not; he prefers to make toys. Vanderhof says Poppins ought to come and live with them, and soon Poppins does, joining Alice's father and another man, an ice man, who came to make a delivery nine years earlier and stayed. When Tony and Alice sit in the park one night some children teach them a dance that is sweeping the country. They pin a sign that says "Big Apple" on Alice's back; the reverse side says "Nuts." She is wearing the "Nuts" sign when she encounters Tony's parents in an expensive restaurant. They are nuts, and happy, in a way that the rest of the conventional diners are not.

When Tony manipulates his stuffed shirt parents into visiting the Vanderhof household, everyone is arrested because the fireworks have gone off in the basement. When they are all in jail, democracy and the irrational are linked in opposition to business and convention. Kirby rages against the "scum" in jail, who are a racial mixture of lower-class people. When Kirby tosses his cigar on the floor, the poor people dive for it. As Kirby rages, Vanderhof tells him he might be better if his business ventures failed so he could concentrate on what is important. Kirby tells him, "Man, you're crazy." This equation makes retaining sanity an economic enterprise. For Kirby, if one's goal is not profit, then one is crazy. Kirby Sr. tries to cement his relationship with his son by making him president of the munitions company, trying to make economics equal family. But Alice responds to the Kirbys' snobbery by running away, and Tony quits his job at his father's bank. Kirby's effort to recover his son reintroduces the money-sanity equation, but now revises Kirby's view. Kirby shows up at Vanderhof's home asking for advice on how to recover his son. Tony is upstairs in the home pounding on Alice's door trying to reconcile. Vanderhof advises Kirby to sit down and play a duet with him on the harmonica, by Kirby's lights a completely irrational response to his problem. When Vander-hof insists, he complies, and both children, Alice and Tony, respond to the nonverbal signal and come downstairs. By getting underneath logic and appealing on a sensual level, the music has enabled Kirby to recover Tony. At its most philosophical, screwball means casting off capitalist conventions and trusting ones instincts, as surely as disap-pearing into Shangri-La, this gets one back to a natural state.

8

The American Contradiction

CLASS INTEREST AND THE PRESS

LOUIS BRANDEIS ONCE REMARKED THAT "WE CAN HAVE DEMOC-
racy in this country, or we can have great wealth concentrated in the
hands of the few, but we can't have both." If one applies this logic to
America's journalistic institutions in the 1930s, embodying as they do
by that point in American history an almost mythic role as the voice
of democracy, one can see the dilemma posed for thirties journalists,
working as they did for capitalist magnates, and for the American
people, having as their source of information material sifted through
the hands of the wealthy. Summarizing the consequences of this circumstance, A. J. Liebling asserted, "Freedom of the press belongs to
the man who owns one." Throughout the twenties and thirties, columnist Walter Lippman struggled with this innate contradiction in a democratic society, often returning to theorizing about ideals journalists,
who were pulled in various directions by competing interests, ought
to meet. Writing with Charles Merz, he contended, "does it not follow
that a constant testing of the news and a growing self-consciousness
about the main sources of error is a necessary part of the democratic
philosophy." Later Lippman wrote, "When you consider how pro-
foundly dependent the modern world is upon its news, the frailty of
human nature becomes an argument not for complacency and apology,
but for eternal vigilance." In 1931 he added, a journalist ought "to
remain clear and free of his irrational, his unexamined, his unac-
knowledged prejudgments."[1]

Nevertheless, Lippman's concerns for journalistic standards were
not universally shared in the thirties. A sensational New York rape and
murder case in 1935 suggested how far from Lipmann's standards some
journalists of the period would depart and how much capitalist self-
interest could influence the news. After John Fiorenza, an uphol-
sterer's assistant, was convicted of the murder, a Hearst paper, the
Daily Mirror, "began a six-part daily feature called 'Fiorenza's Own
Amazing Story.' " But soon the district attorney reported that "no

Hearst representative had seen Fiorenza in Tombs Prison." Fiorenza's "only three visitors, his lawyers and his mother, swore they had told the *Mirror* nothing." Further, "the prison psychiatrist was quoted as saying that Fiorenza told him, 'I never gave an interview to anybody from a paper.' " *Time* magazine concluded, "Hearst's fake is so abhorrent it shames the whole newspaper business."[2] Nor is the Hearst incident an aberration in newspaper history. In his 1936 memoir, *Personal History*, foreign correspondent Vincent Sheean describes reporters he met in the Ruhr: "the older correspondents derived pleasure from the manipulations and treacheries of the politicians. It pleased many of them . . . to know something that the public did not know; to observe, and then conceal, the degradation of governments. . . . the press and most of the politicians of continental Europe were on sale to the highest bidder."[3]

While the newspaper business had, by the 1930s, acquired a long history of yellow journalism and stunt reporting, the contradiction in the nature of the country's fourth estate ran deeper than just manipulation of the facts. While the press from colonial times was perceived as speaking for the people when the people might have no other voice in the halls of power, the thirties brought on concerted attacks on the press in charges it was an ally of the privileged. Thomas Jefferson had once remarked, "Were it left to me to decide whether we should have a government without newspapers, or newspapers without a government, I should not hesitate a moment to prefer the latter."[4] But, by the 1930s, the contradiction between American faith in a history of a democratic press and a press answerable to the influential had fully materialized. Hammering away at the gap between the press's advertised function and what he saw as its real function, Harold Ickes, Roosevelt's Secretary of the Interior and head of the Public Works Administration, attacked the press for what he perceived to be its violation of its own American identity: "with regard to the press, we are in the same dilemma as medieval man was in relation to the feudal aristocracy. Theoretically, the feudal barons, being specialists in violence, were supposed to protect the people against robbers and marauders. But in reality, these barons, having a monopoly of the instruments of violence, themselves became oppressors of the people."[5]

That the press often failed to live up to its advertised claims of objectivity and being the people's voice was not a new phenomenon in the thirties, but the circumstance of the Depression, throwing the masses into a crisis, made the need for representation from the press acutely felt. That portion of the populace most threatened by the trauma of depression most needed a voice that could speak for them to financial and political leaders. But often the press seemed to be one among many

special interests. And its reporters, caught between pressure to produce for profits and to not run afoul of the politics of wealthy publishers, were restricted in what they could actually write. In 1938,
George Seldes, a longtime foreign correspondent himself, noted that in
the 1936 presidential campaign "the lay reader might have found cause
for thought in the report . . . that the overwhelming majority of the
correspondents traveling with both Landon and Roosevelt, most of
them writing Republican or pro-Landon news, would vote for the reelection of the President." He adds, "The reader might have wondered
how it was possible to write one way and vote another." But news-
papermen "knew that most Washington news is cut to fit editorial policy . . . there are . . . numerous instances of distortion and suppression
of their telegrams . . . news is frequently colored, sometimes faked in
the home office." The effect on reporters, he argues, is that "correspondents are cynics who do not themselves believe much in the bun-
combe they send and which their publishers use to fool the American
people."[6]

   Studies of the press in the early decades of the century were finding
how un-democratic the press could be. *The New Republic* remarked
that there was "an irrepressible conflict between the newspaper as an
organ of public information and as a mechanism for private profit."[7]
In their 1929 study of Middletown (Muncie, Indiana), Robert and
Helen Lynd found that the economic clout of the business class persistently outweighed a paper's desire or ability to present the news in
an unbiased fashion. In 1890, a paper that had "carried 108,715 lines of
advertising" by 1923 carried "604,292 lines." This shift intensified the
obvious result that "The growing profit in controlling the agencies of
news diffusion has developed yet another use of the press — that of but-
tressing the interests of the business class who buy advertising." The
Lynds quote an editorial from "a small outlawed weekly," which
charges the major newspapers "protect higher-ups and ruin the reputations of those without influence."[8] Returning to Middletown in the
mid-thirties, the Lynds trace developments in the contradictory situation occupied by the press: "obligated on one side by a tradition of a
'free press' with the high obligation to report all the news . . . confined
on another side by the financial controls over Middletown and by its
own dependence upon commercial advertising."[9] This dilemma is intensified by economic concerns, since even the issue of profit contains an
internal contradiction. The Lynds note that "the operation of a prof-
itable newspaper depends upon securing . . . maximum circulation . . .
and maximum advertising." But 70 percent of Middletown is working
class and only 30 percent is from the business class. Thus the paper has
to couch its business class pandering in carefully chosen language in

order to keep both working-class subscribers and business-class advertising. Therefore, labor struggles are attached to movements that are locally disdained; it is socialist and communist agitators who are causing unrest. When a front-page photo shows the police battering strikers, the text characterizes them as "putting down an . . . anarchistic brute threat." Discussing layoffs and wage cuts, the paper skirts businesses options and remarks, "It's pretty sad to relate that labor costs are down, but a man out of work would rather work for low wages than not to work at all."[10] Ickes sums up the plight of the populace when he remarks, "We are, therefore, in a dilemma. We cannot control the press without losing our essential liberties, and yet our newspapers . . . are often out of sympathy with, and have different interests from, the majority of the people."[11]

Films of the thirties reveal an era obsessed with newspapers, in part because the papers brought news of each new development in the Depression economy. If someone powerful was causing the Depression or delaying recovery measures, the press was a place to look to for disclosure of the truth. But its own divided interests corrupted its potential as an ally to the people at the bottom. Films of the period provide a decade long meditation on the patent ways press practices contradict implied and overt claims made by newspapers. Some of the most somber films of the period dissect the genesis and growth of newspapers, as though exposing the special power interests entwined in the creation of newspapers will somehow change reality. Some of the angriest films lash out at the press for not living up to the myths that surround a democratic fourth estate. Other films derive their comic logic from focusing on the predicament of power-weak reporters and the colossal cynicism that results. And, finally, one subcategory of films examines the amorphous or entirely absent line between the rising establishment of publicity agents and the supposedly objective press. At a moment of national trauma, the press provided the American public a paradigm for the deeper contradiction that marked the U.S. system, that of a democracy run by plutocrats.

CREATION STORIES

Harrison Otis, the first owner of the *Los Angeles Times,* by virtue of having squeezed his partner out, insisted on being called the "General" (having been a brigadier), called his work force "the Phalanx,"and the *Times* building "the Fortress." With a sense of impending doom triggered by union developments of the period, Otis kept fifty rifles and a large quantity of ammunition inside the Fortress. He insisted on his reporters being trained for war. As Mark Dowie points out, when unions contacted his pressman about organizing, he responded by driving around L.A. in a car with a cannon mounted on top.[12] Calling the shots at the *Times,* the General wrote his own bombastic editorials, which he placed on the front page of his paper, calling his enemies names and reprinting articles that had provoked libel suits. Among his targets was the rival paper, the *Daily Times.* In search of a way to squash the *Daily Times,* Otis teamed with one of his former paper carriers, the entrepreneurial Harry Chandler, who had monopolized paper distribution and offered a scheme for driving the *Daily Times* out of business. Chandler suggested inviting all of the *Daily Times* delivery boys out into the desert for a picnic, where he intended to strand them for a week, leaving their paper undelivered. Chandler and Otis believed subscribers would become enraged and the paper would risk folding. The two carried this plan out quite effectively. Dennis McDougal points out that "Chandler's scheme worked so well that [the *Daily Times*] was forced into bankruptcy."[13] Meanwhile Otis inquired to see who held the lien on the *Daily Times* presses. One step ahead of Otis, Chandler had already bought up the liens. They had succeeded in driving their rival out of business. They then proceeded to knock out other papers, establishing a near monopoly in southern California. In the process of establishing the *L.A. Times,* they also began to acquire huge tracts of land around Los Angeles, "a wall-to-wall urban industrial complex reaching from the Tehachapis to the Mexican border, and laterally 'from the mountains to the sea.' " Dowie adds, "News became secondary to the dream, and the *Times* became little more than a booster pamphlet for Los Angeles expansion. . . . Land became Harry's obsession, so preeminent in his mind that he would say to editorial page writers, 'Before you write, think of what is good for real estate.' "[14]

In events that would serve as the plot substance for the 1974 film *Chinatown* (notably set in the thirties), in 1904 Chandler and Otis sent out a covert agent, who represented himself as a Bureau of Land Reclamation officer. Their agent persuaded local farmers to relinquish water rights, which were to then be used in a project that would irrigate the valley and benefit everyone. Once the rights were secured, Otis and Chandler "used the *Times* to convince Los Angeles voters to support a bond issue to finance an aqueduct from the Owens River to the San Fernando Valley. An 'enemy of the city' is how a Chandler editorial described anyone who would vote against aqueduct bonds."[15] Meanwhile having bought up parched land, Otis and Chandler gained millions upon millions in reselling it once the land was irrigated. Not surprisingly, Ickes described Chandler's *Los Angeles Times* as "the most rabidly reactionary and savagely anti–New Deal newspaper in California, with the possible exception of *The San Francisco Chronicle.*" He adds, "When a publisher has so much wealth and so many investments it would be quixotic to expect him to use his newspaper to advance the general welfare when it conflicts with his personal interest."[16]

The Otis-Chandler history serves to illustrate the internal workings and power interests of the contradictory nature of America's fourth estate. And this point becomes a central issue in plot constructions of films of the thirties, which examine the contradiction in the American system. Such films become part of a larger, decade-long discourse on the American economic establishment and its relationship to a democratic system. Coming at the outset of the Depression, both Edna Ferber's novel (1930) and the film versions of *Cimarron* (1931) look back to the creation of a newspaper in late nineteenth-century Oklahoma as an important factor in establishing a new civilization. In Ferber's novel pioneer Yancey Cravat wants to start a newspaper that will print "all the news, all the time, knowing no law but the law of God and the government of these United States." Referring to the murdered editor who preceded him, Yancey remarks, "Because Pegler had the same idea I have—that here's a chance to start clean, right from scratch. . . . Clean politics instead of the skullduggery all around; a new way of living and thinking, because we've had a chance to see how rotten and narrow and bigoted the other way has been."[17] But the newspaper of the pioneer west gives way to the compromised history of the turn of the century and the ensuing three decades. One can tell that *Unholy Partners* (1941) comes at the tail end of the Depression, in the era of *Sergeant York* rather than in that of *The Lost Squadron,* for as the film opens with Bruce Corey (E. G. Robinson) returning from World War I, his old job is still waiting. Coming as it does at frightening moment for Americans at the onset of World War II, it presents tradition and established business in a manner more respectful than did the early thirties films, which bitterly portrayed returning veterans who were quickly forgotten by employers and politicians. Before the war, Corey worked for a newspaper, the *Sentinel.* But he does not want his old job back; he wants to start a new paper. Starting from this plot point, *Unholy Partners* becomes an investigation into how modern journalism went wrong. And it becomes an exposure of the mistake men on the make made in departing from American tradition and compromising on what it presents as accepted values. Rather than offering a character analysis, as does *Citizen Kane,* it creates a black-and-white allegory of moral mistakes made by newspaper entrepreneurs willing to ignore morality to build empires. Corey tells his old editor that the new paper he envisions will cut through all of the old slow processes of the *Sen-*

tinel. He blames the war for changing people: "war has done things to people. We've made life cheap. That's made emotions cheap. You know death has lost its dignity. There's no privacy left. As far as this generation's concerned keyholes were made to look through and what they can't spy out personally, they want to read about or see in photographs." He argues that papers need to publish news as it happens, which means compromises in the care with which they handle the truth. His editor refuses to go along, maintaining the importance of the traditional values embodied in the *Sentinel.* Responsibility for a new, slippier morality, as this film presents it, rests not with traditional centers of power, but with a populace that has let its morality erode in hard times.

Another way of putting this would be to say that this film is closer to T. S. Eliot's conservative characterization of the public as a "mob," rather than to the view of Robert Riskin, who consistently sees the masses embodying American decency. Corey becomes a case in point of what happens when one gives in to the temptation to abandon traditional morality by giving the mob what it wants. He does not want to cover the news to inform people who, in a democratic society, need to comprehend the complexities of the times in order to best govern themselves. Rather he substitutes exploitation of a too willing marketplace for the values of the *Sentinel.* The film then embodies this lesson in the person of a gangster, Merrill Lambert (Edward Arnold).

Unable to get financing from legitimate sources to start his paper, Corey makes an "unholy alliance" with Lambert, who becomes his silent partner. Lambert wants influence in the papers to keep the press from being the power that limits his illegal activities. This film participates in a discourse that questioned the rise of organized crime that took place throughout the twenties. Here organized crime is presented not as the result of environmental forces which overcome people (as it was presented in *The Doorway to Hell* and *Paid),* but rather it's part of a giving in to temptation, strictly an individual choice, like that of Corey's departure from the *Sentinel.* At a moment in history when collective cooperation with authority has become a necessity triggered by crisis, this film demonstrates the social ills that result from departing from traditional authority. The film offers a major scene meant to illustrate the consequences of such a departure from tradition. Desperate for some new incident he can transform into a screaming, paper-selling headline, Corey hears of a potentially sensational murder. He orders a "sob sister" be sent to the scene to get the emotional angle (summoning up a whole history of yellow journalism).[18] He goes to the murder site himself and finds the body has already been removed. He instructs his secretary to lie down on a bed, cover her face, and hike up her skirt. He then photographs her as the murdered woman. Soon he has headlines screaming about the case. Unfortunately his gangster partner does not stay silent for long. In an episode recalling William Randolph Hearst's use of his newspaper empire to promote the movie career of his mistress, Marion Davies, Lambert brings in a chorus girl he wants promoted in the papers. Their eventual fight over the paper leads to Corey's killing Lambert, fleeing, and apparently crashing his plane intentionally. The film's final scenes suggest that any tainted departure from the imagined tradition represented by the *Sentinel* will lead to compromise and disaster. The film demonstrates that Corey is not so corrupt that he will stand for anything, but it presents his tragedy as the result of moral weakness.

If *Unholy Partners* seeks to create a morality tale that places full blame for newspaper abuses and gangsterism on the individual, *Citizen Kane* employs the methods of Freudian psychoanalysis to make its point about the compromises made to achieve American success. Commenting on the film's unwillingness to completely trash William Randolph Hearst, upon whom Charles Foster Kane is modeled, in his review of the film Otis Ferguson remarked, "I could, and would if the editor were not afraid of libel, give you quite a list of Hearst's undesirable qualities not possessed by Kane."[19] The film both exposes Kane's abuses as owner and editor of the *Enquirer* and accords him a sympathy that assigns responsibility for his actions to forces larger than himself. At the heart of *Citizen Kane*'s interest in its subject lies the issue of self-interest. While Walter Lippman espoused objectivity in journalism, *Citizen Kane* cannot believe in its possibility. Referring to the camera and magic tricks that characterize this film, Pauline Kael asserts, "I think what makes Welles' directorial style so satisfying in this movie is that we are constantly aware of the mechanics . . . the pleasure *Kane* gives doesn't come from illusion but comes from our enjoyment of the dexterity of the illusionists, and the working of the machinery."[20] These camera tricks work to repeatedly take viewers into Kane's subjective mind, visually reinforcing the lesson that subjective interest is inescapable. This lesson, while it is tied up in a work marked by pop psychoanalysis, also intersects with press and Hearst family history. This makes *Citizen Kane* more than a character study; it's what connects it to the preoccupation with the press during the Depression.

A series of requests the young William Randolph Hearst made of his father, at the time the younger Hearst had just taken over the *San Francisco Examiner,* demonstrates the way self-interest intrudes into the world of journalism, not in spite of journalism's being a capitalist enterprise, but because American journalism cannot be anything but a

As the account of Kane's ownership of the newspaper unfolds, slowly the story's attention shifts from the paper to himself (*Citizen Kane*, RKO, 1941).

part of a system of capitalist self-interest. This film will argue that as one cannot escape one's subjective self, journalism cannot escape its capitalist environment. Between 1887 and 1889, young Hearst was writing to his then–Senator father requesting the elder Hearst use his considerable political and economic influence to help the younger Hearst in his fight with San Francisco rival newspapers, especially the *Chronicle*. He wanted his father to go to New York to meet with the influential men who ran the Pulitzer-owned *World*. He writes, "make friends with these powerful eastern newspaper men. They would appreciate a visit from a U.S. Senator, they would feel flattered. . . . Then the first thing you know they will do anything they can for us." David Nasaw remarks, "At the age of twenty-four, Hearst had developed a ruthless, scheming side to him which he now presented to his father." Later when the younger Hearst "learned that the *Examiner* was not getting its fair share of government contracts . . . he asked his father to do what he could to remove the director of the Port of San Francisco and the California surveyor from office."[21] When Hearst took over the *Examiner* from his father, it was an ailing enterprise. He saved it, in part, by ruthless methods. Those methods had little to do with journalistic objectivity, but the journal itself would not have existed without them, another example of the contradiction embodied by the press. The film asserts the closely related point that Kane cannot be either separated or understood apart from his own subjective self-interest.

Citizen Kane arranges the order of our learning about Kane to intentionally foreground the problem of first absolute truth, then absolute objectivity, in the press. It accomplishes this by starting with a scene of Kane dying. We are caught in his deeply subjective moment, and despite witnessing it, we have no immediate way of understanding. The dying Kane is holding a small globe that contains a pleasantly domestic-looking little house set in a rustic snowy environment, complete with a snowman. As he dies, the globe rolls out of his hand and smashes. We then move, not further into his subjective mind, but entirely away from it; and our guide is the press, in the form of a *News on the March* newsreel. Presented in the authoritative voice of its narrator, it soon reveals its inability to go beneath the surface. Subjective truth is unavailable to us. We can only see what we (and the camera) can see. Feeling the inadequacy of the newsreel account of Kane's life, a reporter investigates to learn the meaning of his last word "rosebud." He encounters and interviews the people who knew Kane. He learns Kane was aware of the problem of subjective interests interfering in journalism's desire for objectivity. Kane writes a "declaration of principles" for the paper, one of which states there will be no "special interests" influence on reporting. But when Kane brings dancing girls to a staff party in which Kane is calling for war with Spain, the focus of the party subtly shifts to being about Kane himself. One of Kane's old employees, Leland (Joseph Cotten), tells the reporter that Kane never believed in anything except himself. This point underscores the problem of dismissing one's own interests in favor of objective truth. Leland recalls the shift in Kane's view when he remarked "People will believe what I tell them to believe." When Leland accuses Kane of caring about people only on his own terms, Kane is directly faced with the dilemma of objectivity and self-interest. He responds, "My terms? The only terms anybody knows." After Kane has tried using the paper to promote, and misrepresent, his mistress's skills as a singer, he rises to the occasion of objective reporting by allowing Leland to write a negative review, which Kane finishes.

The incident demonstrates that one can sometimes rise above one's subjective interests, but such a position, the entire film demonstrates, cannot be absolute. As one flashback reveals, Kane has been separated from his mother when he was a child; something she allowed to get him away from an abusive stepfather. His dying reference to rosebud, the name on his childhood sled, takes him back to his childhood and memories of his mother. His own subjective boundaries all relate back to that moment; they provide the subjective boundaries of his entire life and dramatize this film's interpretive position on the impossibility of pure journalistic integrity—and on decades of a marred newspaper history.

THE PERSONS BETWEEN AS PARADIGM

In the newspaper business in the thirties, in between the publishers and the public fell the reporters and editors. Noting that in principle "the American press is free," Ickes asserted, "Nevertheless, there is a considerable amount of suppression, fabrication, and distortion, for none of which the government or the people are responsible." He charges, "all of the censorship, that exists in this country is self-imposed by the editors and publishers themselves."[22] He then cites several examples of press suppression and fabrication. In Chicago in 1933 there was an "outbreak of amoebic dysentery." But this fact was kept suppressed for five months out of fear that it would damage business at the world's fair. He cites "an important metropolitan newspaper [which] confesses the possession of a 'Censorship Department.' " When columnist Hugh S. Johnson praised labor leader John L. Lewis his column "was quickly excised." On April 4, 1934, the *Detroit Free Press,* which opposed Roosevelt's PWA housing projects, "Carried a front-page photograph of two men seemingly fishing in a pool of water in the gaping foundations of a PWA housing project in Detroit." However, the original negative of the picture revealed only two men standing near the house's foundation looking into the water. It was later discovered the poles and line had been inserted into the photograph by the art department, with the intention of discrediting federal housing. Ickes recounts how some twenty years earlier the *Chicago Tribune* went to war with Hearst's Chicago paper, an event Ickes credits with initiating "the reign of gangsterism in Chicago." The *Tribune* hired a group of gangsters who would "lay in wait at strategic points for the agents of Hearst's *Examiner.*" When the Hearst people showed up, the *Tribune* men opened fire. "The Hearst forces then resorted to counter-ambushes with a delivery truck as a decoy. Newsboys, some of them crippled and unable to scamper to safety, were shot. Passing women were clipped with bullets." The same gangsters terrorized union people. James Keely, a managing editor of the *Tribune,* testified about anti-union violence before a Senate Committee. He told of one man who was beaten up, thrown down an elevator shaft, then shot. "Some of the press room men or stereotypers picked up the man and took him over to a big wash basin and started to wash the blood off him, and then the fellow who was after him came down . . . with a gun and shot at him." When a *Tribune* reporter who had been peddling influence in the newspaper was murdered, the *Tribune* sought to intervene in the investigation, partly at this point to obtain a conviction. The police arrested one Leo Brothers. But they did not take him to jail. Rather, police officers and *Tribune* employees took him to a hotel where for several days they attempted to torture a conviction out of him.

In a radio broadcast in early 1939, George Seldes pointed out that newspaper publishers, unlike their enemies, "never commit adultery, they are rarely divorced, they know nothing of the 'love-nests' the press talks about; they never sue anyone, they are never sued." Columnist Westbrook Pegler explained, "publishers who had intimate affairs . . . protected themselves, proving that they knew it was dirty pool to treat others so." Referring to reporters on Colonel McCormick's *Chicago Tribune,* Ickes concludes, "They receive directions that are sometimes veiled, to write according to their employer's prejudices."[23] In this atmosphere, and within this set of power relations, reporters and editors had to function in the thirties. Their resulting cynicism was so absolute, it was comic.

The movies, some of which were written by ex-reporters (notably Ben Hecht), use the reporters' plight as a comic version of being trapped by economics in a set of power dynamics beyond one's control. Once one gives oneself over to this circumstance, cynicism results. In the Capra films, *Mr. Deeds Goes to Town* and *Meet John Doe,* cynical city reporters are made to reconnect to traditional American values, to shed their cynicism. It is notable that in his attack on the *Chicago Tribune* Ickes has to reach back some eighty years to an earlier attack made by Abraham Lincoln on that same paper. Having traveled so far into the amoral labyrinth of the newspaper world, Ickes seems compelled to grab onto Lincoln as proof that some evidence of American morality once existed. Capra's characters, confronted by newspaper cynicism, make this same move repeatedly, visiting national monuments or summoning up the names of the founding fathers, then uttering them almost as a mantra to ward off their discoveries of power economics and exploitation of the American democratic promise attached to the fourth estate, as does the compromised editor in *John Doe,* when he discloses to Doe that the reporter Doe loves has made common cause with an industrialist and newspaper publisher (who, like Harrison Otis, has his own private army) to initiate a fascist takeover of the White House.

Nothing Sacred (1937), however, in its title and in its entirety conveys the deeper entanglement of newspaper ethics in capitalist society, and in so doing accords with a general cynicism felt by the American public over their own vulnerability in the face of the Depression. It matters in *Nothing Sacred* that news of Hazel Flagg's terminal illness makes the papers. She feels trapped in her small hometown. The film begins with words on the screen which lay out the terms of its patent cynicism: "This is New York, skyscraper capital of the world ... where the slickers and know-it-alls peddle gold bricks to each other ... and where truth, crushed to earth, rises again more phony than a glass eye."

The phoniness the film sees arises from claims to treasuring traditional verities for people to whom only profit matters. In the opening scene, Oliver Stone (Walter Connolly), the editor of the *New York Globe,* addresses a full banquet hall as he dedicates the *Globe*'s new museum. The *Globe*'s honored guest is a sultan. Soon a black woman and several children arrive and identify the sultan as the woman's husband, the children's father, and a bootblack. The incident, based on an actual hoax of the period, is the first in a series of frauds that permeate the film. Wallace Cook (Frederick March), the reporter responsible for the stunt, is demoted. To regain status he pitches the idea that the *Globe* feature a series of articles on dying small-town girl, Hazel Flagg (Carole Lombard). We see Hazel learn that she is not dying after all; her Norman Rockwellesque doctor is an alcoholic who has misdiagnosed her. Cook arrives in Hazel's town to be treated rudely by a series of locals: children in the back of a wagon throw garbage at him, and shortly thereafter a small boy rushes from concealment and bites Cook's leg. Desperate to get out of the town, Hazel allows Cook to take her to New York, where she is to be feted for her courage. She attends a wrestling match, which is clearly faked, then endures the fraudulent emotions of a nightclub emcee, who uses her case and that of famous women in history to slightly cloak a burlesque act. The mayor, civic leaders, and Stone all capitalize on Hazel's terminal illness. When they learn she has been faking to avoid losing face in public, they fake her death, hold a funeral, and laud her in the papers. While the film seems to condemn reporters for lacking ethics, the environments of both the small town and the city are composed of hucksters and malcontents on the make. Everyone in the film has a fraud to perpetrate. Newspaper reporters aren't society's demons; they merely emerge from society. *Nothing Sacred* is to the thirties what Tennyson's *In Memoriam: A.H.H.* was to the nineteenth century. The notion of a universe running on love had been undermined for many by theories of evolutionists. Tennyson saw a "nature, red in tooth and claw" in the place of the old benign nature. *Nothing Sacred* sees cherished American democratic freedoms as by then in the service of predatory self-interest and profit.

The humor of many of the newspaper films of the decade derives from a cold abandonment of traditional scruples, a circumstance provoked by reporters desperate, nearly obsessed with beating the competition, at a moment when unemployment is a frightening threat. Their cold bloodedness follows because they have no control over the rules of their game or the demands made of them. In *Back in Circulation* (1937), reporters come upon a railroad wreck. Railroad officials want to keep all but medical people out to protect the families of the dead from suffering shock by learning of their losses in the papers. Reporter Timmie Blake (Joan Blondell) and her reporter pals lie and say they are doctors, then coldly collect names of the dead, which they plan to publish. Later an editor remarks of the wreck photo, "best picture we've had since that dame worked on Willie Guffy with a sash blade." Later, when the editor refuses to be seen publicly with Timmie, she attributes it to the time she lied for him on the witness stand in a libel suit. The extent to which abandoning ethics hardens reporters accounts for a group of reporters making jokes about the impending execution of murderer Earl Williams in *His Girl Friday* (1940). Soon they haggle with the sheriff over moving up the execution so they can make the early edition with the story. When an insurance man (Ralph Bellamy) tries to take star reporter Hildy Johnson (Rosalind Russell) away from the paper to marry her, her editor and ex-husband, Walter Burns (Cary Grant), plants a watch on him and has him arrested for theft. The circumstance of the reporters who are to serve as the voice of the people is so entangled in the predatory capitalist enterprise that they have lost all moral bearings.

This circumstance makes them useful to the powerful. In *The Girl from Missouri* (1934), Tom Paige (Franchot Tone), the son of a rich industrialist, wants to marry a commoner, Edie Chapman (Jean Harlow). Opposed to the marriage, Tom Sr. (Lionel Barrymore), has a man break into Edie's apartment, then he sends reporters in after him to photograph the two in an apparent love tryst in order to smear Edie. The reporters' cooperation is too automatic to even be an issue. One need only wave sleaze in front of them and they are there. In *What Price Hollywood?* (1932) as movie actress Mary Evans (Constance Bennett) grieves over the suicide of a longtime friend, predatory reporters climb through her upstairs window to snap photos. *Five Star Final* (1931), the angriest of the newspaper films of the thirties, connects this development to the unscrupulous behavior that had come to be associated with yellow journalism and the tabloid press. Early in *Five Star Final,* the tone is set when newspaper thugs assault a paper vendor for not selling their paper. A copyboy remarks that the editor, Joseph Randall (E. G. Robinson), has taken to calling the paper's owner "the Sultan of Slop." While employees argue about getting more girls in underwear into ads to sell papers, a flat-chested secretary is

Having been smeared by the papers, Edie turns the table and uses the soullness reporters to smear her enemy (*The Girl from Missouri*, MGM, 1934).

fired and the paper hires an attractive and clearly loose woman to replace her. Lacking a sensational story to stir up circulation, the paper publisher orders the editor to dig up an old story concerning a woman, Nancy Vorhees, who was tried and acquitted of murdering her husband for infidelity. Their specialist in such cases, Ichabod (Boris Karloff) impersonates a reverend to get the woman and her new husband to talk. Nancy's daughter is about to marry a society boy, and the scandal will ruin her. To endure the rottenness of the smear they are perpetrating on Nancy, both the newspaper's secretary and Ichabod get, and stay, drunk through most of the film. When Nancy and her husband commit suicide, reporters climb through the window to get pictures of their bodies. Unable to control the paper's publisher, and nauseated at the paper's tactics, Randall quits. The film's last scene of the suicide victims' mourners on the front page of the paper, which then blows into a gutter and floats toward a sewer grate. In its angry indictment of newspaper tactics, *Five Star Final* connects a central development in the late nineteenth and early twentieth century to the frenzied effort to profit by getting lurid headlines into the papers.

This development was explained by a magazine publisher in the late nineteenth century. Addressing a group of manufacturers, Cyrus Curtis, publisher of *Ladies Home Journal*, remarked, "Do you know why

Reporters sneaking in a back window to take a picture of a woman grieving over a friend's suicide (*What Price Hollywood?* RKO, 1932).

we publish the *Ladies Home Journal?* The editor thinks it is for the benefit of American women. That is an illusion . . . the real reason, the publisher's reason, is to give you people who manufacture things that American women want and buy, a chance to tell them about your products."[24] *Five Star Final* consistently makes the point that advertising plays an increasing role in decisions concerning the paper. At one point a paper employee remarks that the paper should give the public girls in underwear ads because nobody buys papers to read about politics. The development in the shared history of newspapers and advertising that seemed to take the growing influence of advertising in papers to its next logical stage was the birth of the public relations man—the publicity agent. Notably many of the pioneers of public relations, such as Ivy Lee, had first been newspaper reporters.[25] And many reporters had first learned about the power of PR from running publicity campaigns for the government during the First World War.[26] Michael Schudson's referring to the rise of public relations as "the decline of 'facts' in journalism" accords with the treatment given publicity agents in films of the thirties: journalism gives way to advertising then to pure publicity, and finally to moral chaos.[27] At a touchy moment in American economic history, the public was treated to a nightmare for a capitalist democracy, albeit from the shaky security of their art deco theater seats.

BOMBSHELL

A monument still stands in Ludlow, Colorado, bearing the names of some eighteen people, the youngest of whom was listed as three, who died violently in a union dispute on April 20, 1914.[28] In that year striking Colorado coal miners, along with their wives and children, had erected a tent village that would resemble the later Depression-era Bonus Army village in Washington, D.C. In 1914, the Colorado Fuel and Iron Company was engaged in an acrimonious dispute with their laborers over the effort the workers had made to join the UMWA. On the twentieth, coal company guards, hired thugs, and Colorado militia descended on the makeshift village and poured kerosene on the tents. Inside the tents the miners had built crude foxholes to protect their families from the line of gunfire. Many of the family members were later discovered still in the foxholes burned to death. While no one associated with the mining company was ever charged in the incident, several miners were arrested and many were blackballed from the coal industry. Far removed from the event by geography, the Rockefeller family nevertheless had a stake in the potential public relations disaster that seemed about to result because they owned the mines. To ward off this possibility, the Rockefellers hired Ivy Lee, a former reporter who had made a name for himself as the first publicity director of the Pennsylvania Railroad. Lee quickly sent out some nineteen bulletins to people of influence, many of them containing false information about the events of the massacre and causes of the strike.[29] Lee was not reporting the news; he was presenting the Rockefeller side of the conflict in the best possible light. In effect, he was selling that position.

Several developments in the early part of the twentieth century account for the emergence of public relations as a significant force in American life. By the 1930s a degree of nervousness and pessimism over democracy had set in. Several journals questioned whether the democratic system would survive.[30] Harold Laski told readers of the *American Political Science Review* in 1932 that representative democracy had fallen into an "institutional malaise."[31] Roscoe Pound, Dean of the Harvard Law School, saw an erosion of certainty in American thinking, which he attributed in part to the effect of Freudian psychoanalysis: "In place of reason, we have subconscious wishes, repressed desires, rooted behavior tendencies, habitual predispositions which are different for each individual economic unit. In place of enlightenment we have—well, perhaps, glands."[32] Michael Schudson points out, "The distrust of reason Pound spoke of took several forms." Politically it meant a new distrust of governing institutions. In class terms, the concept of "middle class" had been changing. In the mid-nineteenth century, "public opinion" had been the "voice of the middle class against an aristocracy." But by the twentieth century, public opinion had come to mean that of the masses, including immigrants, minorities, and women. These new groups were regarded by the old dominant groups as "incapable of sustained rationality." Therefore, "rather than attribute rationality to them, social scientists and others began to reconceive human nature generally, replacing a term like 'conviction,' which stressed human rationality, with term like 'attitude' and 'opinion,' which indicate that human thought and opinion mix reason and passion." Schudson concludes, "Public relations developed in the early part of the twentieth century as a profession which responded to, and helped shape, the public, newly defined as irrational, not reasoning . . . This had a far-reaching impact on the ideology . . . of American journalism."[33] By 1935, Roland Marchand notes, advertising man Bruce Barton could claim, "Wherever businessmen now congregated . . . public relations was 'very nearly the No. 1 topic of conversation.' "[34]

Writing to John D. Rockefeller, Ivy Lee seemed to have understated things when he said that his coverage of a Rockefeller charitable gift was "not really news," but, regardless, "the newspapers gave . . . much attention to it" due to the way Lee "dressed up" the account. Lee asserted, "It seems to suggest very considerable possibilities along this line."[35] By the twenties and thirties the line between news and public relations had blurred enormously. "Silas Bent estimated that at least 147 of 255 stories in the *New York Times* of December, 29, 1926, originated in the work of press agents." A few years later, "in 1930, political scientist, Peter Odegard estimated that 50 percent of news items originated in public relations work."[36] Reporters not only had to compete for news, but they had to compete with sources who had little or no regard for being influenced in their choices of story. A reporter might attend a press conference that had been largely staged to the advantage of a politician. He or she might find a story on labor blocked by a paper's publisher. And next to an article the reporter wrote another might appear that had been originated by a press agent. At the same time the same press agent might be representing business in campaigns that amounted to advertising. Objectivity became an impossible goal, as did freeing oneself of special-interest pressure. Films of the period record this bitter irony. And no film better dramatizes the commodification of everything in America which ensues from the new circumstance of a society permeated by public relations influence than does *Bombshell* (1933).

Bombshell enacts the tangled processes of advertising people as commodities, showing how the advertised commodity sells, depicting how the advertising occurs, showing how the commodity affects and changes others, and conveying how the person is turned into a commodity. Even as it does so, as a film it plays with its audience, reminding them they are, as they watch, participating in the process they are watching. It opens with a series of images flashed in rapid succession: we are shown magazine covers picturing movie star Lola Burns (Jean Harlow), newspaper headlines featuring her, then a series of faces reading about her, staring at her picture, next we see people using products bearing her name, makeup, nylons, perfume, her name in neon lights, girls and boys daydreaming about her, money raining down through the air, her face on a movie screen with Clark Gable, and people in a theater watching her. The opening establishes relationships between stardom, publicity, money, and newspapers. But the cause-and-effect order of these things is impossible to determine, which is one of this film's points. In a capitalist democracy selling simply is, where it started is obscure.

After its opening shots, the film cuts to Lola's bedroom at 6 a.m. Her maid is waking her up to start her workday. We find out immediately that her image is not merely an illusion dreamed up by a publicity agent, it requires constant work and attention. She is soon contacted by phone by a second assistant director; then a makeup man, who makes her up just for the trip to the studio, where she arrives accompanied by a hairdresser. They are followed by an interviewer. Meanwhile the sycophants who live off of her descend on her with their problems and requests. In the midst of all this, Lola gripes about how the studio's publicity agent, Space Hanlon (Lee Tracy) keeps up a steady stream of nasty and lurid stories about her, which he plants in the papers. When she arrives at the studio, a mob of fans awaits; from their midst a stalker rushes out and insists Lola is his wife.

The film cuts to the publicity man's office where Hanlon is being verbally assaulted by another actress for planting false stories about her sexual escapades in the papers. She tearfully asks what her husband will think. After he convinces her he had nothing to do with the stories, he orders a secretary to get a newspaper photographer after her to construct still another story. As Lola enters her dressing room, she's beset by a mixture of contract and sales people, the difference by now virtually indistinguishable. After she has been remade up, she goes onto the set to reshoot scenes for *Red Dust,* a movie Jean Harlow rather than Lola Burns, made with Clark Gable just a year earlier. For *Bombshell*'s audience, Lola Burns, whose character was based on earlier star Clara Bow, now merges with that of Harlow. This puts a film audience of the day into the midst of the process they witnessed at the film's start. Harlow is the product, the movie's star, the daydream, and they are the consumers, as ticket-buying filmgoers, but also potential consumers for newspapers, magazines, and products that will bear her name.

On the set, Lola's current boyfriend (a marquis), her leeching father, and the director all begin to argue. We then get a demonstration of selling in America. As the men appear ready to come to blows, Space appears. He sells the director on the notion that he is a genius, better than the B-picture directors who fight on the set; he sells the marquis on an idea—that will never transpire—that the marquis advise the studio on European magazines in which they advertise Lola. And he sells her father on the notion that he can advise them on sporting matters. Soon, when Lola and the marquis attend a club, Space has the police arrest him as an illegal immigrant. He's planted reporters on the scene whom he pays off in bottles of Jack Daniels. As Lola sobs at the sight of the departing marquis, he convinces her he had nothing do to with it, even as she spots a newspaper with headlines already screaming news of the marquis' arrest and his involvement with Lola. While she berates him, his counterargument is of interest. He answers that modern newspaper linotype gets the news off so fast that newsreels can get it and put it on the screen so that it's as if the reader or viewer is there. We have just seen the publicity agent at the center of this process. He puts stories into the papers, then covers the reactions of the principals to generate and put more stories into the papers.

When Lola nearly gets him fired for these repeated publicity ambushes, he mollifies her by giving her what she calls "good publicity." He has repeatedly asserted that he, rather than the studio or Lola herself, has created Lola as the "It" girl, which was what Clara Bow was dubbed—the Bombshell. He brings in an interviewer from *The Ladies Home Companion*. The interviewer's questions have an arresting effect on Lola. We see that the act of gaining information for a publicity story is not a one-way process; rather it's fluid. The interviewer's questions began to recreate Lola as we watch. The interviewer manages to summon up an attractive image of domesticity; the image her magazine sells to American women, which, like Lola, is used to then sell them products. Soon Lola shifts to playing the role the interviewer has created. Upon the woman's departure she believes she wants a baby. She tries to adopt one, but her drunken family, the marquis and his lawyer, and Space all arrive at her house as the dowdy orphanage women interviews her. Courtesy of Space, reporters are present for the melee. As the marquis approaches, his lawyer advises him not to speak to reporters because "they'll pay for a signed interview" later.

Enraged at the fiasco, Lola stalks off the picture and heads for a desert resort where she vows she is through with movies. There she meets the son of an old-money Boston family, and they become engaged. But the boy's parents learn she has been in the movies and the three of them shun her. This sends her back to Hollywood and Space. Back at the studio with Space, she overhears the Boston family outside her dressing room. Soon she learns they are hack actors in Space's employ. Even her romance has been publicity. As she drives off in a huff, Space leaps into her car. He has nearly calmed her down when the stalker reappears. Seeing Space he blurts out that they know each other; he too has been a publicity stunt. *Bombshell* demonstrates that buying and selling, influence, and product have become inescapable. When Lola sobbed at the rebuff from the Boston family, she remarked, as the director learned in *Sullivan's Travels,* that there was not "any disgrace in entertaining people, making them laugh, making them cry." She adds that fans are her friends; they send her pictures, ask her advice on their problems. And this is true. Her friendships, romances, family, have ceased to be private matters; they are all part of a public-exchange process that seems without origin. In the world of "glands," to use Roscoe Pound's term, "attitudes and opinion," production and trans-action, become inescapable. If, during the economic trauma of the period, people felt threatened by these things, in the end they proved too powerful to go away.

Notes

1. Ducking Prostitution

1. Thomas Minehan, *Boy and Girl Tramps of America* (New York: Farrar and Rinehart, 1934), 140, 142.

2. Quoted in John F. Bauman and Thomas H. Coode, *In the Eye of the Great Depression: New Deal Reporters and the Agony of the American People* (Dekalb: Northern Illinois University Press, 1988), 83.

3. Ibid., 86.

4. Mirra Komarovsky, *The Unemployed Man and His Family: Status of the Man in Fifty-Nine Families* (1940, New York: Altamira Press, 2004), 40, 81.

5. Robert McElvaine, ed., *Down and Out in the Great Depression: Letters from the Forgotten Man* (Chapel Hill: University of North Carolina Press, 1983), 62, 57–58.

6. Arthur Pound, "Bankruptcy Mill," *The Atlantic Monthly,* February 1932, 173–75.

7. "Vagrant Civil Engineer," *The New York Times,* May 4, 1932; rpr. David Shannon, ed., *The Great Depression* (Englewood Cliffs, N.J.: Prentice Hall, 1960), 90.

8. Errol Lincoln Uhys, *Riding the Rails: Teenagers on the Move During the Great Depression* (New York: TV Books, L.L.C., 1999), 31–32.

9. Tino Ballio, *Grand Design: Hollywood as Modern Business Enterprise, 1930–1939* (Berkeley: University of California Press, 1993), 13–18.

10. Elliott Robert Barkin, *And Still They Come: Immigrants and American Society, 1920 to the 1990s* (Wheeling, Il.: Harlan Davidson, 1996), 50.

11. Thomas Schatz, *The Genius of the System: Hollywood Filmmaking in the Studio Era* (New York: Pantheon, 1988), 69–158.

12. Balio, 23.

13. Rick Altman, "Genre Cinema," *The Oxford History of World Cinema,* ed. Geoffrey Nowell-Smith (New York: Oxford University Press, 1997), 283.

14. Stephen Greenblatt, *Shakespearean Negotiations* (Berkeley: University of California Press, 1988), 113.

15. Quoted in Frederick Lewis Allen, *Only Yesterday: An Informal History of the Twenties* (1931, New York: Perennial, 1959), 225.

16. Ibid., 225–40; a shrewd interpretive account of the place of the Florida land deals in a history of the oncoming stock market collapse and Great Depression can be found in Robert McElvaine, *The Great Depression, 1929–1941* (New York: Three Rivers Press), 41–44; see also William H. Leuchtenburg, *The Perils of Prosperity, 1914–32* (Chicago, Ill.: University of Chicago Press, 1958), 183–85. Gertrude Mathews Shelby participated in the buying frenzy and wrote about it. See "Florida Frenzy," *Harper's,* January 1926, 177–86.

17. McElvaine, *The Great Depression,* 43.

18. Robert E. Burns, *I Am a Fugitive from a Georgia Chain Gang!* (1932; Athens: University of Georgia Press, 1987), 257.

19. "Penitentiary Reform in Mississippi," *Publications of the Mississippi Historical Society* 6 (1902): 111–28.

20. On such labor systems, see John Hope Franklin, *Reconstruction after the Civil War* (University of Chicago Press, 1961), 49–53; and James C. Cobb, *The Most Southern Place on Earth: The Mississippi Delta and the Roots of Regional Identity* (New York: Oxford University Press, 1992), 42–43.

21. See David M. Oshinsky, *Worse than Slavery: Parchman Farm and the Ordeal of Jim Crow Justice* (New York: Free Press, 1996).

22. Pauline Kael, *5001 Nights at the Movies* (New York: Henry Holt, 1984), 264.

23. Cobb, 142.

24. Ibid., 143.

25. Robert Palmer, *Deep Blues* (New York: Penguin, 1981), 28–29; Leroi Jones (a.k.a. Imamu Amiri Baraka), *Blues People* (New York: Morrow, 1963), 17–31; Lawrence Levin, *Black Culture and Black Consciousness* (New York: Oxford University Press, 1978); see as well the essays in Eileen Southern, ed., *Readings in Black American Music* (New York: W. W. Norton, 1983); for blues lyrics which demonstrate Roosevelt's influence on black America during the Depression, see Guido Van Rijn, *Roosevelt's Blues: African-American Blues and Gospel Songs on FDR* (Jackson: University Press of Mississippi, 1997).

26. Burns, 143.

27. Cobb, 143.

28. For an analysis of the facts in the Burns's case, see Matthew J. Mancini, in "Foreword to the Brown Thrasher Edition," in Burns, v–xxiv; for additional material, see William Stott, *Documentary Expression and Thirties America* (Chicago, Ill.: The University of Chicago Press, 1986), 41–45.

29. Karen Horney, *The Neurotic Personality of Our Time* (New York: W. W. Norton, 1937), 34.

30. Bauman and Coode, 73–76.

31. Gerald N. Grob, *The Mad Among Us: A History of the Care of America's Mentally Ill* (Cambridge, Mass.: Harvard University Press, 1994), 101, 176.

32. Ibid., 165–90.

33. Erving Goffman, *Asylums* (New York: Doubleday, 1961), 128.

34. Arthur Schlesinger Jr., *The Politics of Upheaval* (Boston: Houghton Mifflin, 1960), 314.

35. *Three Cornered Moon* (1933) makes an identical point when an upper-class family falls on hard times and the young daughter (Claudette Colbert) goes to work in a factory. Faced with unemployment or sexual harassment, she quits.

36. *Baby Face* (1933) approaches the same point from a different perspective. Having been sold to various men by her father, the film's "baby face," Lilly (Barbara Stanwyck), runs off and makes her way using her sexuality to gain advancement. The film conveys this by having her literally start her employment on the ground floor of a bank, then proceed up a floor at a time as she is promoted. She achieves promotions by sleeping with the right influential men. Once she has gained a measure of power and wealth, she can rewrite her identity and she stops prostituting herself.

37. For example, Pauline Kael remarks, "Apparently Berkeley devised his choreographic spectacles on his own, without reference to the script, and without worrying about whether they would pass as parts of one musical," 398.

38. Wassily Kandinsky, "On the Problem of Form," in Herschel Chipp, *Theories of Modern Art* (Berkeley: University of California Press, 1968), 166.

39. Martin Rubin, *Showstoppers: Busby Berkeley and the Tradition of Spectacle* (New York: Columbia University Press, 1993), 52.

40. Susan Ware, *American Women in the 1930s: Holding Their Own* (New York: Twayne, 1982), 6, 8.

41. This connection is made explicit in the 1938 Laurel and Hardy feature, *Block-heads*, in which World War One soldier, Laurel, literally becomes a "forgotten man" of World War One when he is left behind to guard a trench and no one returns to inform him the war has ended. He remains faithful to his duty until 1938.

42. Ephraim Katz, *The Film Encyclopedia* (New York: Harper, 1994), 119; Schatz, 150.

43. "The Presidency," *Time,* January 4, 1932, 7; David Kennedy, *Freedom from Fear: The American People in Depression and War, 1929–1945* (New York: Oxford University Press, 1999), 111.

44. Paul J. Vanderwood, ed., *Juarez* (Madison: University of Wisconsin Press, 1983), 18.

45. George R. Clarke, "Beckerstown 1932: An American Town Faces the Depression." *Harper's,* October 1932, 586.

46. William Trufant Forster and Waddill Catchings, *The Road to Plenty* (Boston: Houghton Mifflin, 1928).

47. For a discussion of their role in Depression-era economic discourse, see Arthur Schlesinger Jr., *The Crisis of the Old Order* (Boston: Houghton Mifflin, 1957), 134–36.

48. On Eliot's views of the curse of urbanization and the merits of the parish, see his *The Idea of a Christian Society* (1939). Rpr. in *Christianity and Culture* (New York: Harcourt, 1967), 23–26. For Brandeis, see Schlesinger, *Politics of Upheaval,* 219–21.

49. Joseph McBride, *Frank Capra: The Catastrophe of Success* (New York: Touchstone, 1992), 253–58.

2. The War over World War I

1. Matthew J. Mancini, "Foreword to the Brown Thrasher Edition," in Robert Burns, *I am a Fugitive from a Georgia Chain Gang* (1932; Athens: University of Georgia Press, 1997), vi, 37, 38, 44, 46.

2. Herbert Hoover, *The Memoirs of Herbert Hoover: The Great Depression, 1929–1941* (London: Hollis and Carter, 1953), 2.

3. Evelyn Cobley, *Representing War: Form and Ideology in first World War Narratives* (Toronto, ON.: University of Toronto Press, 1993), 5, 10, 12.

4. Clayton R. Koppes and Gregory D. Black, *Hollywood goes to War: How Politics, Profits, and Propaganda Shaped World War II Movies* (Berkeley: University of California Press, 1987), 40.

5. Margaret Drabble, *The Oxford Companion to English Literature* (New York: Oxford University Press, 1985), 813.

6. Maurice Samuels, "Realizing the Past: History and Spectacle in Balzac's *Adieu,"* *Representations* 79 (Summer 2002): 86, 90–91.

7. Robert Weiman, "Realism, Ideology, and the Novel in America (1886–1896): Changing Perspectives in the Work of Twain, Howell, and Henry James," in Donald E. Pease, ed., *Revisionary Interventions in the Americanist Canon* (Durham, N.C.: Duke University Press, 1994), 89–90.

8. Paul Fussell, *The Great War and Modern Memory* (New York: Oxford University Press, 1975), 317–18.

9. Ibid., 8.

10. Ibid., 21.

11. "The Flight of the Bonus Army," *New Republic,* August 17, 1932, 13–15; "Heroes: Bonus Army," *Time,* July 11, 1932, 12.

12. John Maynard Keynes, *Economic Consequences of the Peace* (1920; New York: Penguin, 1995), 260.

13. On Herbert Hoover's offering aid to the Central Republic Bank of Chicago, while simultaneously denying welfare to American citizens, see Robert McElvaine, *The Great Depression: America,* (Boston: Houghton Mifflin, 1957), 89–92.

14. Thomas Berger, *Crazy in Berlin* (New York: Dell, 1958), 45.

15. Arthur Schlesinger Jr., *The Crisis of the Old Order, 1929–1941* (New York: Three Rivers Press), 15.

16. Keynes, *Economic Consequences,* 228, 297.

17. Arnold. A. Offner, *The Origins of the Second World War: American Foreign Policy and World Politics, 1917–1941* (New York: Praeger, 1975), 48.

18. J. B. S. Hardman, *Rendezvous with Destiny: Addresses and Opinions of Franklin D. Roosevelt* (New York: Dryden, 1944), 40.

19. Offner, 104.

20. David Kennedy, *Freedom from Fear: The American People in Depression and War, 1929–1941* (New York: Oxford University Press, 1999), 386–87.

21. Keynes, *Consequences of the Peace,* 251, 43, 45, 143–46, 150–51, 247, 205, 251.

22. John Kenneth Galbraith, *The Great Crash, 1929* (Boston: Houghton Mifflin, 1955), 26–27, 28–29.

23. Offner, 104–5.

24. For accounts of the perceived evasiveness of the European allies to pay war debts to the U.S., see "The Presidency," *Time,* January 4, 1932, 7; "Arms, Men, and Women," *Time,* January 4, 1932, 8; "War Debts: Britain Can't Pay Cash and Won't Pay 'in Kind,' " *News-Week,* July 7, 1934, 29–30.

25. Fussell, 12–13.

26. Morton J. Horowitz, *The Transformation of American Law, 1870–1960: The Crisis of Legal Orthodoxy* (New York: Oxford University Press, 1992), 188–89; Cass Sunstein, *The Second Bill of Rights: FDR's Unfinished Revolution and Why We Need it More than Ever* (New York: Basic Books, 2004), 29.

27. Ibid., 170, 195.

28. Ibid., 187, 155, 166.

29. Sunstein, 24.

30. Ibid., 20.

31. Fussell, 86; Siegfried Sassoon, "Fight to a Finish," *Collected Poems, 1908–1956* (London: Faber and Faber, 1961), 77.

32. Fussell, 86, 27.

33. Ibid., 8–9.

34. Horowitz, 145–56.

35. Kennedy, 248–87.

36. William Leuchtenburg, *Franklin D. Roosevelt and the New Deal* (New York: Harper, 1963), 198.

37. Kennedy, 405–6, 462, 468–69.

38. Carol Christ, *Victorian and Modernist Poetry* (Chicago: University of Chicago Press, 1984), 124, 125, 68.

39. George Lukács, "The Sociology of Modern Drama," in Eric Bentley, *The Theory of the Modern Stage* (London: Penguin, 1990), 442.

3. RACIAL CONSTRUCTIONS OF THE THIRTIES

1. Ric Burns, James Sanders, and Lisa Ades, *New York: An Illustrated History* (New York: Knopf, 2003), 436.

2. "The Charge of the Light Brigade," *Time,* November 2, 1936, 21–22.

3. Harvard Sitkoff, *A New Deal for Blacks, the Emergence of Civil Rights as a National Issue: The Depression Decade* (New York: Oxford University Press, 1978), 268.

4. Quoted in Lawrence James, *Raj: The Making and Unmaking of British India* (New York: St. Martin's Griffin, 1997), 533.

5. Kevin Shillington, *History of Africa* (New York: St. Martin's Press, 1995), 364.

6. Ibid., 364–66.

7. "Ethiopia: Man of the Year," *Time,* January 6, 1936, 13.

8. "The League: Jig Up?" *Time,* July 6, 1936, 18.

9. *The Oxford English Dictionary* cites Abraham Cowley's use of the word to mean "devil": "He's dead long since, and gone to the Blackamores below."

10. "Races: Blacks *"Aflame,"* *Time,* February 10, 1936, 14.

11. "Ethiopia," 13.

12. James.

13. Sitkoff, 6.

14. "Puran Swaraj!" *Time,* January 13, 1930, 27–28; see also, "India: Soul Force Wins," *Time,* October 3, 1932, 16.

15. James, 533.

16. Niall Ferguson, *Empire: The Rise and Demise of the British World Order and the Lessons for Global World Power* (New York: Basic Books, 2002), 329.

17. Ibid., 43–44.

18. James, 32.

19. D. K. Fieldhouse, *Colonialism: 1870–1945* (New York: St. Martin's Press, 1981), 29–30.

20. On the beliefs and practices of this cult, see James, 195–203.

21. Ibid., 511.

22. Ibid., 511.

23. Shillington, 299–300, 311–12.

24. Sitkoff, 268, 280.

25. Ibid., 291–95.

26. Kennedy, 395.

27. Sitkoff, 297.

28. Hans Schmidt, *The United States Occupation of Haiti, 1915–1934* (New Brunswick, N.J.: Rutgers University Press, 1971), 4–6.

29. Arthur and Barbara Gelb, *O'Neill* (New York: Harper, 1962), 438–39. O'Neill also used material from the lives of Henri Christophe (who made himself king in 1811, ruled brutally, established a *corvée,* and eventually shot himself in the head) and Jean Jacques Dessalines. Dessalines was the first black leader of Haiti to have himself proclaimed emperor (thereafter going by the title of Emperor Jacques I).

30. Schmidt, 117.

31. Schmidt explains that "the roping together of workers was especially upsetting to the peasants, since it recalled legends of colonial slave gangs," 101, 119.

32. Neil McMillen, *Dark Journey: Black Mississippians in the Age of Jim Crow* (Urbana: University of Illinois Press, 1990), 237.

33. Stephen Greenblatt, *Shakespearean Negotiations* (Berkeley: University of California Press, 1988), 12.

34. Schmidt, 65.

35. One change in Haitian government forced on Haiti by the occupation of the United States was that outsiders—whites—be allowed to own land in Haiti. Since Dessalines's time, whites had been prohibited from owning land due to Haitian fears of a return to slavery. See Robert Debs and Nancy Gordon Heinl, *Written in Blood: The Story of the Haitian People, 1492–1971* (Boston: Houghton Mifflin, 1978). The three newspaper articles were reprinted in Ralph Ginzburg, *100 Years of Lynching* (New York: Black Classics Press, 1997), 90, 93, 96.

36. Sitkoff, 236.

37. Quoted in Edward Ayers, *Vengeance and Justice* (New York: Oxford University Press, 1984), 187.

38. Vernon Lane Wharton, *The Negro in Mississippi, 1865–1890* (New York: Harper Torchbooks, 1965), 235. Later, certainly by the 1930s, whites were included. In the South white and black prisoners usually experienced some form of segregation; for an historical sense of developments in the system, see "Penitentiary Reform in Mississippi," *Publications of the Mississippi Historical Society* 6 (1902): 111–28; for a study of connections between race and incarceration in the South, see David M. Oshinsky, *Worse than Slavery: Parchman Farm and the Ordeal of Jim Crow Justice* (New York: Free Press, 1996).

39. Ayers, 191.

40. See Robert Palmer, *Deep Blues* (New York: Viking, 1981), 33, 36–39.

41. Harold Courlander, *The Drum and the Hoe, Life and Lore of the Haitian People* (Berkeley: University of California Press, 1960), 23, 190.

42. Greenberg, Cheryl Lynn, *Or Does It Explode?* (New York: Oxford University Press, 1991), 80.

43. Sundquist, 241.

44. "Letters to the Editor," *New York Times*, April 25, 1935.

45. Sitkoff, 3, 15.

46. Ibid., 62.

47. Gerald Horne, *Class Struggle in Hollywood, 1930–1950* (Austin: University of Texas Press, 2001), 52.

48. For example, see Donald Peavy, *Go Slow Now: Faulkner and the Race Question* (Eugene: University of Oregon Press, 1978).

49. Stephen Brier, *Who Built America?* Vol. 2. (New York: St. Martin's Press, 2000), 291–92, 355.

50. Keith L. Bryant and Henry C. Dethloff, *A History of American Business* (Englewood Cliffs, N.J.: Prentice Hall, 1990), 186.

51. Walter Benjamin, *Selected Writings, 1935–1938*, vol. 3, ed. Howard Eiland and Michael Jennings (Cambridge: Harvard University Press, 2002), 94.

52. Walter Benjamin, *Illuminations: Essays and Reflections*, ed. Hannah Arendt (New York: Schocken, 1988), 234.

53. For a contemporary account reflecting the public mind, see "Henry Ford: Individualist," *The New Republic*, September 13, 1933, 115–17.

54. Robert McElvaine, *The Great Depression: America, 1929–1941*, (New York: Three Rivers Press, 1993), 43.

55. Stuart Bruchey, The Wealth of the Nation: An Economic History of the United States (New York: Harper and Row, 1988), 146; see also W. Elliot Brownlee, *Dynamics of Ascent: A History of the American Economy* (New York: Knopf, 1979).

56. Bryant and Dethloff, 134.

57. Thomas Schatz, *The Genius of the System: Hollywood Filmmaking in the Studio Era* 58. Tino Balio, *Grand Design: Hollywood as a Modern Business Enterprise, 1930–1939* (Berkeley: University of California Press, 1993), 15.

59. Paul Buhl and Larry Wagner, *Radical Hollywood* (New York: New Press, 2003), 10.

60. Schatz, 136.

61. Buhl and Wagner, 10.

62. Ibid., 69.

63. Eugene Genovese, *The Political Economy of Slavery: Studies in the Economy and Society of the Slave South* (New York: Vintage, 1967); Elizabeth Fox-Genovese, *Within the Plantation Household: Black and White Women of the Old South* (Chapel Hill: University of North Carolina Press, 1988); Gavin Wright, *Old South, New South: Revolutions in the Southern Economy Since the Civil War* (New York: Basic Books, 1986); Jonathan M. Weiner, "Class Structure and Economic Development in the American South, 1865–1955, *American Historical Review* 84, no. 4 (1979): 970–92.

64. Schatz, 160.

65. Buhl and Wagner, 45.

66. Schatz, 161.

67. Arthur Schlesinger Jr., *The Coming of the New Deal* (Boston: Houghton Mifflin, 1958), 136–51.

68. Horne, 5.

69. Buhl and Wagner, 70–71; Horne, 22–26.

70. Horne, 52.

71. Brier, 329.

72. Press reports of the period were full of accounts of union uprisings. For examples, see J. B. S. Hardman, "How to Break a Union," *The New Republic*, October 21, 1931; 252–5; "Labor: Blood Flows in San Francisco; General Strike Threatened," *News-Week*, July 14, 1934, 5–6; "Labor: A Hundred Cities Experience Strikes and Disorder; While Minneapolis Truckmen Explode, San Francisco Calms Down," *News-Week*, July 28, 1934, 3–5.

73. Raymond Wolters, *Negroes and the Great Depression* (New York: Greenwood Press, 1970), 305–8; Harvey Klehr, *The Heyday of American Communism: The Depression Decade* (New York: Basic Books, 1984), 324–48; *The Complete Report of Mayor LaGuardia's Commission on the Harlem Riot.* (New York: Arno Press and New York Times, 1969), 11, 42; Bernard Sternsher, ed., *The Negro in Depression and War: Prelude to Revolution, 1930–1945* (Chicago: Quadrangle Books, 1969).

74. Lawrence Levine, *Black Culture and Black Consciousness: Afro-American Thought, From Slavery to Freedom* (New York: Oxford University Press, 1978), 255.

4. U.S. FOREIGN POLICY AND RACIAL IDENTITY

1. Marius B. Jansen, *The Making of Modern Japan* (Cambridge: Harvard University Press, 2000), 414–55; Herbert P. Bix, *Hirohito and the Making of Modern Japan* (New York: Perennial), 171–204, 279–317.

2. Wolfram Eberhard, *A History of China* (London: Routledge, 1958), 324–29.

3. Arnold A. Offner, *Origins of the Second World War* (New York: Praeger, 1975), 96–103, 141–62, 185–93; Jansen, 577–90, Bix, 235–44.

4. Iris Chang, *The Chinese in America* (New York: Penguin, 2003), 224–25.

5. See in particular Earl Derr Biggers, *The Black Camel* (New York: Grosset & Dunlap, 1929).

6. On Chinese Exclusion Acts and other restrictions on immigration, see Chang, 77–78, 146–51; Ronald Takaki, *Strangers From a Different Shore* (Boston: Little Brown, 1998), 79–131; Stephen Brier, ed., *Who Built America: Working People and the*

Nation's Economy, Politics, Culture, and Society, vol. 2 (New York: Pantheon, 1992), 57, 70, 114, 153.

7. Sax Rohmer, *The Mask of Fu Manchu* (1932; New York: Pyramid, 1962), 22.

8. The same year Myrna Loy, who apparently looked "exotic" to Hollywood in her early career, played the racially mixed Ursula Georgi in the film version of Tiffany Thayer's *Thirteen Women.* She is seeking revenge on a group of racist former upper-class private-school girls who foisted racial indignities on her as a classmate. The novel uses her earlier experience as a plaything for sailors to titillate its audience. The racism visited upon her seems to function for the same purpose. Film and novel attempt to keep sympathy away from the clearly wronged Ursula character by making her a potential murderer of a young boy, the son of one of the private-school racists. A taste of the novel suffices to convey the freedom with which Asian Indians were regarded (at the time of their officially being regarded in California as the "least desirable race"). When one of the school girls shows up and finds she is assigned to share a room with Ursula, her brother remarks, "Pheeew, Anne, are you gonna sleep with a nigger?" (New York: Triangle Books, 1932), 326. If nothing else, both Thayer's novel and the film illustrate how powerless people of color were perceived to be by the general public and by some participants in the creation of popular culture.

9. Pearl S. Buck, *The Good Earth* (1931; New York: Simon and Schuster, 1994).

10. Howard Zinn, *A People's History of the United States* (New York: Perennial, 2003), 265–66, 382; Takiki, 80–131.

11. John Kuo Wei Tchen, ed., *Genthe's Photographs of San Francisco's Old Chinatown* (New York: Dover, 1984).

12. G. F. Seward. *Chinese Immigration in Its Social and Economic Aspects* (New York: Charles Scribner's Sons, 1881); Mary E. B. R. S. Coolidge, *Chinese Immigration* (New York: Arno, 1969).

13. Chalsa M. Loo, *Chinatown: Most Time, Hard Time* (New York: Praeger, 1991), 40.

14. On the British opium sales in Shanghai, see Stella Dong, *Shanghai* (New York: Morrow, 2000), 4–9; Ernest O. Hauser, *Shanghai, City for Sale* (New York: Harcourt, Brace, 1940), 34–36; and Harriet Sergeant, *Shanghai, Collision Point of Cultures, 1918–1939* (New York: Crown, 1990), 16–21.

15. Joseph von Sternberg, *Fun in a Chinese Laundry* (New York: Macmillan, 1965), 81.

16. Dong, 44–45, 2.

17. *Webster's Third New International Dictionary* [unabridged] (Chicago: G. & C. Merriam, 1976), vol. 3.

18. Dong, 3, 10, 28.

19. John Colton, *The Shanghai Gesture* (New York: Boni and Liveright, 1926), 235, 186, 188.

20. On the freedom of pre-code Hollywood and the shift to applications of the code by the Hays Office, see Thomas Doherty, *Pre-Code Hollywood: Sex, Immorality, and Insurrection in American Cinema, 1930–1934* (New York, N.Y.: Columbia University Press, 1999); Mick LaSalle, *Complicated Women: Sex and Power in Pre-Code Hollywood* (New York: Thomas Dunne Books, 2000); Leonard J. Leff and Jerold L. Simmons, *The Dame in the Kimono: Hollywood, Censorship, and the Production Code from the 1920s to the 1960s* (New York: Grove Weidenfeld, 1990).

21. Offner, 148–62; Jansen, 576–624; Bix, 235–78.

22. Elliot Robert Barkan, *And Still They Come: Immigrants and American Society, 1920 to the 1990s* (Wheeling, Ill.: Harlan Davidson, 1996), 45.

23. Loren Grey, in his foreword to his father, Zane's novel, *The Vanishing American* (1925; New York: Simon and Schuster, 1982), v.

24. *Squaw Man* was first a play by Edwin Milton Royle. It was adapted as a novel by Julie Opp Faversham (New York: Grosset & Dunlap, 1906). It was filmed in 1914, 1918, and 1931.

25. Walter Benn Michaels, *Our America: Nativism, Modernism, and Pluralism* (Durham, N.C.: Duke University Press, 1995), 39.

26. Edna Ferber, *Cimarron* (Garden City, N.Y.: Doubleday, Doran, 1930), 356.

27. Blanche Wiesen Cook, *Eleanor Roosevelt, 1933–1938*, vol. 2 (New York: Viking, 1999), 183–84.

28. On the Gentlemen's Agreement, see Ronald Takaki, *Strangers from a Different Shore: The Story of Asian Americans* (New York: Penguin, 1989), 27, 46, 50, 56, 65, 203, 337, 49; Bud Fukei, *The Japanese American Story* (Minneapolis: Dillon Press, 1976), 17–28.

29. On Native American experience in the thirties vis-à-vis the New Deal, see Graham D. Taylor, *The New Deal and American Indian Tribalism: The Administration of the Indian Reorganization Act, 1934–45* (Lincoln: University of Nebraska Press, 1980); Brian Dippie, *The Vanishing American: White Attitudes and U.S. Indian Policy* (Middletown, Conn.: Wesleyan University Press, 1982), 297–321; William T. Hagan, *American Indians* (Chicago: University of Chicago Press, 1993).

30. When the Depression struck, authorities in the United States enticed or forced many Mexicans to return to Mexico. Elliot Barkan remarks, "Thousands of Mexicans and Mexican Americans were rounded up and detained, while those without proper papers were sought out for deportation." Of those who had been enticed to return to Mexico voluntarily, many "were virtually abandoned and left without resources or assistance." *And Still They Come: Immigrants and American Society, 1920 to the 1990s* (Wheeling, Ill.: Harlan Davidson, 1996), 46. Nevertheless, at a time when many countries were turning to fascism, on U.S. screens Mexico and Mexicans were represented quite favorably, as participants in a nascent Mexican democracy. In *Juarez* (1939), Benito Juarez, presented as virtually worshiping Abraham Lincoln, is depicted as trying to build a democracy modeled on that of the United States. Similarly, in *Viva Villa* (1934), bandit Pancho Villa is transformed into a revolutionary general by democratic ideals.

31. Walter Edmunds, *Drums Along the Mohawk* (Boston: Little, Brown, 1937).

32. Kenneth Roberts, *Northwest Passage* (1937; Greenwich, Conn.: Fawcett, 1967).

5. SEXUAL POLITICS AND THE DEPRESSION

1. Susan Cheever, *Home Before Dark: A Biographical Memoir of John Cheever by His Daughter* (Boston: Houghton Mifflin, 1984), 3, 7.

2. "Shining Stars," *Time,* July 24, 1933, 12.

3. George R. Clark, "Beckerstown 1932," 580, 583–89, 591.

4. Robert McElvaine, *The Great Depression: America 1929–1941* (New York: Three Rivers Press, 1993), 106.

5. "Busiest Lady," *Time,* June 12, 1933, 16.

6. McElvaine, 109.

7. For a comprehensive study, see Blanche Wiesen Cook, *Eleanor Roosevelt,* 2 vols. (New York: Viking, 1999).

8. Susan Ware, *Beyond Suffrage: Women in the New Deal* (Cambridge, Mass.: Harvard University Press, 1981), 7.

9. Ibid., 7.

10. Several film historians have reached conclusions compatible with this point. See Norman Zierold, *The Moguls: Hollywood's Merchants of Myth* (Los Angeles: Silman-James Press, 1969); Thomas Schatz, *The Genius of the System: Hollywood Filmmak-*

ing in the Studio System (New York: Pantheon, 1988), 3–66; Neal Gabler, *An Empire of Their Own: How the Jews Invented Hollywood* (New York: Anchor, 1988); Larry May, *The Big Tomorrow: Hollywood and the Politics of the American Way* (Chicago: University of Chicago Press, 2000), 55–99; Paul Buhl and Dave Wagner, *Radical Hollywood* (New York: New Press, 2002), 56–111; Gerald Horne, *Class Struggle in Hollywood, 1930–1950* (Austin: University of Texas Press, 2001), 120–52.

11. Molly Haskell, *From Reverence to Rape: The Treatment of Women in the Movies* (New York: Penguin, 1974), 150, 151.

12. "New Deal Weighed," *Time*, July 3,1933, 16.

13. Mirra Komarovsky, *The Unemployed Man and His Family: Status of the Man in Fifty-Nine Families* (1940; New York: Rowman & Littlefield, 2004), 1.

14. Ibid., 2, 23, 40, 23, 33.

15. James Thurber, "Ivorytown, Rinsoville, Anacinburg, and Crisco Corners," *The Beast in Me and Other Animals* (1947; New York: Harvest, 1974), 220; Burton Bernstein, *Thurber: A Biography* (New York: Ballantine, 1975), 542.

16. For works that set out to address this question, see Alan Brinkley, *Culture and Politics in the Great Depression* (Waco, Tex.: Baylor University Press, 1999); Robert S. Lynd and Helen Merrill Lynd, *Middletown in Transition* (New York: Harcourt, Brace, and World, 1937).

17. F. Scott Fitzgerald, "Bablyon Revisited," *The Stories of F. Scott Fitzgerald* (New York: Scribner's, 1984), 389.

18. Quoted in Gail Collins, *America's Women: Dolls, Drudges, Helpmates, and Heroines* (New York: HarperCollins, 2003), 331.

19. Frederick Lewis Allen, *Only Yesterday,* 1931; 89–90.

20. This remark must have been viewed with skepticism if not outright hostility by audiences in a decade that saw the down-and-out First World War Bonus Army veterans march on Washington in 1932 in the faith that the government would do the right thing by them and give them promised bonuses early, as the collapsing economy meant they desperately needed the money. The unemployed veterans set up shacks in Washington to wait for a decision on their requests from Congress. In response, Herbert Hoover "wanted to bring out the machine guns with which it had greeted the Communist hunger marchers in the previous December." Eventually Congress said no to the bonuses. General MacArthur brought the situation to a crisis, confronting the veterans with tanks, "machine guns hooded, and a column of infantry, with fixed bayonets, steel helmets, gas masks, and at their belts, blue tear-gas bombs." Soon they advanced on the veterans and their families, who had erected makeshift shacks, "tossing gas bombs into little groups of defiant veterans, setting fire along the way to the shacks and barracks lest the inhabitants return . . . Women and children, their eyes streaming with tears, ran frantically from their dwellings." Arthur Schlesinger Jr. *The Crisis of the Old Order* (Boston: Houghton Mifflin, 1957), 258, 262–63.

21. A variation on this point occurs in the *Merry Frinks* (1934) in which the entire Frink family relies on the family matriarch, Hattie Frink (Aline MacMahon) to hold everything together. She inherits money on the condition that she leave her deadbeat family, a move which brings the rest of the Frinks to consciousness and an appreciation of their dependence on her.

22. Komarovsky, 31.

23. Ibid., 26–27.

24. Genevieve Taggard, "Mill Town," *Calling Western Union* (New York: Harper, 1936), 83.

25. For a critical contemporary look at the class divide in the form of an analysis of upper-class women's clubs, see Margaret Cobb, "Three Million Women," *The American Mercury,* March 30, 1930, 319–25.

26. Ware, 34.

27. Ibid., 34–35.

28. Lois Scharf, *To Work and to Wed: Female Employment, Feminism, and the Great Depression* (Westport, Conn.: Greenwood Press, 1980), 100.

29. On the lack of job security for working-class women, see Teresa Amott and Julie Matthei, *Race, Gender, and Work: A Multi-Cultural History of Women in the United States* (Cambridge, Mass.: South End Press, 1996).

30. Quoted in Lisa M. Fine, *The Souls of the Skyscraper: Female Clerical Workers in Chicago, 1870–1930* (Philadelphia: Temple University Press, 1990), 58–59.

31. Scharf, 100–101.

32. The class and economic foundations of a woman's being particularly vulnerable to sexual harassment present themselves in *Three Cornered Moon* (1933), Elizabeth Rimplegar (Claudette Colbert), formerly a rich and idle spoiled brat, is forced by her family's losing their money on the stock market to work in a shoe factory, where she must succumb to the sexual advances of her boss or lose her job.

33. William Henry Chafe, *The American Woman: Her Changing Social, Economic, and Political Roles, 1920–1970* (New York: Oxford University Press, 1972), 52.

34. Chafe, 52.

35. Ibid., 52–53.

36. Ibid., 53.

37. Ibid.

38. Quoted in Fine, 59.

39. Ibid., 59.

40. Ware, 14.

41. Ibid.

42. For a pair of articles that capture the ambivalence of upper-class feminists of the 1930s, consult Worth Tuttle, "Autobiography of an Ex-Feminist," *Atlantic Monthly,* December 1933, 640–49; and, by the same author, "A Feminist Marries," *Atlantic Monthly,* January 1934, 73–81.

43. For a representative example of the differing dynamic of pre-Depression film, see *The Wild Party* (1929), or virtually any Clara Bow film of her "It Girl" period, *Our Dancing Daughters* (1928), or virtually any Joan Crawford film of the 1920s, in which female assertiveness is contained by male authority.

44. An example of the latter case would be *You Can't Take It With You* (1938), in which the world of business, especially as represented by the bank, is conventional and rational, whereas the world of the home, in the thirties the feminine domain, is irrational, screwy, but liberated and a place of natural, intuitive behavior.

45. John Cheever, "The Swimmer," *The Stories of John Cheever* (New York: Ballantine, 1981), 719.

46. Ibid., 722.

47. Ibid., 725.

48. Both Andrew Bergmen, *We're in the Money: Depression America and Its Films* (Chicago: Ivan Dees, 1971), 50–51, and McElvaine, 340, see the image of the prostitute in films as materializing out of an economy that could force women into prostitution. The prostitute at least represents the potential for the trauma of the period to remove one's options.

49. In his study of Busby Berkeley's work, Martin Rubin finds the number so disconnected from the film as a whole that he concludes it cannot "justify its presence in the narrative as a fitting climax . . . The tone and style . . . have little in common with the surrounding narrative." Of the film's visual appearance, Rubin comments, "The majority of the shots employ extreme off-angles . . . Nearly every shot is composed

around a sharply oblique angle that clashes with those of the shots immediately around it." He could just as easily be describing a Picasso or Kandinsky painting. *Show Stoppers: Busby Berkeley and the Tradition of Spectacle* (New York: Columbia University Press, 1993), 128–29.

50. For the dance marathon as a Depression phenomenon, see the documentary, *The Great Depression: The Great Shake-Up,* produced by Jonathan Towers, vol. 1 (New York: Tower Productions, 1998).

6. THE ARC OF NATIONAL CONFIDENCE AND THE BIRTH OF FILM NOIR

1. Malcolm Cowley, "A Farewell to the Thirties," *Harper's,* November 1939, 42.

2. Tyrus Miller, *Late Modernism: Politics, Fiction, and the Arts between the Wars* (Berkeley: University of California Press, 1999), 8.

3. Fredric Jameson, "The Synoptic Chandler," in Joan Copjec, ed., *Shades of Noir.* (London: Verso, 1993), 23; also see James Naremore's discussion of film noir as a modernist art form in *More than Night: Film Noir and Its Contexts* (Berkeley: University of California Press, 1998), 40–95.

4. For studies of connections between art and social developments in Weimar Germany, see Peter Gay, *Weimar Culture: The Outsider as Insider* (New York: W. W. Norton, 2001); Walter Laquer, *Weimar: A Cultural History* (New York: Perigree, 1980); Siegfried Kracauer, *From* Caligari *to Hitler, A Psychological History of the German Film* (Princeton University Press, 1974); Lotte H. Eisner, *The Haunted Screen* (Berkeley: University of California Press, 1973); Bruce Arthur Murray, *Film and the German Left in the Weimar Republic: From* Caligari *to Kuhle Wampe* (Austin: University of Texas Press, 1990).

5. Harris Gaylord Warren, *Herbert Hoover and the Great Depression* (New York: Oxford University Press, 1959), 53.

6. Arthur Schlesinger Jr., *The Crisis of the Old Order* (Boston: Houghton Mifflin, 1957), 162.

7. Paul Johnson, *A History of the American People* (New York: Harper, 1999), 744.

8. William Leuchtenburg, *Franklin D. Roosevelt and the New Deal, 1932–1940* (New York: Harper and Row, 1963), 26.

9. Schlesinger, 171.

10. Leuchtenburg, 28.

11. Schlesinger, 174, 176.

12. "An Angry Rancher's Revolutionary Ideas," Hearings before a Subcommittee of the Committee on Labor, House of Representatives, in David A. Shannon, ed., *The Great Depression* (Englewood Cliffs, N.J.: Prentice Hall, 1960), 122.

13. Schlesinger, 205.

14. Leuchtenburg, 26, 27.

15. Schlesinger, 57.

16. Leuchtenburg, 20.

17. Frederick Lewis Allen, *Since Yesterday, 1929–1939* (1940; New York: Bantam, 1965), 58.

18. John Dos Passos, *1919* (New York: Harcourt, Brace, 1932), 375.

19. Leuchtenburg, 218.

20. David Kennedy, *Freedom from Fear: The American People in Depression and War, 1929–1945* (New York: Oxford University Press, 1999), 387.

21. Robert McElvaine, *The Great Depression: America, 1929–1941* (New York: Three Rivers Press, 1993), 104, 106.

22. Leuchtenburg, 39.

23. Allen, *Since Yesterday*, 178.

24. On the fallen woman genre, see Lea Jacobs, *The Wages of Sin: Censorship and the Fallen Woman Film, 1928–1941* (Madison: University of Wisconsin Press, 1991); for representative studies of the gangster genre, see Jonathan Munby, *Public Enemies, Public Heroes: Screening the Gangster from Little Caesar to Touch of Evil* (Chicago: University of Chicago Press, 1999); John McCarty, *Hollywood Gangland: The Movies' Love Affair with the Mob* (New York: St. Martin's Press, 1993).

25. Johnson, 736, 744.

26. Tino Balio, *Grand Design: Hollywood as a Modern Business Enterprise, 1930–1939* (Berkeley: University of California Press, 1993), 62.

27. Munby, 55.

28. Quoted in Arthur Schlesinger Jr., "When the Movies Really Counted," *Show*, April 1963; rpr. in Gerald Mast, ed., *The Movies in Our Midst: Documents in the Cultural History of Film in America* (Chicago: University of Chicago Press, 1982), 423.

29. Raymond Durgnat, "Paint it Black: The Family Tree of Film Noir," Robert Porfirio, "No Way Out: Existential Motifs in Film Noir," both reprinted in Alain Silver and James Ursini, eds., *Film Noir Reader I* (New York: Proscenium Publishers, 1996), 38, 77–93.

30. Thomas Schatz, *The Genius of the System: Hollywood Filmmaking in the Studio Era* (New York: Pantheon, 1988), 160.

31. Alan Brinkley, *The End of Reform: New Deal Liberalism in Recession and War* (New York: Vintage, 1996), 16.

32. Leuchtenburg, 184–88.

33. Dewey W. Grantham, *The Life and Death of the Solid South* (Lexington: University Press of Kentucky, 1988), 26–58.

34. Brinkley, 141–42.

35. Frederick Lewis Allen, *The Big Change: America Transforms Itself, 1900–1950* (1952; New York: Perennial, 1969), 140.

36. Leuchtenberg, 217–19.

37. Kennedy, 462–63.

38. Allen, *The Big Change*, 143–44.

39. Lloyd Shearer, "Crime Pays on the Screen," *New York Times Magazine*, August 5, 1945, rpr. in Silver and Ursini, eds., *Film Noir Reader 2* (New York: Limelight, 2003), 13.

40. Miller, 27, 42.

41. Phil Hardy, "Crime Movies," in Geoffrey Nowell-Smith, ed., *The Oxford History of World Cinema* (New York: Oxford University Press, 1997), 306.

42. Jacobs, 147, 133–49.

43. Molly Haskell, *From Reverence to Rape: The Treatment of Women in the Movies* (New York: Penguin, 1974), 151.

44. Mirra Komarovsky, *The Unemployed Man and His Family: The Effect of Unemployment Upon the Status of the Man in Fifty-Nine Families* (1940; Walnut Creek, Calif.: Altamira Press, 2004), 23.

45. Susan Ware, *Beyond Suffrage: Women in the New Deal* (Cambridge, Mass.: Harvard University Press, 1981).

46. Owen Young, "New Deal Weighed," *Time*, July 3, 1933, 16.

47. Kennedy, 337.

48. Representative studies of women in film noir include Elizabeth Cowie, "Film Noir and Women," in Copjec, 121–65; James Maxfield, *The Fatal Woman: Sources of*

Male Anxiety in Film Noir (Madison, N.J.: Fairleigh Dickinson University Press, 1996); Frank Krutnik, *In a Lonely Street: Film Noir, Genre, Masculinity* (London: Routledge, 1991); Ann Kaplan, ed., *Women in Film Noir* (London: British Film Institute, 1978); Catherine Jurca, "*Mildred Pierce,* Warner Bros., and the Corporate Family," *Representations* 77 (Winter 2002): 30–51.

49. Daphne Du Maurier, *Rebecca* (1938; New York: Perennial, 2001), 130.
50. Kennedy, 351.
51. Brinkley, 20.
52. Allen, *Since Yesterday,* 19, 58, 246.
53. Ibid., 127.
54. This term belongs to Neal Gabler. See *An Empire of Their Own: How the Jews Invented Hollywood* (New York: Doubleday, 1988); and Norman Zierold, *The Moguls: Hollywood's Merchants of Myth* (Los Angeles: Silman-James Press, 1969).
55. Raymond Borde and Etienne Chaumeton, *A Panorama of American Film Noir, 1941–1953,* trans. Paul Hammond (1955; San Francisco: City Lights Books, 2002), 13.
56. Miller, 11–12.
57. For representative discussions of the city in film noir, see Naremore, 9, 35–36, 44–45; Foster Hirsch, *The Dark Side of the Screen: Film Noir* (New York: Da Capo, 2001), 1–22; David Reid and Jayne L. Walker, "Strange Pursuit: Cornell Woolrich and the Abandoned City of the Forties," in Copjec, 57–96.
58. Brain Truster Raymond Moley ridiculed Brandeis for averting his eyes from urban America while hoping "that if America could once more become a nation of small proprietors, of corner grocers and smithies under spreading chestnut trees, we should have solved the problems of American life." *After Seven Years* (New York: Harper, 1939), 24; Eliot believed urbanization created people "detached from tradition, alienated from religion and susceptible to mass suggestion: in other words, a mob." "The Idea of a Christian Society," in *Christianity and Culture* (1939; New York: Harcourt, 1967), 23; Roosevelt "always did and always would think people better off in the country and would regard the cities as rather hopeless." Leuchtenburg, 136.
59. Donald L. Miller, *City of the Century: The Epic of Chicago and the Making of America* (New York: Touchstone, 1996), 277; Erin Burns, James Sanders, and Lisa Ades, *New York: An Illustrated History* (New York: Knopf, 2003), 237.

7. ESCAPING THE THIRTIES

1. Louis Marin, "Frontiers of Utopia: Past and Present," *Critical Inquiry* 19 (Winter 1993): 419–20.
2. Yi-Fu Tuan, *Escapism* (Baltimore: Johns Hopkins University Press, 1998), 31.
3. T. S. Eliot, "The Idea of a Christian Society," in *Christianity and Culture* (1939; New York: Harcourt, 1976), 25.
4. David M. Kennedy, *Freedom from Fear: The American People in Depression and War, 1929–1945* (New York: Oxford University Press, 1999), 121.
5. Lyle Lanier, "The Philosophy of Progress," in Louis Rubin Jr. ed., *I'll Take My Stand: The South and the Agrarian Tradition* (1930; Baton Rouge: Louisiana State University Press, 1983), 153.
6. Wassily Kandinsky, "On the Question of Form," in Kenneth C. Lindsay and Peter Vergo, eds., *Wassily Kandinsky: Complete Writings on Art* (1912; New York: Da Capo, 1994), 250.
7. Franz Marc, "Aphorisms," in Herschel B. Chipp, *Theories of Modern Art* (Berkeley: University of California Press, 1968), 180.

8. Oskar Koschka, "On the Nature of Visions," 1912; Chipp, 174.

9. Quoted in Colin Rhodes, *Primitivism and Modern Art* (London: Thames and Hudson, 1994), 20.

10. Ibid., 106.

11. Ibid., 32.

12. "Fiscal: New Year," *Time*, July 10, 1933, 14.

13. Franklin Roosevelt, "Inaugural Address," March 4, 1933, in J. B. S. Hardman, ed., *Rendezvous with Destiny: The Addresses and Opinions of Franklin Delano Roosevelt* (New York: Dryden Press, 1944), 40.

14. Thirties films that do advertise such a confrontation include *The Grapes of Wrath, Heroes for Sale, The Lost Squadron, I Am a Fugitive from a Chain Gang, Our Daily Bread, Street Scene, Modern Times, One Third of a Nation, Paid, The Roaring Twenties, Midnight Mary, Fury,* and many others.

15. William L. White, "Pare Lorentz," *Scribner's*, (January 1939): 8.

16. Quoted in Rhodes, 70.

17. George Fitzhugh, *Cannibals All! Or Slaves Without Masters,* C. Vann Woodward, ed. (1856; Cambridge: Harvard University Press, 1982), 15.

18. Frederick Lewis Allen, *Since Yesterday, 1929–1939* (1940; New York: Bantam, 1965), 205.

19. Elizabeth Fox-Genovese, *Within the Plantation Household: Black and White Women of the Old South* (Chapel Hill: University of North Carolina Press, 1988), 39–45.

20. For the origins of such chivalric logic in the American South, see Anne Firor Scott, *The Southern Lady: From Pedestal to Politics, 1830–1930* (Chicago: University of Chicago Press, 1970), 14–15.

21. For example, in his 1934 novel, *Pirates of Venus,* Edgar Rice Burroughs refers to no people "with more lovable qualities than Mexicans who have not been contaminated by too close contact with the intolerance and commercialism of Americans." (New York: Ace, 1978), 16; see also Harvey Fergusson, "Seen and Heard in Mexico," *American Mercury* 20, n. 78 (January 30): 165–71.

22. Stuart Chase, *Mexico: A Study of Two Americas* (New York: Macmillan, 1931), v, 327.

23. Marin, 414–15.

24. Thorne Smith, *Topper* (1926; New York: Random House, 1999), 66.

25. Quoted in Rhodes, 68.

26. Ibid., 18, 22.

27. Ibid., 34.

28. Milton Friedman and Anna Jacobson Schwartz, *A Monetary History of the United States* (Princeton, N.J.: Princeton University Press, 1993), 299.

29. Notably Warner Brothers launched their Looney Tunes cartoon series in the early thirties, logically—or illogically—of a piece with screwball, just as screwball emerged. See Jerry Beck and Will Friedwald, *Looney Tunes and Merrie Melodies: A Complete Guide to the Warner Bros. Cartoons* (New York: Henry Holt, 1989). The purest form of live action irrationality on U.S. screens during the thirties was that of the Marx Brothers, who first starred together on screen in the film adaptation of *Cocoanuts* (1929). They had already made it big in the stage version in 1925. Their brand of irrationality might be better termed farce. The 1925 date for *Cocoanuts* might seem to undermine my point about connections between the phenomenon of the irrational and film in the thirties, until one realizes that *Cocoanuts* was based on the speculation-marked Florida land boom-and-bust of the mid-twenties, which were characterized by Frederick Lewis Allen as a rehearsal for the Great Depression in *Only Yesterday,* (1931; New York: Perennial, 1959), 225–40.

30. Allen, *Since Yesterday*, 124–25, 128–29.

31. Brian McHale, *Postmodernist Fiction* (New York: Metheun, 1987), 12.

32. Raymond Moley, *After Seven Years* (New York: Harper and Brothers, 1939), 374; see also Arthur Schlesinger Jr., *The Crisis of the Old Order* (Boston: Houghton Mifflin, 1988), 20–22.

33. William E. Leuchtenburg, *Franklin D. Roosevelt and the New Deal* (New York: Harper and Row, 1963), 217–18.

8. THE AMERICAN CONTRADICTION

1. Michael Schudson, *Discovering the News: A Social History of American News-papers* (New York: Basic Books, 1978), 154.

2. "Hearst Hoax," *Time*, May 11, 1936, 48–49; see also "The Yellow (Journalist) Peril," *The New Republic*, January 16, 1935, 263–64; "Cooing Hearstlings," *Time*, October 14, 1935; George P. West, "Hearst: A Psychological Note," *American Mercury*, 21, n. 83 (November 30, 1930), 298–308; Walter Millis, "Hearst," *Atlantic*, December 1931, 697–709.

3. Vincent Sheean, *Personal History* (New York: Doubleday, Doran, 1936), 52.

4. Quoted in Harold Ickes, *America's House of Lords: An Inquiry into the Freedom of the Press* (New York: Harcourt, Brace, 1939), 6.

5. Ibid., 6.

6. George Seldes, *Lords of the Press* (New York: Julian Messner, 1938), 294–95.

7. Quoted in Ickes, 137.

8. Robert S. Lynd and Helen Merrell Lynd, *Middletown, A Study in Modern American Culture* (1929; New York: Harcourt, Brace, 1957), 475, 476–77.

9. Robert S. Lynd and Helen Merrell Lynd, *Middletown in Transition: A Study in Cultural Conflicts* (1937; New York: Harcourt, Brace, 1965), 374.

10. Lynd, *Middletown in Transition*, 382–83.

11. Ickes, 8.

12. Mark Dowie, "The Chandlers: L.A.'s First Family," *Santa Monica Mirror*, September 22, 1999; Robert S. Lynd and Helen Merrell Lynd, 28, I am indebted to Dowie's detailed account of the Otis Chandler history throughout my own account. See also Seldes, 71–75; Robert S. Lynd and Helen Merrell Lynd, 5; Dennis McDougal, *Privileged Son: Otis Chandler and the Rise and Fall of the L.A. Times Dynasty* (New York: Perseus, 2001), 25–43; Robert S. Lynd and Helen Merrell Lynd, 43; Mark Arax and Rick Wartzman, *The King of California: J. G. Boswell and the Making of a Secret American Empire* (New York: PublicAffairs, 2003); John Walton, *Western Times and Water Wars: State, Culture, and Rebellion in California* (Berkeley: University of California Press, 1992), 142–54.

13. McDougal, 28.

14. Dowie, "The Chandlers."

15. Ibid.

16. Ickes, 18.

17. Edna Ferber, *Cimarron* (Garden City, N.Y.: Doubleday, Doran, 1930), 107–8, 116.

18. On sob sister journalism, see Marion Marzolf, *Up from the Footnote: A History of Women Journalists* (New York: Hastings House, 1977); Maurine Beasley, Sheila Gibbons, and Sheila Silver, *Taking Their Place: A Documentary History of Women and Journalism* (Lanham, Md.: American University Press, 1993); Phyllis Abramson, *Sob Sister Journalism: Contributions to the Study of Mass Media and Communications*

(Westport, Conn.: Greenwood Press, 1990); for a contemporary account from the period, see "Annie Laurie" [one of the sob sisters], *Time,* October 28, 1935.

19. Otis Ferguson, "Citizen Welles, " *The New Republic,* June 2, 1941.

20. Pauline Kael, *The* Citizen Kane *Book* (Boston: Little Brown, 1971), 61–62.

21. David Nasaw, *The Chief: The Life of William Randolph Hearst* (New York: Houghton Mifflin, 2001), 70–71.

22. Ickes, 43.

23. Ickes, 44, 45, 45–47, 53, 60–61, 62–63, 79–81, 52, 64.

24. Jib Fowles, *Advertising and Popular Culture* (Thousand Oaks, Calif.: Sage Publications, 1996), 37.

25. For a contemporary view of Ivy Lee, see "Ivy Lee," *Time,* August 7, 1933, 21; on his career, see Ray Hiebert, *Courtier to the Crowd: The Life Story of Ivy Lee* (Ames: Iowa State University Press, 1966). On the rise of public relations and publicity agents, see Roland Marchand, *Creating the Corporate Soul: The Rise of Public Relations and Corporate Imagery in American Big Business* (Berkeley: University of California Press, 1998), 202–48; Edwin Emery and Michael Emery, *The Press and America: An Interpretive History of the Mass Media* (Englewood Cliffs, N.J.: Prentice Hall, 1940), 409–15; Edward L. Bernays [one of the early public relations pioneers], *Biography of an Idea* (New York: Simon and Schuster); Fowles, 26–52; Schudson, 134–59.

26. Ibid., 141–43.

27. Ibid., 134.

28. Though the plaque lists some eighteen names, Kirk Hallahan cites the number of deaths in the massacre at fourteen. Kirk Hallahan, "Ivy Lee and the Rockefellers' Response to the 1913–1914 Colorado Coal Strike," *Journal of Public Relations Research,* 14 no. 4, (2002): 265–315.

29. Howard Zinn, *A People's History of the United States, 1492–Present* (New York: Perennial, 2003), 355–57; Irving Bernstein, *A History of the American Worker: The Turbulent Years* (Boston: Houghton Mifflin, 1970), 61–62.

30. "Will Revolution Come?" *Atlantic Monthly,* August 1932, 184–91; "The American Plan: Its Rise and Fall," *The New Republic,* October 2, 1935, 204–7; Ronald A. Egger, "The Collapse of Democracy," *American Mercury,* April 30, 1930, 462–68.

31. Quoted in Schudson, 125.

32. Ibid., 126–27.

33. Ibid., 127, 129, 134.

34. Ibid., 203.

35. Ibid., 138.

36. Ibid., 144.

Bibliography

Abramson, Phyllis. *Sob Sister Journalism: Contributions to the Study of Mass Media and Communications.* Westport, Conn.: Greenwood Press, 1990.

Agar, Herbert, and Allen Tate, eds. *Who Owns America? A New Declaration of Independence.* 1936. Wilmington, De.: ISI Books, 1999.

Allen, Frederick Lewis. *The Big Change: America Transforms Itself, 1900–1950.* 1952. New York: Perennial: 1969.

———. *Only Yesterday: An Informal History of the Twenties.* 1931. New York: Perennial, 1959.

———. *Since Yesterday, 1929–1939.* 1940. New York: Bantam, 1965.

"The American Plan: Its Rise and Fall," *The New Republic,* October 2, 1935, 204–7.

Amott, Teresa, and Julie Matthei. *Race, Gender, and Work: A Multi-Cultural History of Women in the United States.* Cambridge, Mass.: South End Press, 1996.

Altman, Rick. "Genre Cinema." In *The Oxford History of World Cinema,* edited by Geoffrey Nowell-Smith. New York: Oxford University Press, 1997; 276–312.

"An Angry Rancher's Revolutionary Ideas," edited by David A. Shannon, *The Great Depression.* Englewood Cliffs, N.J.: Prentice-Hall, 1960; 121–23.

"Annie Laurie." *Time,* October 28, 1935, 48–50.

Arax, Mark, and Rick Wartzman, *The King of California: J. G. Boswell and the Making of a Secret American Empire.* New York: PublicAffairs, 2003.

"Arms, Men, and Women." *Time,* January 4, 1932, 8.

Atwell, Edward F. *Washington, the Battleground: The Truth about the "Bonus Riots."* Washington, D.C.: Patriotic Publishing Society, 1933.

Ayers, Edward. *Vengeance and Justice.* New York: Oxford University Press, 1984.

Ballio, Tino. *Grand Design: Hollywood as Modern Business Enterprise, 1930–1939.* Berkeley: University of California Press, 1993.

Barkin, Elliott Robert. *And Still They Come: Immigrants and American Society, 1920 to the 1990s.* Wheeling, Ill.: Harlan Davidson, 1996.

Barrios, Richard. *A Song in the Dark: The Birth of the Musical Film.* New York: Oxford University Press, 1995.

Bauman, John F., and Thomas H. Coode. *In the Eye of the Great Depression: New Deal Reporters and the Agony of the American People.* Dekalb: Northern Illinois University Press, 1988.

Beasley, Maurine, Sheila Gibbons, and Sheila Silver. *Taking Their Place: A Documentary History of Women and Journalism.* Lanham, Md.: University Press of American, 1993.

Beck, Jerry, and Will Friedwald. *Looney Tunes and Merrie Melodies: A Complete Guide to the Warner Bros. Cartoons.* New York: Henry Holt, 1989.

Bell-Metereau, Rebecca. *Hollywood Androgeny.* New York: Columbia University Press, 1993.

Benjamin, Walter. *Illuminations: Essays and Reflections.* Edited by Hannah Arendt. New York: Schocken, 1988.

——. *Selected Writings.* Edited by Howard Eiland and Michael Jennings. Cambridge: Harvard University Press, 2002.

Benton, Charlotte, Tim Benton, and Ghislaine Wood. *Art Deco: 1910–1939.* London: V. & A. Publications, 2003.

Berger, Thomas. *Crazy in Berlin.* New York: Dell, 1958.

Bergmen, Andrew. *We're in the Money: Depression America and Its Films.* Chicago: Ivan Dees, 1971.

Bernays, Edward L. *Biography of an Idea.* New York: Simon and Schuster, 1965.

Bernstein, Burton. *Thurber: A Biography.* New York: Ballantine, 1975.

Bernstein, Irving. *A History of the American Worker: The Turbulent Years.* Boston: Houghton Mifflin, 1970.

Biesen, Sheri Chinen. *Blackout: World War II and the Origins of Film Noir.* Baltimore: Johns Hopkins University Press, 2005.

Biggers, Earl Derr. *The Black Camel.* New York: Grosset & Dunlap, 1929.

Bix, Herbert P. *Hirohito and the Making of Modern Japan.* New York: Perennial, 2001.

Bogle, Donald. *Blacks in American Films and Television.* New York: Fireside, 1989.

——. *Toms, Coons, Mulattoes, Mammies, and Bucks: An Interpretive History of Blacks in American Films.* New York: Continuum, 2000.

Borde, Raymond, and Etienne Chaumeton, *A Panorama of American Film Noir, 1941–1953.* Translated by Paul Hammond. 1955. Reprint, San Francisco: City Lights Books, 2002.

Brier, Stephen. *Who Built America?* Vol. 2. New York: St. Martin's Press, 2000.

Brinkley, Alan. *Culture and Politics in the Great Depression.* Waco, Tex.: Baylor University Press, 1999.

——. *The End of Reform: New Deal Liberalism in Recession and War.* New York: Vintage, 1996.

——. *Voices of Protest: Huey Long, Father Coughlin, and the Great Depression.* New York: Vintage, 1983.

Brownlee, W. Elliot. *Dynamics of Ascent: A History of the American Economy.* New York: Knopf, 1979.

Bruchey, Stuart. *The Wealth of the Nation: An Economic History of the United States.* New York: Harper and Row, 1988.

Bryant, Keith L., and Henry C. Dethloff. *A History of American Business.* Englewood Cliffs, N.J.: Prentice Hall, 1990.

Buck, Pearl S. *The Good Earth.* 1931. New York: Simon and Schuster, 1994.

Buhl, Paul, and David Wagner. *Radical Hollywood.* New York: Free Press, 2003.

Burns, James MacGregor. *Roosevelt, 1882–1940: The Lion and the Fox.* New York: Harcourt Brace, 1984.

Burns, Ric, James Sanders, and Lisa Ades. *New York: An Illustrated History.* New York: Knopf, 2003.

Burns, Robert. *I Am a Fugitive from a Georgia Chain Gang!* 1932. Athens: University of Georgia Press, 1987.

Burroughs, Edgar Rice. *Pirates of Venus.* 1934. New York: Ace, 1978.

"Busiest Lady." *Time,* June 12, 1933, 16.

Capra, Frank. *The Name above the Title.* New York: Macmillan, 1971.

Chafe, William Henry. *The American Woman: Her Changing Social, Economic, and Political Roles, 1920–1970.* New York: Oxford University Press, 1972.

Chang, Iris. *The Chinese in America.* New York: Penguin, 2004.

"*The Charge of the Light Brigade.*" *Time,* November 2, 1936, 21–22.

Chase, Stuart. *Mexico: A Study of Two Americas.* New York: Macmillan, 1931.

Cheever, John. "The Swimmer," *The Stories of John Cheever.* New York: Ballantine, 1981.

Cheever, Susan. *Home before Dark: A Biographical Memoir of John Cheever by His Daughter.* Boston: Houghton Mifflin, 1984.

Chipp, Herschel B. *Theories of Modern Art.* Berkeley: University of California Press, 1968.

Christ, Carol. *Victorian and Modernist Poetry.* Chicago, Ill.: University of Chicago Press, 1984.

Clarke, George R. "Beckerstown 1932: An American Town Faces the Depression." *Harper's* October 1932, 580–91.

Cobb, James C. *The Most Southern Place on Earth: The Mississippi Delta and the Roots of Regional Identity.* New York: Oxford University Press, 1992.

Cobb, Margaret. "Three Million Women." *The American Mercury,* March 30, 1930, 319–25.

Cobley, Evelyn. *Representing War: Form and Ideology in First World War Narratives.* Toledo, Oh.: University of Toledo Press, 1993.

Collins, Gail. *America's Women: Dolls, Drudges, Helpmates, and Heroines.* New York: HarperCollins, 2003.

Colton, John. *The Shanghai Gesture.* New York: Boni and Liveright, 1926.

The Complete Report of Mayor LaGuardia's Commission on the Harlem Riot. New York: Arno Press and *The New York Times,* 1969.

"Cooing Hearstlings." *Time,* October 14, 1935, 42.

Cook, Blanche Wiesen. *Eleanor Roosevelt, 1933–1938.* Vol. 2. New York: Viking, 1999.

Coolidge, Mary E. B. R. S. *Chinese Immigration.* New York: Arno, 1969.

Couch, W. T., ed. *These are Our Lives.* 1939. New York: W. W. Norton, 1975.

Courlander, Harold. *The Drum and the Hoe: Life and Lore of the Haitian People.* Berkeley: University of California Press, 1960.

Cowie, Elizabeth. "Film Noir and Women." In *Shades of Noir,* edited by Joan Copjec. London: Verso, 1993, 121–65.

Cowley, Malcolm. "A Farewell to the Thirties," *Harper's,* November 1939, 42.

Cripps, Thomas. *Slow Fade to Black: The Negro in American Film, 1900–1942.* New York: Oxford University Press, 1993.

De Toledano, Ralph. *Little Cesár.* 1930. New York: Anthem, 1971.

Dickson, Paul, and Thomas B. Allen. *The Bonus Army: An American Epic.* New York: Walker & Co., 2004.

Doherty, Thomas. *Pre-Code Hollywood: Sex, Immorality, and Insurrection in American Cinema, 1930–1934.* New York: Columbia University Press, 1999.

Dong, Stella. *Shanghai: The Rise and Fall of a Decadent City.* New York: Morrow, 2000.

Dos Passos, John. *1919.* New York: Harcourt Brace, 1932.

Dowie, Mark. "The Chandlers: L.A.'s First Family," *The Santa Monica Mirror,* September 22–28, 1999.

Drabble, Margaret. *The Oxford Companion to English Literature.* New York: Oxford University Press, 1985.

Du Maurier, Daphne. *Rebecca.* 1938. New York: Perennial, 2001.

Durgnat, Raymond. *King Vidor, American.* Berkeley: University of California Press, 1990.

———. "Paint it Black: The Family Tree of Film Noir." In *Film Noir Reader I,* edited by Alain Silver and James Ursini. New York: Proscenium Publishers, 1996, 37–52.

Eberhard, Wolfram. *A History of China.* London: Routledge, 1958.

Edmunds, Walter. *Drums Along the Mohawk.* Boston: Little, Brown, 1937.

Egger, Ronald A. "The Collapse of Democracy." *American Mercury,* April 30, 1930, 462–68.

Eisner, Lotte E. *The Haunted Screen.* Berkeley: University of California Press, 1973.

Eliot, T. S. *The Idea of a Christian Society* in *Christianity and Culture.* 1939. New York: Harcourt, 1967.

Emery, Edwin, and Michael Emery. *The Press and America: An Interpretive History of the Mass Media.* Englewood Cliffs, N.J.: Prentice Hall, 1984.

"Ethiopia: Man of the Year." *Time,* January 6, 1936, 13.

Faversham, Julie Opp. *Squaw Man.* New York: Grosset & Dunlap, 1906.

Ferber, Edna. *Cimarron.* Garden City, N.Y.: Doubleday, Doran, 1930.

Ferguson, Niall. *The Rise and Demise of the British World Order and the Lessons for Global World Power.* New York: Basic Books, 2002.

Ferguson, Otis. "Citizen Welles." *The New Republic,* June 2, 1941, 47.

———. *The Film Criticism of Otis Ferguson.* Philadelphia: Temple University Press, 1971.

Fergusson, Harvey. "Seen and Heard in Mexico." *American Mercury,* January 30, 1930, 165–71.

Fieldhouse, D. K. *Colonialism: 1870–1945.* New York: St. Martin's Press, 1981.

Fine, Lisa M. *The Souls of the Skyscraper: Female Clerical Workers in Chicago, 1870–1930.* Philadelphia: Temple University Press, 1990.

"Fiscal: New Year." *Time,* July 10, 1933, 14.

Fitzgerald, F. Scott. "Bablyon Revisited." *The Stories of F. Scott Fitzgerald.* New York: Scribner's, 1984, 385–402.

Fitzhugh, George. *Cannibals All! Or Slaves Without Masters.* Edited by C. Vann Woodward. 1856. Cambridge: Harvard University Press, 1982

"The Flight of the Bonus Army." *The New Republic,* August 17, 1932, 13–15.

Forster, William Trufant, and Waddill Catchings. *The Road to Plenty.* Boston: Houghton Mifflin, 1928.

Fowles, Jib. *Advertising and Popular Culture.* Thousand Oaks, Calif.: Sage Publications, 1996.

Fox-Genovese, Elizabeth. *Within the Plantation Household: Black and White Women of the Old South.* Chapel Hill: University of North Carolina Press, 1988.

Franklin, John Hope. *Reconstruction after the Civil War*. Chicago, Ill.: University of Chicago Press, 1961.

Friedman, Milton, and Anna Jacobson Schwartz. *A Monetary History of the United States*. Princeton: Princeton University Press, 1993.

Fussell, Paul. *The Great War and Modern Memory*. New York: Oxford University Press, 1975.

Gabler, Neil. *An Empire of Their Own: How the Jews Invented Hollywood*. New York: Anchor, 1988.

Galbraith, Kenneth. *The Great Crash, 1929*. Boston: Houghton Mifflin, 1955.

Gay, Peter. *Weimar Culture: The Outsider as Insider*. New York: W. W. Norton, 2001.

Gehring, Wes. *Leo McCarthy: From Marx to McCarthy*. New York: Scarecrow Press, 2004.

Gelb, Arthur and Barbara. *O'Neill*. New York: Harper, 1962.

Genovese, Eugene. *The Political Economy of Slavery: Studies in the Economy and Society of the Slave South*. New York: Vintage, 1967.

Ginzburg, Ralph. *100 Years of Lynching*. New York: Black Classics Press, 1997.

Goffman, Erving. *Asylums*. New York: Doubleday, 1961.

Grantham, Dewey W. *The Life and Death of the Solid South*. Lexington: University Press of Kentucky, 1988.

Greene, Graham. *The Pleasure Dome: The Collected Film Criticism, 1935–1940*. New York: Oxford University Press, 1980.

Greenberg, Cheryl Lynn. *Or Does It Explode? Black Harlem in the Great Depression*. New York: Oxford University Press, 1991.

Greenblatt, Stephen. *Shakespearean Negotiations*. Berkeley: University of California Press, 1988.

Grey, Lorne. "Foreword" to Zane Grey, *The Vanishing American*. 1925. New York: Simon and Schuster, 1982.

Grob, Gerald N. *The Mad Among Us: A History of the Care of America's Mentally Ill*. Cambridge, Mass.: Harvard University Press, 1994.

Hallahan, Kirk. "Ivy Lee and the Rockefellers' Response to the 1913–1914 Colorado Coal Strike." *Journal of Public Relations Research* 14, no. 4, (2002): 265–315.

Hardman, J. B. S. "How to Break a Union." *The New Republic*, October 21, 1931, 252–55.

———. *Rendezvous with Destiny: Addresses and Opinions of Franklin D. Roosevelt*. New York: Dryden, 1944.

Hardy, Phil. "Crime Movies." In *The Oxford History of World Cinema*, edited by Geoffrey Nowell-Smith. New York: Oxford University Press, 1997, 304.

Haskell, Molly. *From Reverence to Rape: The Treatment of Women in the Movies*. New York: Penguin, 1974.

Hauser, Ernest O. *Shanghai, City for Sale*. New York: Harcourt, Brace, 1940.

"Hearst Hoax." *Time*, May 11, 1936, 48–49.

Hecht, Ben, and Sidney Zion. *A Child of the Century*. New York: Plume, 1985.

"Henry Ford: Individualist." *The New Republic*, September 13, 1933, 115–17.

"Heroes: Bonus Army." *Time*, July 11, 1932, 12.

Hiebert, Ray. *Courtier to the Crowd: The Life Story of Ivy Lee*. Ames: Iowa State University Press, 1966.

Hirsch, Foster. *The Dark Side of the Screen: Film Noir.* Cambridge, Mass.: Da Capo, 2001.

Herman, Jan. *A Talent for Trouble: The Life of Hollywood's Most Acclaimed Director, William Wyler.* Cambridge, Mass.: Da Capo, 1997.

Hoover, Herbert. *The Memoirs of Herbert Hoover: The Great Depression, 1929–1941.* London: Hollis and Carter, 1953.

Horne, Gerald. *Class Struggle in Hollywood: 1930–1950.* Austin: University of Texas Press, 2001.

Horney, Karen. *The Neurotic Personality of Our Time.* New York: W. W. Norton, 1937.

Horowitz, Morton J. *The Transformation of American Law: The Crisis of Legal Orthodoxy.* New York: Basic Books, 2004.

Ickes, Harold. *America's House of Lords: An Inquiry into the Freedom of the Press.* New York: Harcourt, Brace, 1939.

"Ivy Lee." *Time,* August 7, 1933, 21.

"India: Soul Force Wins." *Time,* October 3, 1932, 16.

Jackson, Guida, and Jackie Pelham, eds. *Fall from Innocence: Memoirs of the Great Depression.* Houston, Tex.: Page One Publications, 1997.

Jacobs, Lea. *The Wages of Sin: Censorship and the Fallen Woman Film, 1928–1941.* Madison: University of Wisconsin Press, 1991.

James, Lawrence. *Raj: The Making and Unmaking of British India.* New York: St. Martin's Griffin, 1997.

Jameson, Fredric. "The Synoptic Chandler." In *Shades of Noir,* edited by Joan Copjec. London: Verso, 1993, 33–56.

Jansen, Marius B. *The Making of Modern Japan.* Cambridge: Harvard University Press, 2000.

Johnson, Paul. *A History of the American People.* New York: Harper, 1999.

Jones, Leroi. *Blues People.* New York: Morrow, 1963.

Jurca, Catherine. "*Mildred Pierce,* Warner Bros., and the Corporate Family." *Representations* 77 (Winter 2002): 30–51.

Kael, Pauline. *The* Citizen Kane *Book.* Boston: Little Brown, 1971.

———. *5001 Nights at the Movies.* New York: Henry Holt, 1984.

Kandinsky, Wassily. "On the Question of Modern Form." In *Theories of Modern Art,* edited by Herschel Chipp. Berkeley: University of California Press, 1968, 155–70.

Kaplan, Ann, ed. *Women in Film Noir.* London: British Film Institute, 1978.

Katz, Ephraim. *The Film Encyclopedia.* New York: Harper, 1994.

Kendall, Elizabeth. *The Runaway Bride: Hollywood Romantic Comedy of the 1930s.* New York: Doubleday, 1990.

Kennedy, David. *Freedom from Fear: The American People in Depression and War, 1929–1945.* New York: Oxford University Press, 1999.

Keynes, John Maynard. *Economic Consequences of the Peace.* 1920. Reprint, New York: Penquin, 1995.

———. *The General Theory of Employment, Interest, and Money.* New York: Harcourt, Brace, 1936.

Klehr, Harvey. *The Heyday of American Communism: The Depression Decade.* New York: Basic Books, 1984.

Komarovsky, Mirra. *The Unemployed Man and His Family: Status of the Man in Fifty-Nine Families.* 1940. New York: Altamira Press, 2004.

Koppes, Clayton R., and Gregory D. Black. *Hollywood Goes to War: How Politics, Profits, and Propaganda Shaped World War II Movies.* Berkeley: University of California Press, 1983.

Koschka, Oskar. "On the Nature of Visions." In *Theories of Modern Art,* edited by Herschel Chipp. 1912. Reprint, Berkeley: University of California Press, 1968, 171–74.

Kracauer, Siegfried. *From Caligari to Hitler, A Psychological History of the German Film.* Princeton: Princeton University Press, 1974.

Krutnik, Frank. *In a Lonely Street: Film Noir, Genre, Masculinity.* London: Routledge, 1991.

"Labor: A Hundred Cities Experience Strikes and Disorder; While Minneapolis Truckmen Explode, San Francisco Calms Down." *News-Week,* July 28, 1934, 3–5.

"Labor: Blood Flows in San Francisco; General Strike Threatened." *News-Week,* July 14 1934, 5–6.

Lanier, Lyle. "The Philosophy of Progress." In *I'll Take My Stand: The South and the Agrarian Tradition,* edited by Louis Rubin Jr. 1930. Baton Rouge: Louisiana State University Press, 1983, 122–54.

Laquer, Walter. *Weimar: A Cultural History.* New York: Perigree, 1980.

LaSalle, Mick. *Complicated Women: Sex and Power in Pre-Code Hollywood.* New York: Thomas Dunne Books, 2000.

Lash, Joseph P. *Eleanor and Franklin.* New York: W. W. Norton, 2004.

"The League: Jig Up?" *Time,* July 6, 1936, 18.

Leff, Leonard J., and Jerold L. Simmons. *The Dame in the Kimono: Hollywood, Censorship, and the Production Code from the 1920s to the 1960s.* New York: Grove Weidenfeld, 1990.

"Letters to the Editor." *New York Times,* April 25, 1935.

Leuchtenburg, William. *Franklin D. Roosevelt and the New Deal, 1932–1940.* New York: Harper and Row, 1963.

———. *The Perils of Prosperity, 1914–1932.* Chicago: The University of Chicago Press, 1973.

Levine, Lawrence. *Black Culture and Black Consciousness.* New York: Oxford University Press, 1978.

Litwak, Leon, ed. *The American Labor Movement.* Englewood Cliffs, N.J.: Prentice Hall, 1962.

Loo, Chalsa M. *Chinatown: Most Time, Hard Time.* New York: Praeger, 1991.

Lukács, George. "The Sociology of Modern Drama." In *The Theory of the Modern Stage,* edited by Eric Bentley. New York: Penguin, 1990, 425–50.

Lynd, Robert S., and Helen Merrill Lynd. *Middletown in Transition: A Study in Cultural Conflicts.* New York: Harcourt, Brace, and World, 1937.

McBride, Joseph. *Frank Capra: The Catastrophe of Success.* New York: Touchstone, 1992.

———. *Searching for John Ford: A Life.* New York: St. Martin's, 2003.

McElvaine, Robert, ed. *The Great Depression: America, 1929–1941.* New York: Three Rivers Press, 1993.

———. *Down and Out in the Great Depression: Letters from the Forgotten Man.* Chapel Hill: University of North Carolina Press, 1983.

McMillen, Neil. *Black Mississippians in the Age of Jim Crow.* Urbana: University of Illinois Press, 1990.

Maland, Charles J. *Chaplin and American Culture.* Princeton: Princeton University Press, 1989.

Mancini, Matthew. "A Foreword to the Brown Thrasher Edition." *Robert Burns I Am a Fugitive from a Georgia Chain Gang!* 1932. Reprint, Athens: University of Georgia Press, 1987, v–xxv.

McCarty, John. *Hollywood Gangland: The Movies' Love Affair with the Mob.* New York: St. Martin's, 1993.

McDougal, Dennis. *Privileged Son: Otis Chandler and the Rise and Fall of* The L.A. Times *Dynasty.* New York: Perseus, 2001.

McGilligan, Patrick. *Fritz Lang: The Nature of the Beast.* New York: St. Martin's, 1997.

McHale, Brian. *Postmodernist Fiction.* New York: Methuen, 1987.

Marc, Franz. "Aphorisms." In *Theories of Modern Art,* edited by Herschel Chipp. 1920. Berkeley: University of California Press, 1968, 180.

Marchand, Roland. *Creating the Corporate Soul: The Rise of Public Relations and Corporate Imagery in American Big Business.* Berkeley: University of California Press, 1998.

Marchetti, Gina. *Romance and the Yellow Peril: Race, Sex, and Discursive Strategies in Hollywood Fiction.* Berkeley: University of California Press, 1993.

Marin, Louis. "Frontiers of Utopia: Past and Present." *Critical Inquiry* 19 (Winter 1993): 397–420.

Marzolf, Marion. *Up from the Footnote: A History of Women Journalists.* New York: Hastings House, 1977.

Mast, Gerald. *Howard Hawks, Storyteller.* New York: Oxford University Press, 1984.

———. *The Movies in Our Midst. Documents in the Cultural History of Film in America.* Chicago, Ill.: University of Chicago Press, 1982.

———. *A Short History of the Movies.* Indianapolis, Ind.: Bobbs-Merrill, 1971.

May, Larry. *The Big Tomorrow: Hollywood and the Politics of the American Way.* Chicago: University of Chicago Press, 2000.

Maxfield, James. *The Fatal Woman: Sources of Male Anxiety in Film Noir.* Madison, N.J.: Fairleigh Dickinson University Press, 1996.

Michaels, Walter Benn. *Our America: Nativism, Modernism, and Pluralism.* Durham, N.C.: Duke University Press, 1995.

Miller, Donald L. *City of the Century: The Epic of Chicago and the Making of America.* New York: Touchstone, 1996.

Miller, Tyrus. *Late Modernism: Politics, Fiction, and the Arts between the Wars.* Berkeley: University of California Press, 1999.

Millis, Walter. "Hearst." *Atlantic,* December 1931, 697–709.

Minehan, Thomas. *Boy and Girl Tramps of America.* New York: Farrar and Rinehart, 1934.

Moffett, Marian, Michael Fazio, and Lawrence Wodehouse. *A World History of Architecture.* New York: McGraw-Hill, 2004.

Moley, Raymond. *After Seven Years.* New York: Harper, 1939.

———. *Are We Movie-Made?* New York: Macy-Masius, 1938.

Mulvey, Deb, ed. *We had Everything but Money: Priceless Memories of the Great Depression.* Greendale, Wisc.: Reminisce Books, 1992.

Munby, Jonathan. *Public Enemies, Public Heroes: Screening the Gangster from Little Caesar to Touch of Evil.* Chicago, Ill.: University of Chicago Press, 1999.

Murray, Bruce Arthur. *Film and the German Left in the Weimar Republic: From Caligari to Kuhle Wampe.* Austin: University of Texas Press, 1990.

Naremore, James. *More than Night: Film Noir and Its Contexts.* Berkeley: University of California Press, 1998.

Nasaw, David. *The Chief: The Life of William Randolph Hearst.* New York: Houghton Mifflin, 2001.

"New Deal Weighed." *Time,* July 3, 1933, 16.

Offner, Arnold A. *The Origins of the Second World War: American Foreign Policy and World Politics, 1917–1941.* New York: Praeger, 1975.

Oshinsky, David M. *Worse than Slavery: Parchman Farm and the Ordeal of Jim Crow Justice.* New York: Free Press, 1996.

Palmer, R. Barton. *Hollywood's Dark Cinema: The American Film Noir.* New York: Twayne, 1994.

Palmer, Robert. *Deep Blues.* New York: Penguin, 1981.

Peavy, Donald. *Go Slow Now: Faulkner and the Race Question.* Eugene: University of Oregon Press, 1978.

Pells, Richard. *Radical Visions and American Dreams: Culture and Social Thought in the Depression Years.* Middletown, Conn.: Wesleyan University Press, 1973.

"Penitentiary Reform in Mississippi." *Publications of the Mississippi Historical Society* 6 (1902): 111–28.

Porfirio, Robert. "No Way Out: Existential Motifs in Film Noir." In *Film Noir Reader I,* edited by Alain Silver and James Ursini. New York: Proscenium Publishers, 1996, 77–94.

Pound, Arthur. "Bankruptcy Mill." *The Atlantic Monthly,* February 1932, 173–75.

"The Presidency." *Time,* January 4, 1932, 7.

"Puran Swaraj." *Time,* January 13, 1930, 27–28.

"Races: Blacks Aflame." *Time,* February 10, 1936, 14.

Reid, David, and Jayne L. Walker. "Strange Pursuit: Cornell Woolrich and the Abandoned City of the Forties." In *Shades of Noir,* edited by Joan Copjec. London: Verso, 1993, 57–96.

Rhode, Eric. *A History of the Cinema: From Its Origins to 1970.* New York: Hill and Wang, 1976.

Rhodes, Colin. *Primitivism and Modern Art.* London: Thames and Hudson, 1994.

Roberts, Kenneth. *Northwest Passage.* 1937. Reprint, Greenwich, Conn.: Fawcett, 1967.

Rogin, Michael. *Black Face, White Noise: Jewish Immigrants in the Hollywood Melting Pot.* Berkeley: University of California Press, 1996.

Rohmer, Sax. *The Mask of Fu Manchu.* 1932. Reprint, New York: Pyramid, 1962.

Rubin, Louis, Jr., ed. *I'll Take My Stand: The South and the Agrarian Tradition.* 1930. Baton Rouge: Louisiana State University Press, 1983.

Rubin, Martin. *Showstoppers: Busby Berkeley and the Tradition of Spectacle.* New York: Columbia University Press, 1993.

Sassoon, Siegfried. "Fight to a Finish." *Collected Poems, 1908–1956.* London: Faber and Faber, 1961.

Scharf, Lois. *To Work and to Wed: Female Employment, Feminism, and the Great Depression.* Westport, Conn.: Greenwood Press, 1980.

Schatz, Thomas. *The Genius of the System: Hollywood Filmmaking in the Studio Era.* New York: Pantheon, 1988.

Schlesinger, Arthur, Jr. *The Coming of the New Deal.* 1958. Reprint, New York: Houghton Mifflin, 1988.

———. *Crisis of the Old Order.* Boston: Houghton Mifflin, 1957.

———. *The Politics of Upheaval.* Boston: Houghton Mifflin, 1960.

———. "When the Movies Really Counted." *Show,* April 1963. Reprinted in *The Movies in Our Midst: Documents in the Cultural History of Film in America,* edited by Gerald Mast. Chicago: University of Chicago Press, 1982, 423.

Schmidt, Hans. *The United States Occupation of Haiti, 1915–1934.* New Brunswick, N.J.: Rutgers University Press, 1971.

Schraeder, Paul. "Notes on Film Noir." In *Film Noir Reader,* edited by Alain Silver and James Ursini. New York: Limelight, 2001, 53–64.

Schudson, Michael. *Discovering the News: A Social History of American Newspapers* New York: Basic Books, 1978.

Scott, Anne Firor. *The Southern Lady: From Pedestal to Politics, 1830–1930.* Chicago: University of Chicago Press, 1970.

Seldes, George. *Lords of the Press.* New York: Julian Messner, 1938

Sergeant, Harriet. *Shanghai, Collision Point of Cultures, 1918–1939.* New York: Crown, 1990.

Seward, G. F. *Chinese Immigration in its Social and Economic Aspects.* New York: Charles Scribner's Sons, 1881.

Sheean, Vincent. *Personal History.* New York: Doubleday, Doran, 1936.

Shearer, Lloyd. "Crime Certainly Pays on the Screen." *New York Times Magazine,* August 5, 1945. Reprinted in *Film Noir Reader 2,* edited by Alain Silver and James Ursini. New York: Limelight, 2003, 9–14.

Shelby, Gertrude Mathews. "Florida Frenzy." *Harper's,* January 1926, 177–86.

Shillington, Kevin. *History of Africa.* New York: St. Martin's, 1995.

"Shining Stars." *Time,* July 24, 1933, 12.

Simmn, Scott. *The Invention of the Western Film: A Cultural History of the Genre's First Half-Century.* Cambridge, UK: Cambridge University Press, 2003.

Sitkoff, Harvard. *A New Deal for Blacks, The Emergence of Civil Rights as a National Issue: The Depression Decade.* New York: Oxford University Press, 1978.

Sklar, Robert. *Movie-Made America: A Cultural History of American Movies.* New York: Random House, 1975.

Smith, Thorne. *Topper.* 1926. New York: Random House, 1999.

Snead, James. *White Screens, Black Images.* London: Routledge, 1994.

Southern, Eileen, ed. *Readings in Black American Music.* New York: W. W. Norton, 1983.

Spoto, Donald. *The Art of Alfred Hitchcock.* New York: Hopkinson and Blake, 1979.

———. *The Dark Side of Genius: The Life of Alfred Hitchcock.* New York: Ballantine, 1983.

Sternsher, Bernard, ed. *The Negro in Depression and War: Prelude to Revolution, 1930–1945.* Chicago: Quadrangle Books, 1969.

Stott, William. *Documentary Expression and Thirties America.* Chicago: University of Chicago Press, 1986.

Strachan, Hew. *The First World War.* New York: Viking, 2003.

Sundquist, Eric. *To Wake the Nations: Race in the Making of American Literature.* Cambridge: Harvard University Press, 1993.

Sunstein, Cass. *The Second Bill of Rights: FDR's Unfinished Revolution and Why We Need it More than Ever.* New York: Perseus Books, 2006.

Susman, Warren. *Culture as History.* New York: Pantheon, 1984.

Taggard, Genevieve. "Mill Town," *Calling Western Union.* New York: Harper, 1936, 83–84.

Takaki, Ronald. *Strangers from a Different Shore: A History of Asian Americans.* Boston: Little Brown, 1998.

Taylor, Graham D. *The New Deal and American Indian Tribalism: The Administration of the Indian Reorganization Act, 1934–45.* Lincoln: University of Nebraska Press, 1980.

Tchen, John Kuo Wei, ed. *Genthe's Photographs of San Francisco's Old Chinatown.* New York: Dover, 1984.

Terrill, Tom E., and Jerrold Hirsch, eds. *Such as Us: Southern Voices of the Thirties.* New York: W. W. Norton, 1978.

Terkel, Studs, ed. *Hard Times: An Oral History of the Great Depression.* New York: Pantheon, 1986.

Thurber, James. "Ivorytown, Rinsonville, Anacinburg, and Crisco Corners." *The Beast in Me and Other Animals.* 1947. Reprint, New York: Harvest, 1974, 208–22.

Towers, Jonathan. *The Great Depression: The Great Shake-Up.* Vol. 1. New York: Tower Productions, 1998.

Trail, Armitage. *Scarface.* 1930. New York: Blackmask, 2005.

Tuan, Yi-Fu. *Escapism.* Baltimore: Johns Hopkins University Press, 1998.

Tuttle, Worth. "Autobiography of an Ex-Feminist," *Atlantic Monthly,* December 1933, 640–49.

———. "A Feminist Marries." *Atlantic Monthly,* January 1934, 73–81.

Uhys, Errol Lincoln. *Riding the Rails: Teenagers on the Move during the Great Depression.* New York: TV Books, L.L.C., 1999.

"A Vagrant Civil Engineer." *The New York Times,* May 4, 1932. Reprinted in *The Great Depression,* edited by David Shannon. Englewood Cliffs, N.J.: Prentice Hall, 1960, 90.

Van Rijn, Guildo. *Roosevelt's Blues: African-American Blues and Gospel Songs on FDR.* Jackson: University Press of Mississippi, 1997.

Vanderwood, Paul J, ed. *Juarez.* Madison: University of Wisconsin Press, 1983.

Von Sternberg. Joseph. *Fun in a Chinese Laundry.* New York: Macmillan, 1965.

Walton, John. *Western Times and Water Wars: State, Culture, and Rebellion in California.* Berkeley: University of California Press, 1992.

"War Debts: Britain Can't Pay Cash and Won't Pay in Kind." *News-Week,* July 7, 1934, 29–30.

Ware, Susan. *American Women in the Nineteen Thirties: Holding Their Own.* New York: Twayne, 1982.

————. *Beyond Suffrage: Women in the New Deal.* Cambridge, Mass.: Harvard University Press, 1981.

Warren, Harris Gaylord. *Herbert Hoover and the Great Depression.* New York: Oxford University Press, 1959.

Weimann, Robert. "Realism, Ideology, and the Novel in America: 1886–1896, Changing Perspectives in the Work of Twain, Howell, and Henry James." In *Revisionary Interventions in the Americanist Canon,* edited by Donald Pease. Durham, N.C.: Duke University Press, 1994, 189–210.

West, George P. "Hearst: A Psychological Note," *American Mercury,* November 30, 1930, 298–308.

White, William L. "Pare Lorentz." *Scribner's,* January 1939, 8.

"Will Revolution Come?" *Atlantic,* August 1932, 184–91.

Wilson, James. *The Earth Shall Weep: A History of Native America.* New York: Grove Press, 1998.

Wolters, Raymond. *Negroes and the Great Depression.* New York: Greenwood Press, 1970.

Wood, Robin. *Hitchcock's Films Revisited.* New York: Columbia University Press, 1989.

Wright, Gavin. *Old South, New South: Revolutions in the Southern Economy Since the Civil War.* New York: Basic Books, 1986.

"The Yellow (Journalist) Peril," *The New Republic,* January 16, 1935, 263–64.

Young, Owen. "New Deal Weighed." *Time,* July 3, 1933, 16.

Zierold, Norman. *The Moguls: Hollywood's Merchants of Myth.* Los Angeles: Silman-James Press, 1969.

Zinn, Howard. *A People's History of the United States.* New York: Perennial, 2003.

Index

Harlow, Jean: *Bombshell,* 203; *The Girl From Missouri,* 198; her onscreen female persona, 113
Harper's, 40, 111, 137
Hart, Sir Robert, 101
Haskell, Molly: on 1930s actresses in film, 113–14
Haste, William, 80
Hawks, Howard, *The Road to Glory,* 57
Hays Code, 20; and film noir, 154, 155; and pre-code Hollywood, 213 n. 20; and *The Shanghai Gesture,* 102
"He Wants His Pants" (song), 23
Hearst, William Randolph: as newspaper publisher, 192–93
Heart of Darkness, 77
Hecht, Ben: as screenwriter with newspaper experience, 196
Heinz, Langlan, 18
Hell's Highway (film), 146
Hemingway, Ernest, 46, 50, 54, 59
Henry VIII, 163
Hepburn, Katherine: *Bringing Up Baby,* 130; her onscreen female persona, 113; *Holiday,* 178
Heroes for Sale (film), 40, 44, 62, 159
Hickok, Lorena: on people of color, 106
High Sierra (film): fatal woman in, 155, 157; 162
Hilton, James: *Lost Horizon* (novel), 173
His Girl Friday (film), 130–32; and amoral reporters, 198
Hitchcock, Alfred: *North By Northwest,* 21, *Rebecca,* 156
Hitler, Adolph, 39, 58, 73, 78, 79, 138
Hobsbawm, Eric, 43
Hohfeld, Wesley N., 56
Holiday (film), 177–81
Holiday (play), 177–78
Hoover, Herbert, 36, 38; and Roosevelt, 142; and the Bonus Army, 47; anger toward, 47, 139; confidence just prior to market crash, 139; criticized for trying to "manage" government, 144; jokes about, 139; offering aid to the Central Republic Bank of Chicago while denying aid to the public, 209 n. 13; on WW I as cause of the Great Depression, 44; proposal

that he become dictator, 39; rugged individualism, 113, 114; social welfare, 43, 51, 52, 88, 89
Hopkins, Harry, 28, 41
Horace, 46, 55, 59
Horatio Alger, 33
Horney, Karen: on "neurotic personality" of the 1930s, 28
Horowitz, Morton: on Legal Realism, 51, 57
Horton, Edward Everett: *Lost Horizon,* 173
Houghton, Walter, 43
House Committee to Investigate Un-American Activities (HUAC), 43, 88, 142; attacks New Dealers Harold Ickes, Frances Perkins, Harry Hopkins, and Federal Theater Project, 152; gains strength after Roosevelt fails in battles with Supreme Court and Southern Democrats, 158
Howard, Trevor: *Mutiny on the Bounty*167
Howard University, 88
Howards of Virginia (film), 66
Howells, William Dean: criticism of apartment buildings, 160
Hurst, Fanny: and racial issues, 86; *Imitation of Life* (novel)
Hurston, Zora Neale, 93
Huston, John: and film noir, 138
Huston, Walter: *American Madness,* 40, *Shanghai Gesture,* 103

I Am a Fugitive from a Chain Gang (film), 24–28, 31, 38, 44, 146
I Am a Fugitive from a Georgia Chain Gang (book), 24, 44
I'll Take My Stand: on an ideal agrarian community, 164; 171
Ickes, Harold, 43, 196; attacks newspaper publishers, 186, 195–96; on newspaper fabrications, 195–96; on the plight of reporters, 196; problem of special interests and the press, 188
Identity: effect of Depression on 15–19, 22
If I Had a Million (film), 15, 32
Imitation of Life (film and novel), 80, 86–93